ADVANCED
CELTIC
SHAMANISM

ADVANCED CELTIC SHAMANISM

D. J. Conway

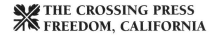 **THE CROSSING PRESS**
FREEDOM, CALIFORNIA

For information on bulk purchases or group discounts for this and other Crossing Press titles, please contact our Special Sales Manager at 800/777-1048.
www.crossingpress.com

Library of Congress Cataloging-in-Publication Data

Conway, D. J., 2000-
    Advanced Celtic shamanism / by D. J. Conway.
        p. cm.
    Includes bibliographical references (p.) and index.
    ISBN 1-58091-076-4 (pbk.)
    1.Mythology, Celtic 2. Celts--Religion I. Shamanism. I. Title
BL900.C657   2000
299'.16--dc21   00-030710
                                                    CIP

I want to thank Tira Brandon-Evans and Maggie Frost for being so gracious with their time, reading the manuscript, and finding the errors I missed in proofreading. This book is dedicated to them both and to the Society of Celtic Shamans for helping to make the Celtic path more available to all who seek it.

Contents

Foreword

There is a land far away, over the sea, under the wave, where you will find the sacred well sheltered within a living grove. Nine hazel trees, in leaf evergreen, in flower ever-white, in fruit ever-ripe, nurture the Well of Segais. Purple-hulled hazelnuts fall like raindrops into that pool. As they drift into dim depths, bubbles of inspiration boil up. Purple spotted salmon rise and break the nuts, feed on the meats, and grow wise. Violet-stained waters flow from the sacred well in five streams. Their names are: Seeing, Hearing, Tasting, Smelling, Feeling. If you would be wise, a master of all arts — a healer, a bard, a warrior, a mystic — you must drink from the well and from each of the five streams. Only then may you truly claim to be *aes dana*, one of the *folk of many arts*.

If you would walk the spiritual paths of the Celtic ancestors, new awareness is waiting for you over the sea, under the wave, in the land that knows no stain or sorrow.

In *Advanced Celtic Shamanism*, D. J. Conway shares with us so that we may each begin our own Great Journey to discover the heart of Celtic tradition. We may each strive to become *aes dana* and, at journey's end, achieve true heart's desire. Enjoy your journey.

Tira Brandon-Evans
Moderator, Society of Celtic Shamans
Sardis, BC—January 2000

Introduction

When I wrote By Oak, Ash & Thorn, I did so knowing that all the information I had to share could not be given in one book. First I needed to open the doors of people's minds to the historical existence and modern applications of ancient Celtic shamanism. I had to make people aware that European shamanism, and particularly Celtic shamanism, actually did exist at one time, even though what records of it there were had been destroyed. A trail of clues runs through the surviving myths of Ireland, Scotland, and Wales like a tiny thread if one is patient enough to painstakingly search for them. These clues prove that the Druids were not the only spiritual system known to the Celts. Legends and myths clearly tell us that many people who had no desire to become Druids knew of a shamanic system that connected them to great spiritual growth and mighty powers.

Shamanism is not a religion. It is a spiritual discipline that can be used in conjunction with any religion. It is also an individual spiritual path that can be practiced in private by yourself. You are not required to join a church or group. All you need is a willingness to learn, practice what you learn, and be dedicated and patient. Success will not come overnight or instantaneously, but it will come if you continue the shamanic methods. However, this book is written primarily to teach those interested in Celtic shamanism in conjunction with Celtic Paganism.

It is very probable that the Druids themselves knew of and used Celtic shamanic methods beyond their practice of Druidism. The stories of Druidic powers point to this. However, both the Druidic and shamanic teachings were sharply curtailed and then expunged under the controlling rule of Christianity.

This is the proper time to restore and renew the Celtic shamanism that once provided strength and hope to a proud and spiritual people. You do not have to be of Celtic lineage to benefit from the teachings of this book. You only need a sincere desire to better yourself, patience to work your way through the paths, and a positive attitude. If you are lacking the positive attitude at this time, be assured that it will come through your efforts and Otherworld journeys. The techniques in this book work best if the reader starts at the beginning and works her/his way through to the end.

I wish for you all the joy and success your heart can hold as you travel the four paths of Celtic shamanism.

CHAPTER 1

UNDERSTANDING CELTIC SPIRITUALITY AND MAGIC

No one knows for certain exactly where the Celtic peoples originated, although there are more than enough writers and historians willing to go out on a limb to make a definitive statement. All we know is that all countries visited by the Celts speak of them as coming "out of the East" in great waves. Even the Hindu histories of India report the same origin. If the Celts came "out of the East" to India, where did they come from? Unfortunately, we do not have clear evidence of their land of origin.

The Celts were composed of many clans of peoples, all speaking dialects of the same language and basically having the same religious structure. They were skilled in building roads and chariots, in raising crops and breeding animals, and in making some of the most beautiful metalwork ever seen. Each clan had specially trained people who were responsible for remembering and preserving the clan's history, genealogies, and laws. A great clan that is almost constantly on the move could not afford to be burdened with written documents that could become lost or destroyed, and it is likely that there was a prohibition against written information, so certain clan members were trained to commit everything to memory.

As individual clan-groups, they traveled through much of the Middle East and the Mediterranean area before settling in France, Britain, and Ireland. Although poorly organized as clans, the Celts had little trouble taking over territory during their moves. At the height of their power, their territory and influence stretched from Turkey to Britain. Their warriors, both men and women, were so courageous and fierce that they were feared even by the disciplined legions of Rome. Even after their settlements became permanent, the Celts continued to trade with far-flung cultures, and many of their warriors were, like the Vikings, hired as paid mercenaries by Mediterranean rulers.

A dynamic, fearless, brilliant people, the Celts learned from all the other civilizations with which they came in contact. For example, legends point to the possible use of yoga techniques and a knowledge of the chakras, or light centers, of the astral body. Although many of their laws were reminiscent of those of Greece, they went a step further and granted their women more rights than any other patriarchal culture.

They used the Greek alphabet for ordinary correspondence, saving the ogham alphabet for religious and magical purposes. Much of their culture laid the foundation for later European civilization.

The Celts were adventuresome and daring in nature. They not only explored vast areas of the earth, but also ventured inward to other planes of existence. There, they discovered the strength and knowledge that enabled them to face any test of character thrown at them by life and circumstances.

The most prominent part of the Celtic religion was the Druidic order, which was comprised of Druids, Bards, and Ovates. The ethics of Druidic teaching were to worship the gods, do no evil, and be strong and courageous. They taught the doctrines of reincarnation and karma, but said that the gods did not punish people in a hell after death. They were familiar with and taught the triune[1] aspects of both gods and goddesses, long before Christianity borrowed the idea. They also allowed women into the Druidic order and permitted both priests and priestesses to marry if they wished.

Once settled in a more permanent place, the Celts began to write down some of their histories, myths, and laws. Some writers state that the Celts had no written records at all, but this is not true. The Church itself recorded that St. Patrick personally burned almost one hundred and eighty Irish books in the Celtic language. We will never know how many other books were destroyed by religious zealots.

The Celts were a very spiritual people, as well as some of the best warriors history has ever seen. Spirituality was not something they did only on special occasions; they incorporated their religious beliefs into their daily lives, right down to the mystical jewelry they created. They valued learning and knowledge, which was fortunate, for during the European Dark Ages, Ireland managed to keep alive centers of learning for medicine, history, and science, while the rest of Europe slid backward into ignorance.

When the basic Druidic practices were ruthlessly stamped out by the rising faith of Christianity, many of the Celts simply shifted their personal devotions and spiritual seeking to the ancient shamanic practices, while giving lip service publicly to the new, dominant religion. However, with the passage of time and the continuous harassment by the monks, even the shamanic arts faded away. Undoubtedly, it became a crime to practice or teach shamanism, just as had happened with other Pagan beliefs. All we have left is a thin trail of clues that runs through the ancient Celtic myths and legends.

Even if we did have complete ancient records of the practice of Celtic shamanism, which we do not, they would not be valid for today's society. Any religion that becomes locked into performing outdated rituals becomes stagnant and will eventually die. Life requires constant changes and adjustments in everything, just as nature does. Only those willing and able to adapt to changing circumstances will continue to thrive. The information in this book is an adaptation of old practices, changed to fit into modern living.

As we know from historical evidence of the Druids, there was more than one level of knowledge and adeptness in this order. Students worked their way through a series of lessons in order to be at the top of their grade or to pass into another level of mysticism. Since this book is not about Druidism, I wondered if shamanism had the same requirements. The degree of adeptness in shamanism appears in other cultures and must have been known in the Celtic societies. I searched the legends until I found the answer. It came in the form of stories about people who excelled in a number of different methods, the more powerful ones being adept in several or all of these methods at one time.

The Celtic shaman must be a healer, bard, warrior, and mystic. These are the four paths of the truly dedicated Celtic shaman, the four paths that she or he must walk to fully appreciate and know the universe in all its forms and creations. The fifth path, which is not actually a path at all, is the center, or balanced spirituality. The center can only be reached after the shaman walks the four paths and brings her or his life and spirit into harmonious balance. Even the balance cannot be held static, however. Humans go through life in a perpetual dance, approaching, then retreating from the balance point. When out of balance, the Celtic shaman can retreat to the four paths of knowledge. By renewing energy and purpose through the disciplines of these paths, she/he can once more reach the calm center.

The purpose of Celtic shamanism is not only to teach spiritual balance, but also to teach knowledge that will affect everyday life in a positive manner. When one's own life is spiritually balanced, it has a harmonious effect on the lives of others. This influence can ripple outward, with the potential of touching whole areas and societies. The Celts believed that everything in creation and in this universe is connected—everything, without exception. By strengthening and bettering your own life, you are creating positive cosmic ripples that cannot help but influence every corner of the universe.

Although many of the subjects in this book may seem to be disconnected from one another, they are not. The use of herbs and oils for healing teaches you to be compassionate toward others as well as aware of your own physical body and its responses. Learning about the ancient Celtic calendar and festivals helps you look at the seasons of the year from a new viewpoint, thus aiding you in learning to flow with the yearly energy tides. With divination techniques, you open yourself to your inner voice as well as to the voices of Deity and your guides. Meditations teach patience and persistence, while the study of symbols opens up a dialogue with your subconscious mind, which speaks only in symbols. The goal of all the paths is to reach a greater sense of spirituality.

The four paths of Celtic shamanism can be traveled at your own speed. There are no time limitations or teachers to make sure that you do not skip over the information. Only you are responsible for taking the time to study and to follow each step properly. Information in one path will build your knowledge for the next path, even though you may think at the time it has little to do with the path you are studying. A thread of connectedness binds all the paths.

If you care enough to start the study of the paths of Celtic shamanism, please care enough to do it right and to finish it. The rewards are great for a job well done. Who knows? Perhaps you will build a better future for this world and pay off some of your negative karma along the way.

---

1. The triune aspects originated with the Great Goddess in Her triple role of Maiden, Mother, and Crone. Later, the Great God was understood to be triple, as in Father, Savior Son, and Warrior.

Chapter 2

The Way of the Healer

The healer was one of the first specialists to appear in any ancient civilization, along with the priests who were responsible for spiritual guidance. Without a healer, clan members would die of disease or injury, thus weakening the whole clan, possibly dooming the clan to extinction. Every life was too precious to lose prematurely. The first healers were likely priest-shamans, a necessary combination until the clan expanded to the point that the expenditure of time and energy made it expedient to divide the positions. Even after this division of priests and healers, there still remained an aura of spirituality to the healers.

From very ancient times, Celtic healers, particularly those in Ireland, were renowned for their skillful use of herbal remedies and magical healing. Their skills extended beyond physical healing into the realm of mental, emotional, and spiritual healing as well. They were so highly regarded that Celtic Irish physicians were entitled by law to sit with the nobility at the royal table. They wore special robes to denote their profession and were usually surrounded by a crowd of carefully chosen pupils. At one time Ireland had the greatest medical colleges in Europe. Pupils came from all over Europe to study there.

We know from surviving records that the most renowned of Irish healers used a variety of practices in their healing, including herb lore, cauterization, trephination, cupping, probing, Cesarean delivery, bone setting, and some surgeries. They knew the effect of the mind and the emotions on the physical body, as well as the effects certain unhealthy habits or conditions could have. They also knew of and treated smallpox (*bolgoch*), consumption (*angobracht* or *anbobracht*), diseases of the bladder and kidneys (*galar fuail*), ophthalmia or conjunctivitis (*galar sula*), palsy (*crith lam*), and ague.

Even though healing methods were taught by masters of the craft, the best physicians were said to have gained their knowledge originally from the Otherworld or the land of fairies. Stories say that the healers journeyed into the Otherworld where they were taught methods that set them apart from others of their profession. The descriptions of all of these Otherworld journeys fit perfectly into the shamanic mode. Celtic healers must have been well-trained shamans.

Ireland is rich in herbs that have healing properties. Every invader of Ireland took advantage of this and used these herbs for healing. Ancient stories say that the Tuatha Dé Danann healer Dian Cécht diagnosed fourteen diseases of the stomach alone, for which he prescribed remedies made of vegetables and herbs. "Dian Cécht's Porridge" is the oldest known remedy in Ireland; it has been used down through the ages for colds, phlegm, sore throats, and worms. The Porridge consisted of hazel buds, dandelions, chickweed, and wood sorrel boiled with oatmeal and eaten in the morning and again at night. Another old remedy is a poultice of yellow baywort tied around the neck for sore throats.

In later Irish history, several families continued the ancient family tradition of healing. Among these were the O'Hickeys, the O'Lees or Lees, and the O'Shiels. The physicians of each of these families originally received Otherworld training, and then passed down the knowledge to other members of their family. The Lee family (O Laoi in Irish)[1] produced generation after generation of healers. As late as the seventeenth century, Muirchertach O Laoi went on a journey to an Otherworld island off Galway where he was taught healing methods by the fairies. Not only did Muirchertach go on the journey, but he also returned with a book on healing, a book that still exists today in the Royal Irish Academy of Dublin.[2]

In Wales there is a similar story of the physicians of Myddfai and a lake maiden of Llyn y Fan Fach, a small lake near the Black Mountains district of Carmarthenshire. During the twelfth century, a young farm lad saw a lake maiden on the banks of the lake combing her long golden hair. He wooed her and eventually married her, accepting her stipulation that he never hit her, even in jest. After several years and several sons, the man playfully struck his wife on the shoulder three times and she disappeared back into the lake. The sons continued to visit the lake, hoping to see their mother. One day she appeared at Llidiard y Meddygon (the Physicians' Gate) and told Rhiwallon, the oldest son, that they must become healers. She gave Rhiwallon a bag full of instructions and medical remedies, and continued to teach her sons the art of healing until they became the best-known physicians in Wales. The sons taught their sons this Otherworld ability until the line died out with Dr. C. Rice Williams of Aberystwyth in the late eighteen hundreds.[3]

In Wales, medicine and healing were considered as one of the three civil arts and one of the nine rural arts[4] practiced before the time of Prydain ab Aedd Mawr. The laws of Dyvnwal Moelmud mention this.[5] The priests and teachers, called the *Gwyddoniaid* ("men of knowledge"), combined the study of healing with religion, astrology, and medical botany. They also were skilled in magic and divination.

Minor healers left the surgeries and more difficult cases to the professional physicians. However, these lesser healers were very skilled in administering herbal remedies, laying on of hands, and other practices. One such healer in the seventeenth century was Valentine Greatrakes, who was renowned for curing sores, cancers, deafness, and dim sight by touch alone. My own great-grandfather had people coming for miles to be healed of warts. Unfortunately, most of these healing secrets have been lost within the last two or three generations. Ridiculed as superstition, the families dropped the practice of teaching the new generation the old secrets.

Fairies were said to cause some illnesses. The Celts believed that many diseases were attributed to "fairy strokes," or *meillteorcacht*. Fairy stroke was thought to be any sudden, inexplicable disease that caused a physical wasting of the body (such as a stroke) or a mental deterioration that showed no evidence beforehand. Forge-water was a recommended cure for many of these problems. The best method was to have the water sprinkled by a blacksmith or the seventh son of a seventh son. Blacksmiths were said not only to be healers, but also to have great magical powers. They could also remove warts by rubbing the wart with a stone, then casting it away.

The Irish believed that the soul, heart, and mind needed to be in balance before the body could be healthy. This is the threefold pattern of the Celtic soul. They called the body the *coich anama*, or soul-shrine, and said that vigor (*anam*) for living came from proper health of the breath and the blood. Since the soul was influenced by the mind and the heart, a soul or mental sickness affected the body as surely as a physical ailment or injury. Therefore, if the body was sick, it affected the soul. If the soul was sick, it affected the body. Irish healers tended to treat the whole person—body, mind, emotions, and soul—something just being acknowledged today in the medical community.

Since the original Celtic healers cared for the clan from the cradle to the grave, and the Celts believed strongly in the survival of the soul, it was not unusual that the practice of soul leading (*treoraich anama*) evolved. This praying over the dying for guidance into the Otherworld was not done by any clergy or church, but by an *anam-chara*, or soul-friend. The relationship between the dying person and the *anam-chara* was a spiritual link that had existed for several lifetimes and would not be broken by death. It was considered a great honor and privilege to perform such a task, and still is in many parts of Ireland today.

The part of the shamanic healer that makes the journeys into the Otherworlds is the astral body. Sometimes, the astral body is referred to as the double or co-walker in Celtic literature. Believers in reincarnation and soul travel, the Irish said that the astral body could leave the physical body and journey into the Otherworld. There, one could visit with the ancestors, fairies, and old deities, regaining lost knowledge and gaining aid for present and future events. This journeying is a shamanic practice, not used by many today.

The idea of the co-walker (Scottish Gaelic, *coimimeadh*), or double, was widespread throughout the Celtic realms. The description of the co-walker, given by the Scottish clergyman Robert Kirk,[6] fits what is now called the astral body. In Scotland, if people saw this co-walker, they assumed it to be a message of ill omen or even death. The Irish believed that this co-walker could appear as a bird just before a person died. Many Irish families still believe in this death-omen and express dread when unusual bird activity appears near their homes. For them, this omen has proved correct too many times to disregard it. For other Irish families, the wail or appearance of the banshee (*bean-sídhe*) heralds a death.

The acceptance of the appearance of an Otherworld messenger of death is quite common in Celtic societies. In Scotland, the banshee is called the Caoineag, or Weeper. Tradition says that she was heard wailing the night before the massacre at Glencoe.[7] In Wales, the banshee is known as the cyhyreath, although originally she was a goddess of streams. This Otherworld being appears, not in retribution or anger, but in sorrow because of her connection with a particular family. These death-omens point to a strong connection between the families involved and beings of the Otherworld.

Sometimes, however, a soul would leave the body because of shock from a physical injury or a mental or emotional crisis. When the soul did not want to return to the body, the healer was required to take a journey to the Otherworld and retrieve it.

Signs of complete soul-loss are very drastic: coma; total detachment with no response to exterior stimuli; simply not "being present."

Soul-loss is not possession and should not be treated as such. Actual possession by some foreign entity is very rare. In fact, actual, complete soul-loss is not common either. Soul-loss, or possession for that matter, also does not occur from meditation, trances, or the use of talking-boards, such as Ouija. This falsehood is promulgated by orthodox churches to keep independent people from exploring other spiritual paths. The shamanic procedure for soul retrieval is given in more detail later in this chapter.

Celtic healers were also aware of the possibility of soul-displacement, or soul-fragmentation. The Brehon Laws acknowledged this and laid down a penalty for this loss, which can be caused by jealousy, great emotional stress or trauma, mental anguish, and even deep hatred. Although some of the symptoms are similar to those found in complete soul-loss, in this case only pieces of the fragmented soul are missing. To correct this problem, the healer-shaman is required to journey into the Otherworld and retrieve the soul fragments, returning them to the affected person.

There are certain characteristics that indicate possible partial soul-loss to the healer. These are: chronic depression; apathy that remains for any length of time; difficulty in resisting illnesses; memory gaps; mental disorientation; uncontrollable emotions; difficulty in reestablishing a normal life after a crisis, such as a death in the family or divorce; severe illness as a child; addictions in a person who wants to be free of them;[8] constantly being discontented with one's lot.

When retrieving soul-fragments, you will need a crystal used just for this purpose alone. The same crystal, however, may be used to retrieve the entire soul when it has been stolen or leaves. This crystal, called a soul-catcher in shamanic terms, should be stored in a soft, dark-colored bag when not being used.

The procedure for retrieval and return of the soul or parts of a fragmented soul are quite simple when you use meditation as a springboard into the Otherworlds. You do not need anything other than your soul-catcher crystal and a recording of the basic steps of meditation to help you make the journey. However, the subconscious mind responds most favorably to symbols, so you might wish to have a special comfortable robe and/or specific pieces of jewelry that you wear while "traveling."

The healer always should begin the practice of soul-retrieval by working on herself/himself. All of our souls fragment at times from the stress of a fast-paced world and the emotions arising from crises. Most of the pieces eventually return home without help. However, some pieces remain fragmented until retrieved and returned.

Usually the pieces of a fragmented soul will retreat to the Middleworld, or the alternate of this world. It is inhabited by many astral creatures, such as fairies, elves, and banshees. You may have to search in many places before you find all the pieces. It is not uncommon to take more than one such journey before all the pieces are found and coaxed back where they belong. Returning too many fragmented pieces of a soul at one time also can create too much emotional stress for the patient, so do not try to retrieve too many pieces on a journey. Sometimes, a piece of a soul will retreat to the Underworld but this is not a common occurrence. The Underworld, however, is the most likely place to find a lost soul that has completely vanished.

Traveling to the Otherworld

Learning and practicing meditation is an absolute must for anyone on the Celtic spiritual paths. Regular meditation, not less than one time a week, keeps you balanced and more able to cope with unexpected happenings. It also opens you up to true messages from the ancestors, guides, and others from the Otherworld. These messages may come during meditation or through later dreams.

Each of the meditations given in this book can be read into a tape recorder at a moderate speaking rate and replayed to aid in meditation. In this way you do not have to take your mind from the meditation to remember where you want to go. It is helpful if you have a background of soft instrumental music on the meditation tape. This music will help you relax and also will keep you from being distracted by background noises. You may record the meditations word for word or make changes in the wording to suit your needs.

These meditations are all shamanic in nature. They introduce you to the various areas of the Otherworld and the inhabitants who live there as you progress through the meditations given for each path.

It is preferable to establish a certain place for meditation. In this area or room you can have a white, blue, or lavender (not purple) candle and burn incense sticks or cones if you wish. When burning incense, however, make certain there is adequate ventilation, or the smoke will irritate your throat and lungs. Good, all-purpose incenses are sandalwood or frankincense and myrrh. You also need a comfortable chair to sit in.

After you have become accustomed to meditating on a regular basis, you will find that the places you visit and the sights you see may well change from time to time. When this occurs, let the meditation take you where it will. Do not go with any preconceived ideas about what you will experience. As to the messages from Otherworld beings or the ancestors, you must learn to distinguish between hearing what you want to hear and hearing what is truth. Facing the truth is a mark of a true seeker on the Celtic spiritual path.

To begin any meditation, shut off the telephone and put a "Do not disturb" sign on the door. Sit in your chair in a comfortable position, with your hands in your lap and your feet flat on the floor. Lying down does not work well as you tend to go to sleep. For a soul-retrieval, have your soul-catcher crystal in your lap or nearby. Turn on your recorder if you have recorded the meditation.

Remember, you are *never* trapped in a meditation. You can leave any time you wish. Just think of your physical body and open your eyes. Also, you do not need to worry about some "evil" being taking over your body and refusing to let you return. It cannot happen.

If you want to record this meditation, begin with the next paragraph. Be certain to leave brief periods without any talking so you can explore and experience.

Soul-Retrieval Meditation

Close your eyes and visualize a brilliant white light over your head. As you inhale deeply, feel this light coursing through your body, from your head down to your toes. Feel your muscles relaxing, beginning with your feet and working up to your head. The deep sense of peacefulness moves up through your legs, into your body and arms. You feel the tenseness flow out of the muscles in your shoulders, neck, and head. You are completely relaxed.

Before you now is a river. Take all the problems in your life and throw them into the swiftly moving water. The problems are quickly carried far away from you. Leave them there. Turn and walk away. You will be constantly protected during this meditation. Absolutely nothing can harm you.

Now see yourself in ancient Ireland, long, long ago when there were just dirt paths passing through the thick forests of oak, pine, ash, and yew. These are the days of the early Celtic warriors and the Druid priests and priestesses with their vast knowledge of the universe and the earth itself.

You are standing on top of a low hill before two great monolithic stones. As you walk up to the stones, you can see the carvings of circles and spirals on them. You stretch out your hands to touch the stones. They are very ancient, and you can feel the energy pulsing deep within them.

As you start to walk between the stones, you feel your crystal in your hand. It will remain with you and be available at a single thought.

The landscape beyond the two monoliths is very similar to that of this world. You are standing in a lush meadow, rich with tall grass and wildflowers. There is a forest on the distant hills, and you hear the songs of birds as they fly overhead. Coming toward you through the meadow grass is a man dressed in a blue tunic, tan trousers, and a multicolored cloak that swirls about his body as he walks. From his belt hangs a leather bag with symbols painted on it. You know instantly that he is a Celtic healer.

As he stands before you and holds out his hand in greeting, he tells you his name. You tell him why you have entered the Middleworld. He asks you a few questions about the person whose soul has been fragmented. You answer the best you can.

The healer takes a small crystal ball out of his healing bag and cups it in his hands. You both gaze down into the crystal and see several scenes of landscapes and buildings where fragments of the soul are hiding. Then he takes your hand and, with the power of his mind, transports you to the first place you saw in the crystal.

You find the soul in human form hiding in the shadows and speak gently to it. You ask why it left. It may or may not give you an answer. You feel your soul-catcher crystal in your hand and coax the soul to enter the crystal. When it is safely inside the crystal, the healer takes you to another place.

The healer takes you to other destinations where soul-fragments are hiding. Some of the soul-fragments may not return with you at this time. Do not try to force them into the crystal. If they do not enter of their own accord, their return will not have a positive effect. Continue your journey until you have retrieved all the fragments that want to return at this time.

The healer talks with you for a time, giving information and advice and answering questions you may have for him. When the conversation is finished, he takes you back to the two monolithic stones.

As you stand before the stones, you hold the crystal in both hands and visualize the person whose soul-fragments are within it. Chant "Return, return. Your body-house welcomes you." You see the soul-fragments fly from the crystal into the body to which they belong. You feel a sense of great peace come over you.

You say farewell to the healer, then step back between the tall stones. You think of your physical body and find yourself within it. The meditation is ended.

The Celts considered soul-theft an even greater crime against the body and spirit. Soul-theft occurs when someone deliberately drains off another person's vitality or manipulates another person's life force so as to put that person under their control.

Any person can be guilty of the theft of vitality; they may do this only on occasion, consciously or subconsciously, although usually the offending person has practiced this habit for a lifetime. These perpetrators are frequently referred to as psychic vampires. As friends, acquaintances, or coworkers, they appear on the scene, depressed and low in energy. Within a short period of time, their mood rises and their vitality soars, while you are left feeling listless and drained. Since most of this draining is done without conscious motive, you can protect yourself from the side effects by wearing protective jewelry, talismans, or something set with black onyx. Those persons who practice this deliberately are another matter, as are those who practice soul-theft.

The idea of soul-theft appears frequently in Celtic myths and legends. This happens when someone deliberately uses their power to intimidate another person, steal their vitality or virtue, or bind them to do as the thief wishes. What this amounts to is a manipulation of another person's life force. When we say that someone is under the power of another person, meaning they are doing and saying things not reflecting their usual nature, we actually mean soul-theft. We see this most frequently among family members, friends, lovers, or those who wish someone to love them. A dominant, self-centered individual controls another, or others around her/him, to such a degree that the people being victimized are afraid to do anything without consulting the controller. The Celts considered this action to be very negative and dangerous. The Celts also considered this domination a trait of fairies, particularly if they had been insulted in some manner.

In Celtic myth and legend, stories of soul-theft most often involve the fairies, or Otherworld beings. Fairies were quick to take retribution for insults or lack of respect from mortals. One such story in *The Mabinogion* of Wales tells the story of Rhiannon and her son Pryderi who were taken away by a magician-fairy named Llwyd Cilcoed, because of an unintentional intrusion by Pryderi into a building. Manawyddan, husband to Rhiannon, finally trapped the magician's wife who had shapeshifted into a mouse. He bargained with Llwyd by threatening to hang the mouse unless his wife and stepson were returned to him.[9] Stories of Celtic retrievals frequently involved many trials and much bargaining.

At other times a coma can be declared to be soul-theft. The soul wanders from the body because of a shock and becomes trapped by the shock itself or is held captive by negative entities. This can be caused by dark magic, ill-wishing, or the evil eye. First, the soul has to be tracked to the place of its imprisonment, freed from the spell that binds it, then coaxed back home. The Celts had various methods of counteracting this negative magic, usually involving weaving, the making of knots, or a mirror.

In the Highlands of Scotland the evil eye was called the *droch shuil*. Being under the spell of the evil eye usually produced a wasting sickness. To break this control, the Celts took water from under a bridge where both the dead and the living crossed, that is, a bridge crossed to reach a cemetery. The Celts blessed the water and touched the ears of the afflicted person without saying the person's name. This action returned the evil to the sender.

Another Highland charm, called *Eolais na T-Snaithnean* (Wisdom of the Threads), was used to break the power of the evil eye. It involved the plaiting or braiding of three threads while reciting a charm. This was then tied around the afflicted person's neck. Sometimes nine knots were also tied in the thread.

In Ireland the Celts frequently used the theme of twisted threads in their art, metal, and stonework as a precautionary practice to avoid ill-wishing and soul-loss of any kind. They also wore the image of twisted threads enameled or engraved on their jewelry. This thread of life that we admire in the beautiful twisting, weaving Celtic art was deliberately used to hold the soul-power where it belonged and to avert anyone causing it to go astray.

Although healers went on shamanic journeys to find a soul and return it to the body, they never tried to do it without the help of the deities and other helpful spirits. They called upon their spiritual teachers and animal allies to help them track down the soul, retrieve it, ward off any negative spirits, and return the soul to its rightful body.

The Irish Celts believed that two deities functioned as soul-guardians: Angus mac Óg and Brigit. In legends Angus is frequently connected to the guarding of souls. When Diarmait Ua Duibne was killed, Angus breathed his soul back into the body, then took him to *Bruig na Bóinne* for safekeeping. For a time the soul of the beautiful Étain resided in a soul-house made for her by Angus. Newgrange[10] (*Bruig na Bóinne*), the house or *sídhe* of Angus mac Óg, is decorated with the triple spiral, a symbol of the threefold soul.

The goddess Brigit is also connected with threefold symbols of the Celtic soul. She is a threefold goddess in her own right, and is also associated with weaving together the mental, emotional, and psychic threads that make up the soul and give meaning to life. Her mantle is called the web of life, and represents the power that can keep the soul within the body. To "weave Brigit's mantle" is an expression that describes the reciting of the *caim*, a protective prayer against many kinds of danger. Any words will do as long as Brigit's name is invoked.

The word *caim* actually means "loop, bend." However, in Irish tradition it refers to a protective circle made by the forefinger of the right hand. The person reciting the *caim* points the finger at the person or object to be protected while walking *deosil* or sunwise around them saying the prayer. The *caim* can be used on anything or anyone, including oneself.

In Scotland the *caim* was usually said and performed by a woman. Tradition says that the woman who has the power of "the *kaims* of care" and a mirror has supreme power and can deflect any enchantment.

As part of their belief in reincarnation, the Celts believed that, although the body was different with each birth, the basic personality and being of a person remained the same. This not only allowed a person the opportunity to carry latent talents, but also the tendency toward certain diseases. A true Celtic healer has to understand the past lives of patients so she/he can instruct them to avoid certain types of lifestyles. The healer accesses this information through Otherworld journeys and talks with the ancestors and Otherworld beings. Also, a shamanic trip to the cauldron of Cerridwen[11] can yield insight.

As you can see, a healer was required to know many things besides the properties of herbs. The Celtic healer had to know how to enter the Otherworld realms on a shamanic journey, retrieve parts or all of a wandering soul, and communicate with the ancestors, deities, and Otherworld beings in order to have all the information needed to bring about a cure for a patient. The requirements of a Celtic healer today are still much the same. Healing includes the whole person: body, mind, emotions, and spirit. All those who walk the path of the healer must be prepared to use herbal remedies, psychic counseling, magical incantations, and spiritual journeys in the quest for healing.

Healer Traits

There are certain traits a healer must cultivate to be effective in treating patients and at the same time not take on their illnesses. The healer must have patience, compassion, detached emotions, discrimination, and a willingness to keep learning and to accept responsibility.

Patience must be cultivated before one can be successful in any endeavor, particularly healing. Herbal and emotional healing are not instantaneous, but build up over a period of time to finally manifest in wellness. No one can be patient all the time, during every circumstance. Patience is an ongoing lesson that will bring great benefits, not only in this life, but in the next one also.

Compassion for one's fellow humans is essential in a healer. You cannot think of yourself as above anyone for any reason. Even though you must admonish a patient for an unhealthy lifestyle or habits, you must not think of yourself as better because you have none.

Detached emotions are very important. This does not mean the healer does not care or feel deeply for the sick person. The healer must not get caught up in overriding emotions that will attract negative energy and possibly the patient's illness into the healer's surrounding aura. You cannot function properly or efficiently if your emotions control you.

Discrimination has two meanings for the healer. First, the healer must be able to see the truth behind the story of the patient's illness. No one wants to be sick, but some people use their sickness to control others. Deep down they have no sincere desire to be well, as they would lose this dubious form of control. Second, the healer must not speak to others about a patient's illnesses or problems. Gossip should have no part in a healer's life.

The healer must always be prepared to keep learning. No one ever knows all there is to be learned about a craft or profession. If you keep adding to your field of knowledge, you will not become stagnant, egotistical, or "old." It is a fact that elders who keep learning something new tend to be healthier and happier than those who do not. The same applies to all humans. Never fall into the trap of thinking you are a master. Someone will always come along to prove you wrong.

Being on a spiritual path does not mean dispensing with the

practical actions of day-to-day life. Therefore, the Celtic healer must understand how to heal her/himself and be prepared to take care of immediate family members before she/he helps others. To be truly spiritual means that one seeks a spiritual path, but keeps that seeking in balance with personal and familial duties. The healer must work to provide an income for living, take care of spouse and/or family, abide by local and national laws, and do all the things everyone else does to provide for bodily needs. Celtic healers do not leave their families to fend for themselves. Neither do they depend upon others as a source of income. Being responsible is the key word for all paths of Celtic spirituality.

Mythic Healers

Dian Cécht, the great physician of the Tuatha Dé Danann, is the best known of the mythic healers. His daughter Airmid is also associated with herbal healing, as is Miach, her brother.

In the story of the Second Battle of Mag Tuired, Dian Cécht, his son Miach, and daughter Airmid joined together to sing healing songs over the well of Slane. Then Dian Cécht put one of every herb in Ireland into the well. When mortally wounded Tuatha warriors were brought to the healers, they plunged the warriors into the well and they emerged whole and well again. The Fomorians knew they must stop this process, so they sent Rúadán, son of Bres, to spy on the healers. He returned to report what the healers were doing and also spoke about the unbreakable weapons forged by Goibniu, the smith. The Fomorians sent Rúadán back to kill Goibniu. He did so by casting a spear through the smith. However, Goibniu plucked out the spear and was healed by the water of the well. The Fomorians then determined to destroy the well. They sent a group of warriors to cast stones into the well until it was filled, making a cairn of stones in its place. This is now called Octriallach's Cairn or Loch Luibe (from the word *lub*, or "herb").

Nuada, the king of the Tuatha Dé Danann, lost his hand in the fierce fighting that followed. Although Dian Cécht, with the help of the three craftsmen of the Tuatha (Goibniu, Credne, and Luchta), made a silver hand for Nuada, he had to step down as king. Bres, who was half-Fomorian, half-Tuatha Dé Danann, was appointed in his place. However, Bres was arrogant and cruel. The Tuatha wanted Nuada as king, but the laws forbade it because of the loss of his hand. It made him imperfect.

One day as Nuada sat in his hall, two young people came toward the palace. The young doorkeeper, who only had one eye, met them on the green and asked their business. When they told him they were healers, he challenged them to prove it by giving him a good eye. They replaced the damaged eye with a cat's eye, which proved to be a mixed blessing. When the young man wanted to sleep, the eye would open at the squeak of a mouse or the twittering of a bird. But he was impressed enough to take them to Nuada.

The healers revealed to the king that they were Miach, son of the great Dian Cécht, and Ormiach, another healer. Miach made another arm of flesh for the king. Ormiach set it into place, while Miach gathered herbs to heal it to the body. Thus, Nuada became king again. However, Dian Cécht was furious with his son and attacked him out of jealousy. Three times Dian Cécht wounded Miach, and each time the young man was able to heal himself. The fourth time Dian Cécht damaged his brain, and Miach died.

After Miach was buried, his sister Airmid visited his grave mound. There, she found a great variety of herbs growing out of the grave. She spread her cloak on the ground and began gathering the 365 herbs, carefully placing them on the cloak to match how they grew on the grave. She instinctively knew the placement of the herbs was vital to new information on healing. Just as she finished, her father Dian Cécht arrived. Still furious that his children might be greater healers than he was, Dian Cécht deliberately scattered the herbs so Airmid could not remember their placement.

Another time Dian Cécht was called upon to destroy an evil baby born to Mórrígán. This child had a heart filled with three serpents that could kill anything. Dian Cécht destroyed the child, cut open its heart, and burned the serpents. When he cast the ashes into the nearest river, they were still so deadly that the water boiled, and everything in the river died. Today that river is called the Barrow (boiling).

The goddess Brigit, daughter of the Dagda, is also connected with healing. Folklore relates that Brigit had her own place at what is now Kildare. Just before she entered the *sídhe* with the rest of the Tuatha Dé Danann, she established an all-female center at Kildare for her priestesses to tend the sick and dying. Her nineteen priestesses, whose number represents the nineteen-year cycle of the Celtic "Great Year," kept an ever-burning sacred fire in their compound. These priestesses knew the healing power of the voice. They sang healing songs for the sick and sleep-songs for dying. Brigit's name is still associated with many of the Irish healing wells. Brigit was such a popular figure of healing that the people refused to give her up when Christianity arrived. The Christian Church made her into a saint.

The hero Cú Chulainn was a great warrior, yet he used the power of his voice and the intent of his mind for healing as well. On one occasion, the goddess Mórrígán was wounded. Cú Chulainn healed her by wishing her good health and the blessings of the gods. Later, when Cú Chulainn himself was wounded in battle, Lug mac Ethnenn of the *sídhe* sang him to sleep for three days and nights while he dropped herbs upon the hero's wounds.

In later legends, the chief Criomhthann heard that there was a great Druid named Trostan who lived among the Cruithnigh (Picts). Now Criomhthann was having trouble in his battles against the Tuatha Fiodhgha because their weapons, which were steeped in poison, were killing a vast number of his men. He sought out Cruithnigh and asked the Druid to help. The Druid ordered a vat filled with the milk from one hundred fifty white, hornless cows. When a man was poisoned by the enemy's weapons, the Druid bathed him in the vat and cured him.

Other deities associated with healing were Áed Abrat, Belenus, Beli, Clídna, Coventina, Cuilenn, Dana, Don of Wales, Epona, Fand, Goibniu, Gwydion, Lludd Llaw Ereint, Lugh, Myrddin, and Scáthach.

Stones

Although the Celts did not build the stone circles or dolmens or erect the solitary monoliths, they recognized the power that came from them. They were a people with close ties to the earth and all nature, sensitive to the world around them and to every psychic flow of energy that emanated from nature. History mentions the wide use of various stones in jewelry and sword and dagger hilts, plus stones that were worn as amulets and talismans. Since the Celts maintained an extensive trading system, they obtained many precious and semi-precious stones that could not be found in Ireland itself. It is reasonable to assume that Celtic healers and shamans used various stones as part of their healing practices. In fact, a specific healing stone, sometimes called the *clock-omra*, was kept in the Fitzgerald family for generations and used on both humans and cattle. A similar stone was kept by the MacCarthy family, while another was preserved in a church in Donegal.

There are several methods for using stones in healing. The stones can be placed directly on the body for periods of time, allowing the aura to soak up needed corrective energy. Stones can be worn in jewelry, thus providing a steady stream of energy for various purposes, from healing diseases to protection. The healer also can make an elixir from stones to add to the patient's bathwater or to give her/him to drink.

Elixirs are made by submerging certain stones in a small amount of purified water. Although some stones cannot be immersed in water without damage, the stones listed here can safely be washed or used to create elixirs. Clean the stones you plan to use by physically removing all dust, dirt, and debris. Pass the stones through frankincense incense smoke. Then, on a full moon, place the stones in a container of the base liquid to be used. Cap it tightly and set in a cool, dark place until the next full moon. Remove the stones and clean them again. Label the bottle and decant the liquid, as needed, into dark-colored bottles with eye-droppers.

Good stones to use for these elixirs are amethyst (general purification and balance), citrine (detoxifying), emerald (general healing as well as the immune and nervous systems), ruby (circulatory system and for vitality), and sapphire (the entire glandular system). Put three to six drops of this type of elixir into a bathtub or a glass of water for drinking. The elixir should be used only once a day.

Sometimes a patient needs a steady flow of certain stone energies to begin the road to recovery. It is not wise to tape stones directly onto the body and leave them, as the patient can get an overdose of the stone's energy that will cause further problems. The best way to impart stone energies without harm is for the patient to wear the needed stone or stones in jewelry of some kind. The following is a list of stones that are reasonably priced and accessible.

Agate, Blue Lace: Arthritis, fractures, digestion, calming of the nerves

Agate, Moss: Protection of the aura, calmness, reducing fever, and skin diseases

Amber: General purification, depression, the endocrine glands

Amethyst: General pain, headaches, insomnia

Bloodstone: Bladder problems, blood disorders

Carnelian: Diseases of the pancreas and spleen, colds, allergies

Garnet, Red: Strength, the blood, depression, and general purification

Hematite: All blood disorders

Lapis Lazuli: Infection, fever, burns, dizziness, stroke

Malachite: Liver, gallbladder, birth labor, the immune system

Marble, Connemara: Calms the nerves and soothes the mind; Connemara marble is from Ireland

Obsidian, Black: The eyes, calming

Onyx, Black: Bone marrow

Quartz, Clear Crystal: All illnesses

Quartz, Rose: The heart

Quartz, Smoky: Depression, insomnia; known in Scotland as cairngorm

Tiger's-Eye: General purification, the throat, reproductive organs

Turquoise: All illnesses

The stones listed with the ogham alphabet in Chapter Four also may be used in healing to bring the power of any month to the patient.

Herbs

The use of herbs in healing has been a cornerstone in every civilization's search for good health. Herbs work more slowly than modern drugs but usually are much safer. Also, through the use of herbs, both the healer and the patient develop closer psychic ties with Otherworld beings.

The Celtic healers carried a *lés* (plural, *lésa*), or medicine bag, with them. In this *lés* were bags of herbs, jars of salves, bottles of potions, and other objects for healing. The lés was like a modern emergency first aid kit.

Herbal ointments were made by steeping herbs for several days or weeks in melted fat or oil. Today, the healer would use canola or almond oil in place of animal fats because animal fats tend to go rancid in a short time.

The Celts were noted for cleanliness.[12] They bathed much more often than most other people of that time. Every household had a wooden tub for nightly bathing, and they made scented soaps, such as elder flower, which softened, cleansed, and soothed the skin. Honey soap was made with soft soap, honey, and sweet marjoram. Honey was a logical ingredient in soaps as it was thought to be a great healer for cuts, wounds, and dry skin.

As part of their healing methods, the Celts also used special steam houses made of stone and roofed with heather and turf. Inside, there were wooden troughs of water into which hot stones were dropped to produce steam. Steaming was prescribed for chest congestion and rheumatism, just as saunas are today.

The Celts traded with the settlements on the European continent, as well as with the Phoenicians and other people from the Mediterranean area. Therefore, they had access to many spices and herbs that were not native to Ireland, Scotland, or Wales. Some of these spices came from as far away as India and China. This gave their healers a wide range of choices for medicinal preparations. Texts hint that they even knew of and used aromatherapy.

The Celtic women knew of and used several beauty products. They made an astringent lotion by infusing rosemary, elder flowers, and sage with wine vinegar for about three weeks. After straining the liquid, they added two tablespoons of the infusion to warm water for the skin or to use as a hair rinse. They also made a hair rinse of birch twigs infused in water. Perfumes were prepared from flower petals or herbs. A mixture of thyme and honey was chewed to sweeten the breath. Ladies darkened their eyebrows with sloe berries and colored their lips and cheeks with other berry juices.

The Celts used dandelion leaves and roots in cleansing tonics for the bladder. Lavender steeped in white wine vinegar with a pinch of rosemary was dabbed on the temples for headaches. Blackberry leaves made a good poultice for infected wounds, while the boiled roots produced an orange-yellow dye for wool. They gathered betony for fevers, bugle for ulcer poultices, and mallow root for burns and cuts. An infusion of willow leaves and bark yielded a natural form of aspirin for pain. Barley broth or water was given to the sick or infirm as a nourishing drink.

The Celts believed there were seven herbs of great benefit: ground ivy, vervain, eyebright, groundsel, foxglove, elder bark, and young hawthorn. Healers also believed that there were seven other herbs that nothing supernatural could touch or hinder: vervain, St. John's Wort, speedwell, eyebright, mallow, yarrow, and self-help. Yarrow was considered to be the best for all-round healing. All herbs gathered on May Day, or Beltane, were said to hold sacred healing powers.

While preparing the herbs or ointments, healers should use their wands[13] to draw the ogham sign of the month in the air over the preparation. This will bind the energies of the month to the medicine. If the month's energies do not seem appropriate, the healer can draw the ogham sign for Beth-Birch, or any other sign, instead. Beth-Birch is for new beginnings and works well.

All healers should encourage every patient to see a qualified medical doctor, even though the healer may be treating them at the same time. *Never* discourage anyone from seeking orthodox medical treatment. This gives the patient the best of both worlds, and keeps the authorities from arresting the healer. Shamanistic methods are complementary to orthodox methods, not opposed to them. The following list of herbs does not include any that are dangerous. Warnings are listed where appropriate.

Alder: An infusion of alder bark can be used as a gargle for sore throat or mouth infections. The bark is astringent and can cauterize sores.

Anise: For gas in adults and colic in infants, make a tea by bruising one teaspoon of anise seed in the mortar and steeping this seed in one cup of hot water for ten minutes. Give an infant only small amounts from a spoon.

Basil: Leaves can be steeped in wine as a tonic for gastrointestinal problems.

Betony: Add the leaves with other herbs to make healing creams. Added to tea, it can assist in relieving migraines. The Celts believed that betony had the power to expel evil spirits, nightmares, and depression. It was often burned for purification and protection.

Blackberry: Dried blackberries, broken into a powder, are useful in counteracting diarrhea. Add a teaspoon of the dried powder to a small amount of water and drink.

Borage: The flowers are edible and can be added to salads. Boil a handful of the leaves in two cups of water. Strain carefully through a cloth as the leaves have a hair-like covering. Sweeten with honey, and drink or gargle for hoarseness.

Catnip: A tea from this herb can be used for relaxation, much the same as chamomile. The tea is also good for shortness of breath. Celtic warriors believed that chewing catnip just before battle increased their fierceness and determination. *Do not* give to pregnant women, as this herb promotes menstruation.

Chamomile: Tea from chamomile flowers is a mild but wonderful sedative for those suffering from insomnia. It also helps with digestive troubles or calming nervousness. Add two tablespoons of flowers to a teapot for each cup of tea. Drink hot.

For stomach and intestinal upset, blend 1 oz. of chamomile flowers, 2/3 oz. of peppermint leaves, 1 oz. caraway seeds, and 2/3 oz. angelica. Steep one teaspoon of the mixture in a cup of hot water for ten minutes. Strain and drink.

Cloves: Oil of cloves helps kill the pain of toothache until one can get to a dentist. Bruised cloves can be added to chamomile tea to relieve depression. Bruised cloves added to other herbal teas can aid in relieving nausea, gas, and indigestion.

Comfrey: Beat the roots into a poultice to ease swollen joints and gout.

Dandelion: Dandelion leaves neutralize the acids in the blood and act as a cleansing tonic to the body. Put a handful of blossoms and leaves into a pint of boiling water for a tea; you may add honey to disguise the slightly bitter taste. This tea is used to reduce swelling in the ankles. Break a dandelion stalk and rub the juice directly onto warts or corns to remove them. Repeat every day. Also see Milkweed.

Dill: Bruise dill seeds with a mortar and pestle, then add the seeds to teas; this helps relieve gas, stomach cramps, and digestive troubles.

Elder Flowers: To make a soothing cream for dry, irritated skin, put five fluid ounces of almond oil and an ounce of lanolin in a kettle. Heat over hot water until the two oils melt together. Then add elder flowers until they are just covered with the oil. Heat this mixture for half an hour, stirring gently, then strain, add a little honey, and pour into sterilized jars.

Eyebright: The Celts thought this herb increased clairvoyance. Soak one tablespoon of flowers in a cup of pure water overnight. Rub a small amount on the eyelids to gain Otherworld sight during meditation.

Garlic: Peel and slightly crush a handful of garlic cloves. Boil in two quarts of pure water until one quart of the liquid has boiled away. Strain. Add a pint of honey to the hot liquid. Take a teaspoonful at a time for any cough, asthma, or shortness of breath.

Ginger: Tea made with this herb is good for treating colds and flu, as it promotes perspiration. It will also ease gas and nausea. Gelatin capsules of powdered ginger can be carried anywhere in case of stomach upset. Caution: do not use if you have a history of gallstones.

Hops: Make a small pillow containing this dried herb. It will help with insomnia and restless sleep.

Horehound: A tea made of two cups of boiling water and two tablespoons of horehound leaves will help alleviate coughs and respiratory problems.

Horsetail: To flush out an existing kidney or bladder infection, blend

1 oz. horsetail, 1/2 oz. green goldenrod, 1/2 oz. birch leaves, 1/2 oz. lovage root, and 1/4 oz. thyme leaves. Gently simmer one to two teaspoons of the mixture for fifteen minutes. Strain and drink the tea. The patient should continue to drink this tea for two weeks. *Do not* use if the patient is allergic to goldenrod.

Juniper Berries: Juniper ointment is helpful in treating scratches, itching, and festering sores. To make, you need two cups of juniper berries, two cups of almond or canola oil, and three tablespoons of beeswax. Soak the berries overnight in water, then strain them out. Simmer the berries in the oil, taking care not to let them burn. Strain out the berries and add the beeswax. Pour into small, sterilized jars. *Do not* use juniper remedies on pregnant women, as it can cause miscarriage.

Lemon Balm: A calming tea mixture can be made with 1 oz. lemon balm leaves, 1 oz. green passionflower, 2/3 oz. chamomile flowers, and 2/3 oz. St. John's Wort. Steep one to two teaspoons in a cup of boiling water for ten minutes. Strain and drink. This mixture is safe for children. The juice of the fresh leaves will also ease bee stings.

Marigold: Ointment made from marigold petals will soothe chapped skin and varicose veins. It is also helpful for dry eczema. To make, heat 2 1/2 cups of dried marigold petals with eight ounces of almond or canola oil. Simmer gently for several hours. Strain out the petals. Slowly melt two tablespoons (2 oz.) of beeswax into the oil. Pour into small, sterilized jars. The ointment is ready when the mixture sets up in a semi-hard condition. If it does not harden, reheat and add more beeswax. The Celts made marigold water from the blossoms and rubbed the mixture on their eyes to see fairies.

Marjoram: Tea made from the leaves of this herb can soothe nerves, help with colds and headaches, and promote menstruation. *Do not* use on pregnant women.

Milkweed: Rub the fresh juice from a milkweed stalk directly onto a wart to remove it. Repeat at least once a day.

Mullein: For earache, slightly warm mullein flower oil in a spoon. Dip a cotton ball in the oil and put into the ear.

Onions: Juice an onion; add the juice to a half pint of honey. Take a teaspoon of this several times a day for coughs, colds, and flu.

Peppermint: Make a tea from peppermint leaves or add peppermint leaves to other teas to aid digestion and dispel some types of headaches. It is also good for muscle cramps. To settle an upset stomach, blend 8 oz. of peppermint leaves, 8 oz. lemon balm leaves, and 8 oz. fennel seeds. Steep one teaspoonful of the mixture in a cup of hot water for ten minutes. Strain and drink.

Poplar, White: Use the juice from fresh leaves to heal skin eruptions.

Raspberry Leaves: To have an easier labor, pregnant women should drink tea made from raspberry leaves daily for the last three months of their pregnancy.

Sage: Sage tea is useful as both a rub and as a drink for fevers. To make a rub, steep 2 1/2 cups of sage leaves in a pint of hot water. Strain out the leaves. Rub over the body to reduce the fever. You can also dispel the odor of eaten onions or garlic by rubbing a fresh sage leaf across your teeth. Compresses of hot sage leaves will help with varicose veins or leg ulcers.

Sage can also be used as a tea-gargle for sore throats. Blend together 1 oz. sage leaves and 3/4 oz. fennel seeds. Pour one cup of boiling water over 2 teaspoons of the mixture. Steep for ten minutes, then strain. Use as a gargle for sore throat, or drink the tea for infections of the mouth and throat.

St. John's Wort: Internally, this herb is very good for nervous exhaustion and depression. Externally, it is made into paste with a little hot water and applied to wounds, inflammations, and sprains. The Celts of Scotland wore this herb to protect against fairy influence.

Thyme: For a sore throat and postnasal drip, drink thyme tea with a teaspoon of honey in it. This remedy will also loosen phlegm and help with shortness of breath. Hot thyme tea will also help a headache. For boils or abscesses, make a paste of moist thyme leaves and hot water; apply hot, but not burning, to the boil.

Vervain: Bladder and kidney stones should be treated by a professional. However, once they are flushed out of the body, vervain tea will aid in keeping them from reforming.

Yarrow: Yarrow tea, splashed over the body, is a good insect repellant. The flowers, added to other herbal teas, also help with canker sores. To stop bleeding and prevent inflammation, bruise the leaves and apply to wounds. *Do not* use this herb internally on pregnant women.

For more in-depth information on herbal healing, study as many books on herbs as you can find. Many good books are listed in the bibliography. Be cautious in using those herbs that can have cumulative, dangerous effects, such as wormwood or goldenseal. Avoid using the very dangerous herbs, such as foxglove, which contains digitalis. Learn all you can before prescribing for others. And never be too proud to double-check an herbal remedy.

Aromatherapy

Aromatherapy falls under the herbal category, as it relies upon the scent of essential herbal oils. These oils should not be taken internally. Instead, it is safer to use the essential oils in massage, in bathwater, or heated in special terra-cotta or ceramic vaporizers to gently scent a room. A little essential oil goes a long way, while overuse can have an adverse effect on a condition. Sweet almond oil is the best carrier when making massage oils.

Be certain to buy essential oils specifically marked for use in aromatherapy, as they are produced differently than regular essential oils.

When using essential oils in bathwater, never add more than the amount listed. Blend the oils with a little almond oil and a very small amount of alcohol so that the oils will dissolve better in the warm water. The bathwater itself should be comfortably warm and not too hot. After the bath, wrap up warmly and relax for an hour if possible.

Before using any essential oils in massage or bathwater, pretest a small amount on the skin first. People with fair hair, light skin, or those who redden quickly in the sun may be very sensitive to certain oils. It is best to start with the more gentle oils, such as chamomile, lavender, and rose.

Oils such as basil, chamomile, clary sage, cypress, fennel, hyssop, juniper, lavender, marjoram, myrrh, peppermint, rose, and rosemary will stimulate menstruation. Therefore, it is best to avoid these oils during pregnancy. Diluted oils of chamomile, lavender, and mandarin are safest for children. However, you must take care that they do not rub their eyes with oil on their hands.

It only takes a few drops (two to four drops) of oil in approximately 1 3/4 cups of water or almond oil to be effective. Too much oil can burn the skin. When using an aromatherapy diffuser or lamp, follow directions from the manufacturer. Again, a small amount of oil works best.

Abscess: Make a hot compress with lavender or tea tree oil in it, and place directly on the swelling.

Arthritis: Make an equal blend of lavender, rosemary, and tea tree oil. Add four to six drops in a bath.

Bronchitis: Put five drops of tea tree oil on a damp, warm cloth. Put this cloth on the chest and cover it with a dry towel.

For a vaporizer, use a mixture of three drops of sandalwood oil to one gallon of warm or hot water. Inhale the vapors.

Bursitis: Make a hot compress with lavender oil and apply over the affected area.

Calming: Add four to six drops of lavender oil to the bath. Use lavender-scented massage oil, particularly on the soles of the feet.

Chicken pox: There is nothing worse for a child than the itch that comes with chicken pox when the sores scab over. Most children cannot help scratching at them in this stage of the disease, which can lead to scarring. To bring some relief from the itch, mix three drops of bergamot oil and eucalyptus oil with one tablespoon of a water-based gel. Apply several times a day to the sores and scabs.

Colds and Flu: Make an equal blend of eucalyptus, lavender, and tea tree oil. At the first sign of a cold, take a hot bath with four to six drops of this oil in it. This blend can also be used in a diffuser to scent a room.

Tea tree oil is a wonderful antiseptic. It helps strengthen the immune system and prevents colds and flu or shortens the symptoms of these diseases. Use eight drops of this oil in a tub of bathwater and inhale the fumes as you bathe. The scent will help to open a stuffy nose and loosen phlegm in the lungs.

Rosemary has a crisp, clean scent when added to bathwater. Its odor is helpful in disinfecting the nasal passages and clearing the bronchial tubes. It also increases circulation and eases aches caused by fever.

Thyme oil is another wonderful antibacterial agent for use in baths. It helps with respiratory infections, colds, flu, and bronchitis.

For sinus infections, mix four drops of tea tree oil, one tablespoon of almond oil, four drops of lavender oil, and four drops of peppermint oil together. Use in a bath at the onset of the first symptoms of a sinus infection.

For encouraging sweating and to help the body eliminate toxics during a case of the flu, mix one cup of sea salt with four drops of eucalyptus oil and four drops of rosemary oil. Use this in a bath just before bedtime.

At the first signs of a cold, combine five drops of thyme oil, three drops of eucalyptus oil, and three drops of lemon oil. Put this mixture in an aromatherapy diffuser or lamp.

Disinfectant: Add several drops of tea tree oil to warm water and use to wash surfaces and the floor. This works well during cold and flu season.

Earache: Make a hot compress with lavender oil and apply to the ear.

Energy: Mix five drops of thyme oil and seven drops of bergamot oil with four tablespoons of almond oil or sea salt. Add to bathwater to stimulate the circulatory system.

Headache: Blend an equal amount of eucalyptus, lavender, and rosemary oils. Place in a small bottle and inhale as necessary. This can also be used in a diffuser.

Carry a small bottle of rosemary oil with you if you suffer from frequent headaches. Simply smelling the odor in the bottle will many times lessen or cure the headache.

Insect Bites: One drop of lavender oil to the bite will help stop itching.

Menstrual Cramps: Mix six drops of geranium oil, three drops of jasmine oil, and two drops of clary sage oil into 1 to 1 1/2 cups of whole milk. Stir into bathwater and soak in the mixture for thirty minutes.

Nasal Congestion: Inhale the scent of eucalyptus oil, and place a few drops in a diffuser to scent a room.

Pain: For neuralgia (nerve pain), mix ten drops of lavender oil with two tablespoons of St. John's Wort oil. Rub it gently onto the painful area.

Stress: Put five drops of mandarin oil and three drops of bergamot oil into a diffuser or aromatherapy lamp to scent a room.

Tension: Blend equal amounts of geranium and lavender oils. Add four to six drops in a bath. Massage oil blended with these oils can be rubbed into the neck and shoulders.

For more in-depth information on healing with aromatherapy, study as many books on the subject as you can find.

Moon Calendar and Festivals

It is important for the healer to be aware of the phases of the moon, especially the new and full moons. Many people will suffer depression and anxiety at these times. They also may contract diseases more easily, or existing diseases may take a turn for the worse during these moon phases. The seasons also affect some people, as has now been proved in scientific studies. The darker months of the year and the lowered amount of sunlight may cause depression for some. Statistics show that elders, for example, take a turn for the worse or even die more often between Samhain and the Spring Equinox. The healer must take into account as many mitigating factors as possible when working with a patient.

The ancient Celts had close connections with the land. They knew the power that flowed through the earth and manifested itself in power spots such as sacred groves or stone circles. They realized that the phases of the moon often intensified this power. They learned to watch the moon and observed how it affected people and their herds. Since the Celts' definition of wealth was the number of cattle each man had, their yearly activities revolved around their herds.

It is not surprising, then, that the Celts used a thirteen-month calendar. At first this calendar was based on the moon itself under various names. Later it became connected with the trees and their ogham alphabet. Twelve months were twenty-eight days long, with the thirteenth month being only a few days. They reckoned the count of their days from sunset to sunset, rather than from sunrise to sunrise, and celebrated all of their religious holidays the night before. They also loosely divided their year into two parts: the light half and the dark half. The light half began with Beltane and the dark half with Samhain.

Many writers cite the Coligny Calendar as Druidic. However, I agree with Robert Graves who dismissed this calendar as too Romanized to be truly Celtic.[14] The Coligny Calendar, a collection of bronze calendar plates, was found in eastern France in 1897. Robert Graves[15] was close to the truth when he reasoned that the *Lebor Gabála Érenn* held the key to the thirteen moon months of the Celts. In this tale, the bard Amairgin sets his right foot on Irish soil and declaims a poem containing thirteen images that begin with "I am."

Poem of Amairgin

I am the wave of the sea
I am the sound of the sea
I am the stag of seven tines
I am a hawk on the cliff
I am a teardrop of the sun
I am a raging boar
I am a salmon in a pool
I am a lake upon a fair plain
I am a spear that roars for blood
I am a god of inspiring fire

Each image he recites describes the characteristics of one month. Since moon months are counted from full moon to full moon, no listing would be correct except for the year in which it was made. To avoid confusion, I have corresponded each moon month in the following list to the name of a solar month. The new Celtic year always began right after the festival of Samhain, known today as Halloween.

By understanding the energy tides of each month, the healer can call upon those energies while casting spells to intensify the power of the herbs or oils and to bind those energies to the patient's body.

The Celtic Moon Months

The Cliff (October 29–31): The Celts held a close association with the sea, particularly in Ireland, Scotland, and many of the islands along Scotland's shores where the winter waves crashed against the rocks and cliffs in a thunderous noise. It is not surprising that Tech Duinn (the House of Donn, god of the dead) was believed to be on a rocky, inhospitable island off the southwest coast of Ireland. It is during this shortened "month" of only a few days that the great Celtic festival of Samhain falls. Samhain was connected with the ancestors and communicating with the dead. Another name for this month was Mid-Samonios, which means "middle of end of summer" or "Middle of Seed-Fall." The last of the seeds of wild plants fall with the harsh autumn winds and weather. The animal name for this month is Sow Moon.

The Tide (November): Irish tradition speaks of *thar naoi dtonn*, or "beyond nine waves." This refers to the idea that beyond the ninth wave lay the fluid dividing line between this world and the Otherworld, particularly the treacherous, dark power of the Fomorians, which came from their House of Tethra (*buar Tethrach*) beneath the ocean. Another name for this month was Dumannios, or "The Deepest Darkness." Dumannios also means "black month" or "dark month." During the dark of the year everything lies fallow and unproductive. However, out of this darkness of the land, animals, and even the human spirit, come the fertile seeds that will begin life anew in the spring. The animal name for this month is Bear Moon.

The Stag (December): The word *dam* in Amairgin's poem can mean either "stag" or "bull." In Modern Irish, the word means "ox." The underlying meaning of this word symbolizes struggle and victory. Stags, particularly white ones, frequently appear in Celtic legends. As magical animals, they lead the hero or heroine into the Otherworld where they encounter mystical adventures and learn important knowledge. These stags are spiritual messengers, bringing hope out of darkness. Another name for this month was Riuros, "Time of Coldness." Riuros also means "frost month"; sometimes this name is interpreted as "month of the great feast." During this month, the Celts celebrated Winter Solstice and the return of the dying sun. The animal name for this month is Wolf Moon.

The Flood (January): The Celts believed that all water originated in the Otherworld, and that this world would have no fertilizing, life-giving water unless it was released from the Otherworld realms. Water was also associated with wisdom, as in the story of the well of Segais, which was surrounded by hazel trees and their nuts of wisdom. Deities of water, especially of wells and rivers, were almost always female. The goddess Bóann tried to drink from the well of Segais and accidentally released its water, thus creating the River Shannon. Sinann was the goddess of the River Shannon itself. In a sense, the release of the waters or flood symbolizes the fertilization of the goddess of the land. Another name for this month was Anagantios, "Inability to Leave the House," or "not-going." The animal name for this month is Raven Moon.

The Wind (February): As the year moves toward the Spring Equinox, strong winds are common. The Celts believed that the health of the breath not only determined the health of the physical body, but it also was connected with the spirit or spiritual body. In Old Irish *anatlon*, "breath," is related to *anatia*, "soul," and the soul is connected in various ways to the Otherworld. The *Lebor Gabála* says that the Tuatha Dé Danann appeared out of the air or wind, borne on clouds. Thus, the Tuatha Dé Danann were viewed as spiritual beings from the Otherworld. In Welsh legend, the cauldron of the goddess Annion is kept simmering by nine maidens blowing on the fire, again the symbol of breath. The rebirth of the land and everything in it was celebrated on February 1 at Imbolc, which is closely associated with the birth of new lambs and new beginnings. Another name for this month was Ogronios, "Ice Time." Ogronios also means "end of the cold." The animal name for this month is Otter Moon.

The Sun-Tear (March): When Amairgin says he is a "drop of the sun," he is referring to the growing light of spring. The sun represents the element of Fire, a necessary spiritual ingredient in any process, physical or metaphysical, to bring life and energy to a project. The word "tear" symbolizes the gentleness of the Fire element rather than the full force of it. At this time of the year new life could not survive under the full strength of the sun, just as a new metaphysical manifestation cannot survive the full force of the Fire of energy in the beginning. Although the god Lugh symbolizes the hot summer sun, the sun goddess Grian is more appropriate for the gentle spring sunlight. Spring Equinox falls during this month. Another name for this month was Cutios, or "Wind Time." Cutios may also mean "beginning of rain." The animal name for this month is Crow Moon.

The Hawk (April): The Old Irish term *séig* was used to describe a number of different birds of prey. The dark half of the year is fast drawing to a close in March and will switch to the light half at Beltane in May. Many personal and place names in Celtic legends translate into the name of a species of hawk. One such example is found in the story of the Second Battle of Mag Tuired, where Brigit's son by Bres Mac Elathan is called Rúadán, which means "red one" or "kestrel." In the Welsh tale *Culhwch and Olwen*, the man *Gwalchmei*, or Hawk of May, helps the hero win the Flower Maiden. Another name for this month was Giamonios, "Showing Shoots." Giamonios also means "end of winter" or "end of the dark half." The animal name for this month is Heron Moon.

The Flowers (May): The newly awakened Goddess transforms Herself into the Bride and Mother at this season. The land and all creatures in it ripen and reproduce. Beltane was the beginning of the light half of the year. The fertility festival of Beltane was celebrated on May 1. Another name for this month was Simiuisionios, "Brightness Time." Another meaning for Simiuisionios may be "halfway through summer." The animal name for this month is Hawk Moon.

The Fiery God (June): The element of Fire is now at its most potent, symbolized by the blazing, hot summer sun. The light of the sun has been growing in strength since the Winter Solstice, and the days grow longer. Now the sun reaches its peak and begins its slow decline toward darkness once more. The Celts celebrated the Summer Solstice during this month. Another name for this month was Equos, which means "Horse Time" or "horse month." The animal name for this month is Eagle Moon.

The Spear (July): At this time of year the waning sun appears to cast a destructive shadow over the land. The harvest ripens and the green stalks turn brown. The spear was one of the four mystical treasures[16] that the Tuatha Dé Danann brought with them to Ireland. The spear symbolizes the lightning; the celestial spear that signals summer rains. Another name for this month was Elembiuos, or "Claim Time." Another meaning of Elembiuos may be "deer month." The animal name for this month is Horse Moon.

The Salmon (August): The sacred salmon of knowledge is one of four animals mentioned by Amairgin in his poem. Connected with the well of Segais that bubbles up from the Otherworld to become the River Boyne, the salmon ate the nuts of wisdom that fell into the well. This symbolism represents the physical harvesttime, when grain and other foods are stored for the winter ahead. Lughnasadh, on August 1, was celebrated in honor of the god Lugh and his foster mother Tailtiu. Another name for this month was Edrinios, "Arbitration Time." Edrinios also means "end of the heat," and was the first month of harvest. The animal name for this month is Hound Moon.

The Hill of the Bards (September): The very last of the harvest was gathered before the coming rains of autumn. People were now able to take part in assemblies where they listened to the bards recite ancient legends. Craft fairs were held for the purchase and exchange of goods. There was free time for song and dance while the good weather held back the crisp winds to come. The festival of the Autumn Equinox was celebrated at mid-month. Another name for this month was Cantlos, "Song Time" or "song month." The animal name for this month is Stag Moon.

The Boar (October 1–28): The last of this month marked the beginning of the dark half of the year. Cattle that could not be fed through the winter, and were not good breeders, were slaughtered and the meat salted or dried. Another name for this month was Samonios, which means "Seed-Fall." At this time of year all types of ripened seeds fall to the ground in preparation for a new crop the next spring. Samonios also means "end of summer." The animal name for this month is Salmon Moon.

In time, when the Celts became settled in one place and grew crops, they began to use the lunar and solar calendars together. However, with a lunar calendar of 364 days in a year, this left an odd day in comparison with the solar calendar. This accounts for the very old phrase of "a year and a day." To reconcile the two calendars, the Druids added an extra day every three years or so at the close of their year, which ended with Samhain.

Their original four sacred festivals were timed to the cattle rearing, seasons, and the land, and based on lunar calculations. These early religious festivals were Samhain (October 31), Imbolc (February 2), Beltane (May 1), and Lughnasadh (August 1).

Four Sacred Festivals

Samhain (October 31): This ancient feast of the ancestors survives today in the misinterpreted antics and commercialized ideas of Halloween. To the Celts, Samhain signified the end of the light half of the year and the beginning of the dark half. The veil between the world of mortals and the Otherworld was said to become very thin, allowing the spirits of the dead to temporarily return to earth and communicate with their descendants. Fairies also chose this night to ride abroad on their journeys from one *sídhe* to another. No blackberries were picked from Samhain until the next May, for tradition said they would be filled with evil spirits (negative energies). Bonfires were lit, especially at the sacred site of Tlachtga, about a dozen miles from Tara. Common hearth fires were extinguished, and then relit with embers from one of the bonfires. Doors and windows were left unlocked so that the spirits of the ancestors could enter. Food was set out in their honor. In Wales, this "feast of the dead" was called *bwyd cennad y meirw*. The apples we now use as entertainment (bobbing for apples) were a symbolic connection with the dead, for the deceased were said to eventually reach Emain Abhlach, "land of apple trees." Deities associated with this festival were Cerridwen and Mórrígán.

Imbolc (February 1): Although many people believe that this name originated from the word for ewe's milk, there is another possibility. It may have derived from *i mbolg*, which means "in the belly," an apt description for the pregnant animals. The birth of lambs heralded the first signs of the coming spring and renewed fertility of the land. Although we associate spring with green, growing things, the Celts believed everything began in darkness and moved toward the light. This is the reasoning behind their counting the days from sunset to sunset. Therefore, the new life signs that appear at Imbolc, even though they are subtle and must be sought, do signal that spring has begun. Straw dolls representing Brigit in her Mother aspect were dressed in children's clothing and laid by the hearth, a way of honoring the goddess and inviting her into the home. The threefold goddess Brigit was connected with this festival.

Beltane (May 1): Beltane ushers in the light half of the year. This was a fertility festival, as seen by the phallic maypole and the sexual freedom allowed to the young people. Irish legend says that the first Beltane fires in honor of the god Bel or Belenus were lit at Uisneach by the Druid Mide. In Welsh tradition, this festival is associated with Blodeuwedd, the Flower Maiden, who married Lleu Llaw Gyffes, a solar deity. In Ireland the Flower Maiden was called Bláthnat, which means "little flower." She was the figure of contention at one time between the hero Cú Chulainn and the king Cú Roí, who ruled over an Otherworld castle. Deities of this celebration were Bel, Blodeuwedd, and Llew Llaw Gyffes.

Lughnasadh (August 1): This festival marks the end of the four ancient feasts and most of the harvest. There were great feasts and competitive games, such as horse racing and martial arts contests. Irish tradition says that the god Lugh originated this celebration in honor of his foster mother Tailtiu, the Fir Bolg queen who died after clearing the great forests from County Meath. So the games and contests were actually funeral games, continued through the years in her honor. The Tailtiu fair (*óenach Tailten* in Old Irish) continued to be held in Teltown (named after the queen) as late as 1770. At one time this fair was the principal gathering of the O'Neill clan. Teltown marriages were sanctioned at this festival; such a marriage was a formal agreement to wed for a year and a day. The oath could be renewed, formalized into a regular marriage, or ended the next year.

Later, as the Celts settled in one place instead of roaming, they added four solar-based religious festivals, bringing the total to eight. These solar festivals were the Spring and Autumn Equinoxes, and Summer and Winter Solstices. These eight holy times were positioned on the eight-spoked Year Wheel, which symbolized the Celtic sacred world.

The Celtic calendar was not calculated differently because they were isolated and ignorant of the rest of the world. The Celts were familiar with the ideas and languages of the Greek and Roman civilizations. Although the Celts were familiar with the calendars of other cultures, they chose to adhere to a calendric dating system that was much older than other calendars, and which they brought with them from their original homeland. For example, the Druids understood the theory of the Greek Meton cycle, which is based on 235 lunar months—the time it takes the sun and moon to return to the exact same days and positions they held nineteen years before. The Druids also used a cycle based on dating from the Second Battle of Mag Tuired in Ireland. This was called a Druidic Cycle and was composed of six Lustres (thirty years).

The Celts continued the use of their own lunar-solar calendar until the arrival of the Christian Church, which then forced the use of the Roman calendar.

Sacred Wells

There are thousands of sacred wells, lakes, and other bodies of water in the Celtic lands. There are about 3,000 holy wells in Ireland alone.[17] One of the first references to a sacred healing well is found in the story of the Tuatha Dé Danann physician, Dian Cécht.

According to Irish folklore, however, not all places bearing the name of "well" are actually wells. Some are actually *bullauns*, manmade bowl-like hollows in flat stones where rainwater collects. A few are hollows in the stump of a tree; most of these are the remains of oak, ash, or hawthorn. Others are natural rock basins of fresh water along the seashore, and can be covered by the high tide.

Many of the natural springs or wells that are considered sacred break through the ground at places where powerful energy comes up through the earth. The water is permeated with this energy, thus making it a stronger purifier than usual.

However, all water, unless stagnant or polluted, has healing energy. Life cannot be sustained without water. The Celts knew this and treated water with respect.

Beside and around many of the Irish wells one can find sacred trees and special stones. The trees are primarily hawthorn, ash, hazel, holly, rowan, and yew. Some of the stones are laid out like a chair or bed for the sick to rest upon after making a pilgrimage around the well. A few of the rounded stones found near the *bullauns* were used for swearing an oath or cursing someone. To swear the oath or make the curse, these stones were dipped in the water held in the *bullaun* while reciting the correct words.

There is a concentration of energy at these sites: the rocks are reservoirs of energy, the water is permeated with it, and the trees spread the energy they take through their roots into the air. These sacred sites are powerful distributors and collectors of psychic energy.

There are thousands of other such sites around the world, many of them unknown or no longer used, because of the "superstition" now attached to them. The Celtic healer can sense the tingling power of these sites by standing quietly and opening the senses.

Water also can be blessed by the healer and used in healing ceremonies. Like fairy magic, this action often creates a subconscious reaction in the patient and accelerates the cure. Water is a symbol of the emotions. Blessed water can help to calm nervousness and anxiety. The healer can bless purified bottled water and give a small vial of it to the patient. A few drops of this water are then added to regular drinking water as a psychic tonic.

To bless water, set the purified bottle of water where the light of the full moon will shine upon it. Hold your hands over the bottle, and say a prayer to the goddess Brigit. For example, "Lovely Brigit, goddess of healing and compassion, Bless this water. Fill it with your power, that it may bring healing and wholeness to your children." Leave the bottle in the moonlight for no less than one hour, preferably three hours. Then store it in a cool, dim place.

It is also important that both the healer and patient include water as an important part of their diet and daily health rituals. Drinking plenty of water will flush toxins out of the body. However, the recommended eight glasses of water a day does not work for everyone. Some people simply cannot drink that much without feeling ill. Regular bathing and washing the hands can keep many germs at bay.

Deities associated with water, the sea, rivers, and wells are: Aer (river), Belenus (hot springs), Bóann (wells), Coventina (river), Cyhyreath (streams), Dana (wells and water), Don of Wales (wells), Dylan Eil Ton (the sea), Epona (springs), Lir (the sea), Llyr (the sea), Manannán (the sea), Manawyddan (the sea), Nantosuelta (river), Nechtan (wells), and Sinann (river).

Symbols

Certain symbols are connected with Celtic healing. Images of these symbols can be worn by the healer to denote her/his profession or used to enhance magical healing spells. They also can be used as decoration on the *lés* or clothing.

Ash wand: Shamanic wands were frequently made from ash by the Celts. The wand can be used to draw magical symbols in the ground or the air when casting a healing spell. Together with oak and thorn (hawthorn), the ash made up a triad of magical trees that were connected with the fairy realms. In Scotland and on the Isle of Man, ash wood was used to protect against black witchcraft. One famous ash tree in Irish history was the Tree of Uisneach.

Cauldron: Celtic myth tells the story of the Dagda's magical cauldron, Undry, that was brought from the city of Murias. The goddess Badb was said to have a cauldron from which flowed a constant stream of life, wisdom, and inspiration. In Wales, Cerridwen's cauldron is associated with initiation and inspiration. The gods Arawn and Bran of Wales were also connected with cauldrons. To the healer, the cauldron represents the ability to renew life. It can be used to hold a candle for candle-burning magic or as a mixing vessel when preparing herbal remedies.

Clover: The three-leafed shamrock was known as *seamraog* in Ireland. This sacred herb symbolized the triple aspect of the soul as well as the aspects of triple deities. It particularly represented the Three Mothers. It was considered to be a favorite herb of the fairies. The three-leafed clover symbolizes the healing love of the Triple Goddess and the god Trefuilngid Tre-Eochair, who was called the "Triple Bearer of the Triple Key."

Deer: The stag with its branching antlers is connected with the Lord of the Animals as well as with the Celtic Tree of Life that, like the Norse Yggdrasil, connects all levels and areas of the Otherworld. In Celtic legends, white stags often lead people on journeys into the Otherworld. The doe and stag represent messages from the Otherworld. The goddess Flidais drove a chariot pulled by deer.

Horse: The horse was highly prized by the Celts, next to the cattle. Sacred to such goddesses as Epona and Rhiannon, the horse is a symbol of freedom and stamina. In the shamanic traditions, the horse also represented the means of moving the astral body into the realms of the Otherworld.

Lés: This is the leather bag carried by all Celtic healers. It does not have to be large, just big enough to hold small bags and containers of herbal remedies. Obviously, there would be no need to carry the *lés* while at home. It would be carried while traveling or going out to help a patient. The *lés* can be decorated in any manner you wish, or left plain.

Moon: The moon symbolizes the cycles of this life and the total cycle of all lives lived. Emania, or Moon-Land, was one of the Otherworld places for the dead, before they returned in another incarnation.

The Well of Slane Meditation

General instructions for the meditations in this book can be found earlier in this chapter.

The well of Slane, used in this meditation, was an ancient healing well frequently mentioned in Irish myths. The Tuatha Dé Danann, especially Dian Cécht, Airmid, and Goibniu, used it during the Battle of Mag Tuired.

The Well of Slane Meditation

Close your eyes and visualize a brilliant white light over your head. As you inhale deeply, feel this light coursing through your body, from your head down to your toes. Feel your muscles relaxing, beginning with your feet and working up to your head. The deep sense of peacefulness moves up through your legs, into your body and arms. You feel the tenseness flow out of the muscles in your shoulders, neck, and head. You are completely relaxed.

Before you now is a river. Take all the problems in your life and throw them into the swiftly moving water. The problems are quickly carried far away from you. Leave them there, as you turn and walk away. You will be constantly protected during this meditation. Absolutely nothing can harm you.

Now see yourself in ancient Ireland, long, long ago when

only dirt roads passed through the thick forests of oak, pine, ash, and yew. These are the days of the early Celtic warriors and the Druid priests and priestesses with their vast knowledge of the universe and the earth itself.

You follow a narrow path through the forest. You can hear the birds singing in the trees and see deer watching you. Patches of wildflowers bloom in little open spaces where the sun shines through the trees. You feel at one with all nature.

Soon the path leaves the forest and enters a meadow, lush with tall grass and flowers. A lone hawthorn tree stands in the center of the meadow. You continue to follow the path until you reach the tree. You smell the delicate odor of the hawthorn blossoms as you step into the shade of the tree. Under the tree's wide, sheltering branches, you find a spring of cool water bubbling up into a low, rock-lined, circular depression. The stones are carved with circles and spirals. Green clover grows thickly around the spring, making a soft cushion under your feet.

Seated on the stone wall around this spring is a woman. She is clad in a blue dress with a blue and green woven cloak thrown over her shoulders. The cloak is fastened on one shoulder with a large, circular, bronze brooch. Her long hair is gathered into one braid down her back. On her forehead is a silver band with a crescent moon on it. From the ornate belt at her waist hangs a leather bag. She smiles at you and beckons you to sit beside her.

"This is the well of Slane," the woman says. "Do you come for a healing, or do you come on behalf of others who are in need of healing?"

You tell the woman why you have come to the well. Make your answer as truthful as possible.

The woman takes a silver chalice from the bag at her waist and dips it into the cold water of the well. She stands with the cup between her hands and prays in an ancient tongue you do not recognize. Then she slowly pours the water over your head. The water falls like liquid light over you.

Once more the woman dips the chalice into the well. This time she gives you the chalice to drink. The water tastes different than any other water you have tasted. It is a pleasant taste that fills you with peace and contentment. You feel it affecting every cell in your body with its regenerating power.

When you look up at the woman again, you see that many other men and women stand with her. Some are dressed in ancient clothing like the woman of the well. Others are garbed in different clothing. You may recognize a few of your ancestors in the group.

"You stand at the fabled well of Slane," the woman says as she motions for you to stand. "You have journeyed into the twilight lands, that place where the thin veil hangs between the worlds. Here, you will discover paths that lead far into the Otherworld. When you journey along these paths, you will find those who can teach you knowledge and understanding beyond the ken of your world. If you come with a clear purpose, you may be shown the past, the present, and the future."

You thank the woman and hand her the chalice.

She smiles and beckons to the people behind her. They come to you and introduce themselves. You are free to ask them any question you wish. You may talk with them as long as you want.

When you are ready to leave, you look up to see a white stag waiting on the path behind you. You follow the stag back into the forest until you once again reach the river. You think of your physical body and find yourself within it.

The meditation is ended.

Dress

The healer dressed much like everyone else in her/his Celtic time period. And, like all cultures, the dress mode changed from era to era. The basic dress of the early periods for men was a tunic (*léine*) reaching to the knees[18] with sleeves to the wrists, loose trousers tied at the ankles, leather shoes or ankle-high leather boots, and a cloak (called a *brat* in Ireland) that could be plain in color or a tartan-like weave.[19] The colorful pattern woven into the cloak likely designated the clan from which the healer came. Although tartans are not mentioned as such in the historical tales, evidence in archaeological digs has proven that this pattern was known and used.

Women wore a tunic similar to that of the men; however, their tunic reached to the ankles. Some female healers may have worn trousers and tunics like men, especially if they had to walk in mountainous areas or ride a horse.

The one distinguishing feature of a healer was the leather *lés*, either slung over the shoulder by a leather strap or fastened to the belt at the waist. The *lés* was probably decorated to suit the individual healer and to express her/his feelings about the connection between healing and the spiritual realms. Besides herbs, the *lés* also could contain chosen symbols that had spiritual significance to the healer.

The Celts were fond of jewelry in bronze, copper, silver, and gold. Both men and women wore torcs around their necks, wrist cuffs or bracelets, rings, and brooches. The brooches in particular were often elaborate with enameling in bright colors. The smiths who made the jewelry also fashioned metal belts, fancy buckles, and thin headbands. Much of the jewelry was set with colorful stones.

Each of the four paths is identified by a basic, predominant color. This color can identify the follower of a path to others, or can help the follower identify mentally and spiritually with the powers associated with a specific path.

I have chosen blue as the basic color for healers. Blue is a soothing hue that helps to relieve stress and open the way for healing. A true shade of blue is also associated with calmness and balanced emotions, a necessary ingredient for the healing of body, mind, and spirit.

1. The Lee or MacLee family were hereditary physicians of the O'Flaherties in West Connacht and to Brian Boroihme. Their healing book is dated about 1443. The O'Hickeys were hereditary physicians to the O'Briens, MacBrians, MacNamaras, and O'Kennedys. Their family healing book was written about 1303. The O'Shiels were hereditary physicians to the M'Coughlans and the MacMahons.
2. Dáithí Ó hÓgáin, *Myth, Legend and Romance*.
3. D. Parry-Jones, *Welsh Legends and Fairy Lore*.
4. The three civil arts were medicine, commerce, and navigation. The nine rural arts were healing, astrology, botany, theology, divination, magic, herbal medicine, music, and poetry.
5. C.J.S. Thompson, *Celtic Healing: The Healing Arts of Ancient Britain, Wales, and Ireland*.
6. R. J. Stewart, *Robert Kirk: Walker Between Worlds*.
7. Glencoe was the scene of the 1692 massacre of the MacDonald clan by the Campbells and English troops.
8. Some people with addictions are like those with illnesses who do not want to be healed. The patient must struggle as hard as the healer or the situation will never be remedied.
9. Anne Ross, *Druids, Gods and Heroes*. The trouble started when Pryderi hunted a silver-white boar and followed it into a building where he had no business going.
10. Newgrange is Ireland's best-known prehistoric monument. Found in County Meath, it sits atop a hill near the river Boyne. It is a huge mound 36 feet tall and about 260 feet in diameter.
11. Cerridwen is the Welsh counterpart of the Irish Cailleach. Both goddesses represent the Crone aspect of the Great Goddess and are often associated with the Underworld. The Crone controls death and rebirth, karma and the deeper spiritual mysteries.
12. Ammianus Marcellinus wrote of this practice in the sixth century C.E. As a Roman, he was impressed with Celtic cleanliness, which must have been refreshing after a journey among other Continental tribes.
13. For more information on making and using a wand, see Chapter Five.
14. Robert Graves, *The White Goddess*.
15. Ibid.
16. Ireland, the other three being the sword, the cauldron, and the stone.
17. Patrick Logan, *The Holy Wells of Ireland*.
18. For important occasions, such men as royalty and the Druids wore a tunic that reached to the ankles.
19. A cloak was an unsewn, large, rectangular piece of woolen cloth that was draped or pinned on one shoulder with a brooch to hold it in place, but which left the sword arm free. At night these cloaks or plaids frequently doubled as blankets. In Scottish Gaelic, the word "plaid" was *plaide*, while in Irish Gaelic it was *ploid*.

CHAPTER 3

THE WAY OF THE BARD

The bards came into existence among the Celts because of the clans' frequent moving from place to place. People who had to move to follow their cattle and horse herds from one grazing spot to another could not be burdened with fragile scrolls of written records. Written records were too easily destroyed by natural disasters, fire, war, or mildew. The safest method was to train people to commit this important data to memory. These people could then recite the information needed upon demand.

Myths, legends, and histories frequently mention the bards as an important part of ancient Celtic society. In fact, over one thousand different bards are mentioned in surviving Irish, Scottish, and Welsh literature. Thousands more bards, whose names are not mentioned, were functioning among the Celtic clans, either attached to specific households or wandering freely from place to place.

As with other professions, some bards were more gifted and knowledgeable than others. The very best bards were singled out for special honors, not because of their training or social connections, but because of their skills. Among the Irish bards, it was considered the greatest of honors to be called the Bard of Ireland. However, few were accorded this title. Among the greatest of those listed as the Bard of Ireland were Amairgin and Dallán Forgaill.[1] The greatest bard of Wales was Taliesin.

Bards were not only the keepers of memorized histories, mythologies, and genealogies, they were also trained in other shamanic practices, such as divination and the ability to journey into the Otherworld.

The term "shamanism" was never used by the Celts. Instead, the Irish Gaelic word for "vision poet" was *fili* (fee-lyee), the plural being *filidh*. In Scottish Gaelic, "vision-seer" was *taibhsear* (tah-shar), while in Welsh the term "inspired one" was *awenydd* (ah-wen-ith).

The position of bard was part of the Druid order, which in its entirety consisted of Druid (*druí* in Ireland), Ovate (*fáidh* or *fáith* in Ireland), and Bard (*fili*, singular, *filidh*, plural, in Ireland). The members of these three classes or ranks were the counselors, healers, philosophers, shapeshifters, diviners, and magicians of the Celts. Historical records say that kings frequently consulted with these wise people.

Both men and women could become members of the Druidic order. Among the Continental Celts, the word *druis* was used for a male

Druid, while *dryas* was used for a female Druid.[2] In the Old Irish language, the prefix *ban* meant female. Thus, they called a seeress or poetess a *banfhile* and a Druidess a *bandruí*. A woman satirist was described by the words *bancháinte*, *banlicerd*, and *banrindile*. It was not unusual for a woman to be a member of the Druidic orders, as seen by the frequent mention of them in legends and histories.

These three ranks of spiritual leaders were required to have *fiss* or *imbas*, which was magical and arcane knowledge. The word *fiss* is derived from *im-fhiss*, "complete wisdom." In Irish literature, a wise man was referred to as *fisidh*, which is derived from the same word. These leaders were held in such esteem that the laws demanded the same honor-price for their injuries as that of a king or clan chief. At first the duty lines between these Druidic divisions were strong. With the passing of years the lines became more blurred.

In Ireland there was a further division among the *filidh*, according to the level of training. These professional poets had to receive a total of twelve years of intensive training before they could hope to reach the highest rank, that of *ollam*. At the eighth year of training, the *filidh's* training included prophetic invocation and shamanic seeking of knowledge in the Otherworld. Protected by the law, bards could satirize anyone, king or commoner, if their ethics and behavior were unacceptable.

The Welsh bards also had to endure a lengthy training course. The top level of Welsh poets was the *pencerdd*, or chief poet. The *pencerdd* did not automatically receive this title, but had to win it through skill. The bottom of the grade was the *clerwr*, or minstrel, who usually wandered the country and did not belong to any particular household.

One psychic gift shared by all those trained by the Druidic order was "second sight." Although this talent was more highly developed by the Druids, it seems also to have been a natural, inherited trait in many Celtic people. "Second sight" includes visions, divinatory abilities, highly refined intuition, and communication with Otherworld beings.

Having *dá shealladh* ("two sights") was common in the Celtic world, and still is. It was a gift that could be trained, and once opened could not be denied, though it was often not useful personally. Second sight and divination were highly respected and the user was frequently called upon to answer questions for the clan. The bard also was taught to understand dreams, use the ogham alphabet and stones, study the flight and songs of birds, watch and understand the unusual activities of animals, use psychometry, use the *frith* of Brigit, and contact Otherworld beings.

The bard often was aware of a guardian spirit that accompanied her/him. This spirit was looked upon as a teacher or guide from the Otherworld.[3] Bards also used what we today call power animals or animal allies. Bards took journeys to the Otherworld to discover their animal allies and the nature of their guardian spirits. This seeking first of allies and guardians was a necessary practice and preparation for the longer shamanic journeys to uncover knowledge needed by the clans.

The Celts were one of the few cultures that gave equal importance to their goddesses and their gods. Probably descended from an original matriarchal culture, the Celts clung to certain goddesses long into the Christian era. For example, worship of the goddess Brigit was so deeply ingrained that the Church could not eradicate it, and so made Brigit into a Christian saint and turned her holy site at Kildare into a nunnery.

All bards sought out a goddess when they wanted a spiritual initiation or were in need of inspiration. The Welsh bard Taliesin wrote that all true initiation and inspiration came from the cauldron of Cerridwen, while Irish legends mention powerful goddesses connected with wells of inspiration that flow from the Otherworld.

Irish tradition says that the shadowy god Nechtan refused to let any women near the well he guarded; some myths say this well was the well of Segais, which contained the sacred salmon and was surrounded by the nine hazel trees. Segais was the source of all knowledge, wisdom that was apparently withheld from humans, particularly women. When Nechtan's consort, the goddess Bóann, secretly went to the well and walked three times widdershins (against the sun) around it, the waters of the well burst forth and formed the River Boyne in this world. Symbolically, the wisdom was released into the mortal world. It is not the god Nechtan who is remembered as the giver of wisdom and inspiration, but the goddess Bóann. After the release of the waters of wisdom, Bóann was known as the deity of inspired imagination and the patroness of poets and bards.

A similar legend remains about the goddess Sinann of the River Shannon. Myth says she visited the well of Connla, a source of wisdom that lay in the undersea world of Tír Tairngire. She also released the waters of this well so that the water, and the knowledge it contained, flowed into the physical world of Ireland.

Bards were not only called upon to recite history and genealogies in royal courts or those of clan chieftains. They were an integral part of all Celtic celebrations, as well as entertaining private gatherings in the evenings, particularly during the long, cold months of winter. The bards were trained to accompany their recitations or song-poems with music, because they knew how music affects the emotions and feelings of people. No Celtic gathering or celebration was considered complete without music. Originally, the common instruments were the bodhrán (drum), pipes, and bronze trumpets. Later the bagpipes and the harp were added. Although the harp is only mentioned in the later Irish stories, the bards may have used it or the Greek lyre in earlier times.

Bardic Traits

There are certain traits that a bard must cultivate to be effective in the practice of bardic responsibilities, which includes divination and shamanic seeking. Bards must have a powerful but pleasant speaking voice, an awareness of body language and the moods of those around them, respect for all laws in the country in which they live, an openness to the Otherworld and all of its creatures, and a knowledge of the correct meanings of words.

Mastery of the voice was very important to the ancient bards. Each bard perfected the natural tone of her/his voice until it was pleasant and commanded attention when necessary. The normal speaking voice was not changed into an artificial tone, but simply refined. They studied the effects of soft and loud tones and when to use each to the best advantage. They also knew the power of certain tones and chanted vowels.

All bards were aware of the mood and body language of every person who gathered to hear them. Without this ability, the bard could not hope to keep the attention of the audience. This ability carried with it an added responsibility. The bard had to be careful of the emotions she/he aroused in the audience and not inflame the people into negative action.

Respect for the laws was an important obligation of all Druidic members. No bard would use her/his power to overthrow laws unless they were against the good of the people, and then only after consulting with higher authorities. When such laws were found to be detrimental, no single bard acted alone, but acted in unison with the other Druidic orders. This rebellion against existing laws was never done because of personal opinion. The same behavior applies to any on the Celtic paths today. The opinions of a single person, religious group, or political party should never be forced on the people as a whole.

Every bard had to cultivate an openness to the Otherworld and learn how to travel through all the levels of this parallel realm. Without the essential contact with the Otherworld and Otherworld beings, the bard lost the prime source of information and inspiration. Through sources in the Otherworld, the bard could retrieve lost history, predictions of the future, and other valuable information.

Every bard, ancient or modern, must have an accurate knowledge of words and their correct meanings. Nothing is more fatal to a bard's credibility than the use of unfamiliar words in the wrong context. Words have great power when used properly. The mood the bard creates will shatter at the first misused or mispronounced word. If you are not certain about the meaning of a word, do not use it. No bard should fill her/his speech with elegant sounding words with which the majority of the audience is not familiar. Such action makes the bard appear pompous, a detriment to keeping an audience's interest.

Mythic Bards

Celtic legends have many examples of Druidic prophets. Caicher was a Druid of the Milesians, the invading race that wrested Ireland from the Tuatha Dé Danann. He prophesied that the Milesians would conquer Ireland.

Cathbad was the chief Druid at the court of Conchobar mac Nessa. In the Ulster Cycle he predicted the birth of Deirdre and the troubles that would follow her in life. He also prophesied the luckiest day for Cú Chulainn to take up arms, but added that the hero would die young.

The grandfather of Cormac mac Airt was a Druid who divined the best day for his grandson, Fionn mac Cumhaill, to seek the kingship of Tara. Finnéces ("fair seer") took Fionn as a pupil when the boy was only seven years old. While under his care and tutelage, Fionn ate the Salmon of Wisdom. Later, Fionn mac Cumhaill was initiated by Scáthach, the famous teacher of marital arts.

The most famous and best-known bard is Taliesin Pen Beirdd of the Welsh tradition. It is thought that he was a man who lived in the second half of the sixth century. Through his surviving poetry, Taliesin reveals much about shamanic practices and magical powers. He clearly states that he received his wisdom and power from the cauldron of Cerridwen, a journey which would require visiting the Otherworld.

Another famous Welsh "vision singer" was Myrddin (Merlin), who periodically left civilization to live in the deep forests, communicate with animals, and gain inspiration for foretelling the future. His story is far older than the Arthurian sagas.

Other historic bards were Amairgin of Ireland and Llywarch Hen (Llywarch the Old) from Wales who wove webs of words.

Coinneach Odhar lived during the 1500s in Scotland and was called the Brahan Seer. He was able to see into the future and make accurate predictions. His prophecies included the Battle of Culloden, the Highland Clearances, and the arrival of railroads. However, when he predicted to the Countess of Seaforth that her husband was unfaithful and that the family line would end, the Countess had him burned alive in a tar barrel.

All bards generally received their initiation and wisdom from goddesses or wise women. After this initiation, they regularly journeyed deep into the Otherworld for visions and prophecies. All mortals who frequently took these journeys were known as Walkers Between the Worlds.

Ogham Alphabet

The Celts believed all things were connected and had extremely close ties to everything in nature. Trees held a strong, religious significance for them. All trees were thought to hold memories of history and lore and to be filled with magical energies. These energies often attracted Otherworld beings, which sometimes took up residence in certain trees and groves. For these reasons, trees and groves of trees were very sacred, particularly if they were oak, ash, yew, holly, or hawthorn.

The Celts also had the concept of the Tree of Life, a common shamanic symbol used in many cultures to symbolize the connecting link between all the worlds. However, the Celts in early Ireland took this concept one step further. Each clan chieftain had a specially designated sacred tree within his territory. This tree, or *bile*, was believed to have a direct connection with the Otherworld, the deities and beings who lived in the Otherworld, and the ancestors. The chieftain's royal scepter was made from a branch of this tree to represent his right as ruler. It was a sacrilege to cut down or mutilate this clan-tree. However, when one clan warred against another, the *bile* was often the focus of destructive hostility.

In Scotland today, one can still find certain groves of trees known as Bell Trees, a variation of the old Gaelic *bile*. Tradition says these special trees, always situated near a spring, are the remnants of ancient sacred groves.

In Wales, the name of a sacred meeting hill was a *Gorsedd* in ancient Cymric. A *Gorsedd* was usually crowned with a grove of trees. Parliament Hill in northern London was once such a meeting place; a spring that rose on its flank has since been diverted and the grove was cut down long ago.

At one time oak groves covered almost all of Ireland, providing forage for the wild pigs and protection for other creatures. The oak was considered to have strong magical powers. The Celts used oak wood to make butter churns, stables for their cows, and some furniture. They believed this protected their animals, food, and the people in the house from malevolent influences.

Other trees, such as the holly, yew, ash, and hawthorn, also grew in Ireland. The hawthorn was connected specifically with the fairies, especially if it was a tree growing alone in a clearing or field. These lone hawthorns were never cut for fear of insulting the fairies or Otherworld entities. Today, many people in Ireland still refuse to cut down a lone hawthorn for fear of the bad luck that may follow.

With the Celtic reverence for trees, it is not surprising that the ancient tree calendar of the Celts is connected with their sacred ogham alphabet, which was, according to legend, given to them by Ogma, god of eloquence, and from which this alphabet derives its name. Legend says that this alphabet was first used when Ogma sent a warning to Lugh by writing the letter for birch. This early Irish alphabet can be traced back in usage to circa 600 B.C.E. and is sometimes called the Beth-Luis-Nuin alphabet.[4]

A form of the Celtic ogham is found in northeastern Scotland, or the Kingdom of Argyll, where the Picts carved their version of the alphabet onto stones. As of this date, the Pictish alphabet remains undeciphered.

The ogham alphabet letters are written in straight lines that bisect or meet a central long line or stem. Bards were the primary users, and sometimes employed this alphabet for passing coded messages. However, the alphabet was also considered to be a repository of accumulated knowledge, for the letters were not only linked with trees, but with people, places, and objects. In this context the Druidic orders used the ogham in their magic. (See Appendix 1 for a description of the ogham alphabet.)

Each month of the Celtic year was named for a tree. Each tree-month was represented by an ogham letter. The trees themselves were divided into three classifications: Chieftains, Peasants, and Shrubs. These classifications have nothing to do with size, but rather the importance the Celts ascribed to them. The eight Chieftains are alder, oak, hazel, vine,[5] blackthorn (sloe), furze, and heather. The eight Peasants are birch, rowan, willow, ash, hawthorn (whitethorn), holly, and apple. All other trees are Shrubs. Two of the symbols are not trees: the Grove and the Sea. These symbols are an acknowledgment of the power of the sea, which was ruled by Manannán mac Lir, and an acknowledgment of the extreme sacredness of groves of trees.

The letters are also divided into five groups of five letters each. One grouping is called the Crane Bag and alludes to the sacred crane bag owned by Manannán mac Lir, god of the sea.

Early Irish texts, particularly the *Dunaire Fionn*, tell the story of Manannán who made the bag from the skin of a sacred crane[6] and filled it with the King of Scotland's shears, the King of Lochlainn's helmet, the bones of Assail's swine, Goibniu's smith-hook, his own shirt, and the backbone of a great whale. All these things are actually symbols for the ogham letters in this grouping. These letters in the Crane Bag appear to have been derived from Greek. They supply sounds that were lacking in the Consaine Ogham, the earliest form of this alphabet.

In writing, these straight-line letters were cut along a sharp edge, line, or "stem" into wood or stone. This simple construction of the alphabet letters made it possible to use the alphabet as a sign language, with the nose, arm, shin, or any straight edge used as the stem against which the letters were formed. Legend and history indicate that the Druids used the alphabet in this manner as a symbolic code when they wished to pass along secret messages.

Certain letters do not appear in the Celtic ogham alphabet. The letters J and Y are written as I and are connected with Ioho or Yew, while the letter P is represented by Phagos, or Beech. Z is replaced by the Ss sound found in Straif, or Blackthorn. W (a double U) is connected with Ur, or Heather, and V is represented by Fearn, or Alder. The letter XI of Mór, or the Sea, replaces X. In Gaelic, the letter C is always sounded as a hard "K" (Celtic, *kell*-tik), so it is possible to substitute the ogham letter C for a K.

Some of the ogham letters are not connected with months. They are, however, an important part of the alphabet and divination system.

This alphabet was also used for divination by cutting or painting the letters on flat sticks of wood. The sticks could be drawn and read as one would read the tarot cards or rune stones. This is borne out in the Welsh tales of Taliesin in which the bard says that he was well acquainted with every *sprig* in the cave of the arch-diviner. Ancient Welsh documents tell of the *coelbreni* or *coel bren*, or omen sticks,[7] which were marked with twenty-two of the forty runes listed in the Welsh *Barddas*, a book containing ancient knowledge. These sticks, with the ogham letters cut into them, were cast on the ground and predictions made from the way they fell. The ogham sticks were consulted especially at the eight sacred festivals of the Celtic year.

This method of divination is still applicable today. The ogham letters may be carved or painted on small flat sticks or drawn on squares of stiff paper. After being mixed thoroughly in a bag, the diviner withdraws the required number of oghams. These may be laid out like tarot cards or in any known divination pattern.

Another method is to draw nine sticks. Lay these in groups of threes as they are drawn. The left-hand group is the future, the middle the present, and the right-hand group the past.

Before beginning an ogham reading, the bard/diviner should offer a prayer to either the god Ogma or the goddess Bóann for guidance and inspiration. Questions should not be frivolous. They should be important to the person making the inquiry, such as guidance and direction on certain decisions, goals, or life paths.

Doing a reading with ogham sticks also can help the healer determine what may lie behind a patient's illness. When an illness defies healing, oftentimes the healer must look to past lives for the reason. If possible, the healer should ask the oghams for guidance, then journey into the Otherworld for greater details.

In dealing with illnesses caused by something in a past life or lives, one must first determine what happened, then seek a remedy that goes beyond bodily healing. This takes the healer into the realm of magic, for magical symbols and remedies are the only thing understood by the subconscious and superconscious (genetic)[8] minds of a person. Celtic folklore talks of fairy magic as being able to heal stubborn diseases. This magic is made only with the aid of Otherworld beings.

Ogham letters can also be carved into candles for candle-burning magic or written out on paper when making a request to certain deities. These papers are usually burned on an altar with the requests rising into the Otherworld along with the smoke.

Technically, each tree-month should be divided according to the date of the full moon. However, this varies from month to month and year to year. This makes it impossible for any lunar calendar to be accurate past the current year. To simplify the matter, I have divided the months according to solar months, except for the thirteenth month, which is only a few days long.

The Celtic year ended with Ruis or Elder month, which began on the evening of October 28 and ended on the evening of October 31. The new year began with Beth or Birch month, on November 1. This supports the belief that the Celtic calendar was a lunar one, because most solar calendars begin and end with the Winter Solstice in December.

The Ogham Alphabet

├ *Beth-Birch*

Month: November

Color: white

Class: Peasant

Letter: B

Deity: The Dagda, Gwydion, Myrddin, Taliesin

Planet: Sun

Stone: Clear quartz crystal. Practitioners of the magical arts in medieval Europe believed that if a crystal was cut a certain way, then exposed to the sun, it could make any solid object invisible. Celtic myths tell of Druids using crystals to make themselves invisible and traveling great distances.

Meaning: New beginnings are arriving. A fresh start is now possible; make the most of it. Something or someone different is entering into your life.

├ *Luis-Rowan*

Month: December

Color: red and gray

Class: Peasant

Letter: L

Deity: Banba, the Dagda, Macha, Myrddin, Scáthach, Taliesin

Planet: Uranus

Stone: The Druids use peridot to strengthen the mind and protect.

Meaning: You are protected. You must take care to ward off control by others. Now is the time to gain control in your life.

⨎ *Fearn-Alder*

Month: January

Color: crimson

Class: Chieftain

Letter: F, V

Deity: Badb, Bran, Mórrígán, Scáthach

Planet: Mars

Stone: Ruby is worn to protect against plagues and also to give courage and virility. Red garnet is used for protection, victory, and tranquility.

Meaning: You will receive intuitive hunches and spiritual guidance in making choices.

⨎ *Saille-Willow*

Month: February

Color: bright (Tradition does not elaborate on a specific color)

Class: Peasant

Letter: S

Deity: Anu, Arianrhod, Branwen, Brigit, Dana, Rhiannon

Planet: Moon

Stone: A lucky charm to the Celts and Druids, the moonstone, or selenite, brought victory, prosperity, and wisdom to the owner. They believed that the stone changed color and light intensity with the changing phases of the moon.

Meaning: Secrets are uncovered; be prepared. Balance is needed.

ᚋ Nuin-Ash

Month: March

Color: grass-green

Class: Chieftain

Letter: N

Deity: Arianrhod, the Dagda, Gwydion, Manannán mac Lir, Mórrígán

Planet: Neptune

Stone: The Celts carried coral as a talisman against drowning. Aventurine releases fear and attracts good luck.

Meaning: Circumstances lock you into an event or relationship; you are feeling bound.

ᚆ Huathe-Hawthorn

Month: April

Color: purple

Class: Peasant

Letter: H

Deity: Arianrhod, Cernunnos, the Dagda, Dana, Lugh, Mórrígán

Planet: Vulcan[9]

Stone: The Celts used topaz, associated with the sun, to bring good health, prosperity, long life, and intelligence.

Meaning: You will be frustrated, for no movement is visible. This is a cycle of waiting for change.

ᚇ Duir-Oak

Month: May

Color: dark brown and black

Class: Chieftain

Letter: D

Deity: Beli, Blodeuwedd, Branwen, the Dagda, Myrddin, Taliesin

Planet: Jupiter

Stone: The Irish Druids carried emerald as an antidote to all poisons.

Meaning: Solid protection is all around you. Doors now open that were once closed.

⽇ *Tinne-Holly*

Month: June

Color: dark gray

Class: Peasant

Letter: T

Deity: Anu, Áine, Beli, the Dagda, Dana, Lugh

Planet: Earth

Stone: The word "diamond" comes from the Greek *adamas*, "invincible." The Druids, who knew much about Greek spiritual beliefs, considered the diamond to be associated with supernatural forces. Tiger's-eye protects against ill-wishing and tears away all veils of illusion, revealing the truth.

Meaning: You will be triumphant in an endeavor. You gain confidence to move ahead.

⽇ *Coll-Hazel*

Month: July

Color: brown

Class: Chieftain

Letter: C, K

Deity: Bran, Brigit, Cerridwen, the Dagda, Goibniu, Lugh, Ogma, Scáthach

Planet: Mercury

Stone: A favorite stone in many ancient cultures, red carnelian was used as a talisman against lightning strikes and as a protection against malicious spirits when working within the Otherworld.

Meaning: Intuition will lead you into the way you need to go. Creative energy abounds.

⫲ *Quert-Apple*

Month: none

Color: green

Class: Shrub

Letter: Q

Deity: Arianrhod, Cernunnos, the Dagda, Gwydion, Lugh, Taliesin

Planet: Saturn

Stone: Hematite will break up negativity and help with reevaluation of the life patterns.

Meaning: A choice must be made; you are standing at a crossroads in life.

⫟ *Muin-Vine*

Month: August

Color: variegated

Class: Chieftain

Letter: M

Deity: Brigit, Cerridwen, the Dagda, Lleu Llaw Gyffes, Lugh, Ogma

Planet: Venus

Stone: Like the Greeks and Romans, the Celts believed that wearing amethyst would prevent the owner from becoming drunk. The stone was also carried to improve the memory.

Meaning: This is an important time to plan for the future. Otherworld messages come in dreams and from strangers.

⫠ *Gort-Ivy*

Month: September

Color: sky-blue

Class: Chieftain

Letter: G

Deity: Badb, Brigit, Cerridwen, Dana, Gwydion, Pwyll, Taliesin

Planet: Jupiter

Stone: The opal derived its sinister association with bad luck from the time of the Black Plague. Before that, the ancient cultures looked upon opal as a very lucky stone. The Druids called it a symbol of hope. Lapis lazuli was used in Sumer as long ago as 2500 B.C.E. It increases mental clarity and psychic abilities.

Meaning: A time of introspection, you need to find your personal spiritual path.

 *NgEtal-Reed*

Month: October

Color: grass-green

Class: Shrub

Letter: Ng

Deity: Arianrhod, Bran, the Dagda, Manannán mac Lir, Mórrígán

Planet: Pluto

Stone: Red jasper was considered a powerful amulet for protection. However, the Druids believed that black jasper helped them to raise storms.

Meaning: Upsets or surprises will take you unaware. You must take a stand on a problem or issue that has not been resolved.

Straif-Blackthorn

Month: none

Color: purple

Class: Chieftain

Letter: Ss, Z, St

Deity: Efnisien, Gwydion, Macha, Myrddin, Pwyll, Taliesin

Planet: Neptune

Stone: Azurite cuts through illusions to the truth. It also helps in work toward self-transformation.

Meaning: Because of your refusal to see the truth, you are besieged by lies and illusions.

ⵝ *Ruis-Elder*

Month: the makeup days of the thirteenth month, beginning on the evening of October 28 and ending on the evening of October 31.

Color: red

Class: Shrub

Letter: R

Deity: Badb, Cailleach, Cerridwen, Dana, Donn, Gwydion, Myrddin

Planet: Saturn

Stone: Jet, once called black amber, has been used as an amulet since prehistoric times. The Druids used it to exorcise any malicious spirits. However, it was also used to bring wishes and desires into being. Black onyx was used at least 5,000 years ago. It absorbs negative energy and brings balance.

Meaning: You are faced with the end of one cycle and the beginning of another. Solutions to problems present themselves in an unexpected manner.

ⵞ *Ailim-Silver Fir*

Month: none

Color: light blue

Class: Shrub

Letter: A

Deity: Arianrhod, the Dagda, Manannán mac Lir, Mórrígán, Pwyll

Planet: Moon

Stone: Fluorite helps to connect with the Akashic records.[10] Malachite removes subconscious blockages from other lives.

Meaning: The past holds clues to present problems.

ⵟ *Ohn-Furze*

Month: none

Color: yellow-gold

Class: Chieftain

Letter: O

Deity: Badb, Blodeuwedd, the Dagda, Dana, Taliesin

Planet: Mercury

Stone: Smoky quartz helps with discrimination and getting rid of unproductive parts of life. Red garnet increases the intuition and focus.

Meaning: Important information comes your way. Take action and seek for the answers you need.

‡ *Ur-Heather and Mistletoe*

Month: none

Color: purple

Class: Heather is Peasant; mistletoe is Chieftain.

Letter: U

Deity: Airmid, Bóann, Brigit, Cernunnos, the Dagda, Dian Cécht, Lugh, Miach, Nuada

Planet: Venus

Stone: Amazonite can align the physical, mental, and spiritual bodies. Lodestone attracts good fortune.

Meaning: Healing of the entire body, mind, and spirit is possible at this time. Get a second opinion on important issues.

‡ *Eadha-White Poplar or Aspen*

Month: none

Color: silver-white

Class: Shrub

Letter: E

Deity: Badb, Dana, Macha, Mórrígán, Ogma, Pwyll

Planet: Mars

Stone: Jade helps to solve problems and create harmony.

Meaning: Problems that arise can be quickly solved. You lack trust in yourself or someone close to you.

‡ *Ioho-Yew*

Month: none

Color: dark green

Class: Chieftain

Letter: I, J, Y

Deity: Cerridwen, the Dagda, Dian Cécht, Manannán mac Lir, Ogma

Planet: Saturn

Stone: Amethyst cuts through illusions and gives victory. Tourmaline helps to work through a problem to the end.

Meaning: A complete change in your life path or opinions is upon you. Events bring about a sudden rebirth of optimism or spirit.

✗ *Koad-the Grove*

Month: none

Color: many shades of green

Class: none

Letter: Ch, Kh, Ea

Deity: Badb, Brigit, Cerridwen, the Dagda, Scáthach, Taliesin

Planet: Earth

Stone: Sugilite opens the subconscious mind to higher influences. Moss agate helps in meditation and opening the Third Eye.

Meaning: You can find the knowledge you seek in the spiritual center at this time. Some newly discovered information about past events and circumstances surprises you.

◊ *Oir-Spindle*

Month: none

Color: white

Class: Peasant

Letter: Th, Oi

Deity: Badb, the Dagda, Dana, Myrddin, Taliesin

Planet: Moon

Stone: Chalcedony aids in releasing problems. Smoky quartz breaks up subconscious blockages.

Meaning: Decisions must be made and problems dealt with, or you cannot move forward. Understanding may come in a flash of enlightenment.

Uilleand-Honeysuckle

Month: none

Color: yellow-white

Class: Peasant

Letter: P, Pe, Ui

Deity: Don, Macha, Mórrígán, Ogma, Pwyll

Planet: Mercury

Stone: Bloodstone gives self-confidence. Spectrolite helps to handle improbable situations.

Meaning: Be cautious in what you say or do.

⚲ *Phagos-Beech*

Month: none

Color: orange-brown

Class: Chieftain

Letter: Ph, Io

Deity: Beli, Brigit, Cerridwen, the Dagda, Dana, Taliesin

Planet: Mars

Stone: Goldstone gives energy. Tiger's-eye aids in attracting good luck.

Meaning: New knowledge will help you reach your goals.

⊞ *Mor-the Sea*

Month: none

Color: blue-green

Class: none

Letter: Ae, X, Xi

Deity: Arianrhod, the Dagda, Don, Dylan, Gwydion, Lir, Llyr, Manannán mac Lir, Manawyddan, Mórrígán

Planet: Venus

Stone: Aquamarine clears the mind and banishes doubts and fears.

Meaning: A journey is in the near future. If you are not careful, your emotions may take you for a ride.

Divination

Divination is a process in which a bard listens for the voices of deities or supernatural teachers to access ordinarily inaccessible knowledge in order to see beyond the present into the future. According to Celtic legends, oracular powers many times are opened and intensified after contact with the Tuatha Dé Danann of the Otherworld, because the Tuatha were known as powerful enchanters and magicians.

The Celts had many methods of divination. The association of divination and water is frequently mentioned in Celtic stories. Cauldrons, wells, springs, hot springs, and rivers were thought to be natural containers of liquid that flowed from the Otherworld. Five streams of sacred water were said to flow from the well of Segais; both these streams and the five salmon in the well represented the five physical senses. This well was associated with the goddess Bóann. Deities of inspiration are almost all female, such as Bóann, Cerridwen, and Brigit.

Foreseeing, sometimes called scrying, is an old method of seeing into the future by means of water in a black cup or bowl, a crystal ball, black mirror, or polished onyx slab. By gazing into the scrying object, the conscious mind's attention is diverted and the subconscious mind can evoke pictures or symbols. Some people see scenes in the scrying device itself, while others see the pictures or symbols in the mind.

To use a scrying device, it is best to cover a table or area with a dark colored cloth to act as a neutral background. The color black is the least intrusive. Set the scrying device on this cloth. Be certain that the table is at a height that does not produce strain while you are gazing into the device. Relax, blink your eyes if necessary. Staring without blinking will give you a headache and produce few results. Allow your eyes to defocus and open your mind to Otherworld messages. If you are worried about the truthfulness of the messages or your mental "safety," begin by asking that white light surround and protect you. You may also wish to call upon one of the ancient Celtic deities for aid. The goddess Brigit and the god Ogma are excellent helpers.

Do not practice more than five minutes at a time in the beginning. Do not fret if you see no pictures. Your psychic abilities may be more in the realm of mental impressions or intuition. The scrying device will strengthen your abilities the more you practice.

A small cauldron filled with water can also be used for scrying. The procedure is the same as with a crystal ball or black mirror. The Celts also believed the cauldrons in themselves were very sacred. Because of this identification with the spiritual, cauldron images were used to explain the significance of balance in the human life.

The Celts believe there are three cauldrons, or realms of spiritual insight within each person. The *Anecdota from Irish MS. Vol 5*, or "The Cauldron of Poesy," mentions these three cauldrons. These cauldrons are founts of inspiration and art, directly connected with the soul. The cauldrons are the Cauldron of Warming (*Coire Goiriath*), the Cauldron of Vocation (*Coire Ernma*), and the Cauldron of Knowledge (*Coire Sois*).[11] Few people learn how to access these cauldrons. However, the seeker on the path of the bard should learn to psychically access them. By balancing your own cauldrons, you are better prepared for spiritual insight.

The Cauldron of Knowledge is in the head, and gives spiritual and artistic gifts. The Cauldron of Vocation is in the heart; it gives psychic health and helps to bridge ordinary and Otherworld realities. The Cauldron of Warming is in the belly, and maintains physical vitality and power. All of these are activated by a quest for knowledge and Otherworld journeys.

Bards access these cauldrons in order to bring spiritual balance to their lives. It is extremely difficult to balance another's cauldrons, particularly if that person is not willing to make life changes. If psychic sight reveals that the bard's personal cauldrons are tipped or upside-down, she/he needs to journey to the Otherworld for aid in correcting the situation.

There are three shamanic-type divinations listed in the Celtic legends by which bards gain answers to questions. They were the *imbas forosnair*, the *teinm laída*, and the *dichetal do chennaib*.

The definition of *imbas forosnair* is "great poetic illumination" in Ireland. This divinatory practice involved a meat offering given to the spirits by the poet or bard, and shared by the bard, who then sang a call to the spirits. If they did not give her/him the answer she/he sought, the next step was to lie down in a dark place with the hands over the eyes in preparation for an Otherworld journey. At the end of a specified period, the bard was brought suddenly into the light. Legends say that Scáthach performed this divinatory ritual, as did Fionn mac Cumhaill. In *The Cattle Raid of Cooley*, Queen Medb asks the seeress Fedelm if she can do this.

Modern interpretations of this ancient method are the use of meditation and asking for guiding dreams.

Teinm laída means "burning song or chant," although some writers give the meaning as "chewing the pith." The *fili* sought an answer to a question by trance singing or chanting. She/he sang a repetitive song about the question to bring up images and impressions. Fionn mac Cumhaill used this method by sticking his thumb in his mouth and chewing it in the tales of the Fenian Cycle.

In modern terms, this method is equivalent to chanting an appropriate short verse three or five times before using a divination device, such as the ogham sticks. You may write your own chant or use the following one.

Open the door to the Otherworld. Guide me, I do ask you.
All you gods of the ancient Celts, send me omens true.

The third shamanic method is *dichetal do chennaib*, "extempore incantation." Some descriptions in legends seem to indicate that bards used their finger joints as reference points to interpret the ogham alphabet letters. Each ogham letter had several poetic meanings or allusions. Other legends indicate that this shamanic method is simply the use of psychometry. By touching a person with the fingers, hand, or staff, the bard could use psychometry to seek the answer. Extempore composition was regarded as the only true test of the *fíorfhile* (true poet) in Ireland. In other words, the psychometric message received was changed into verse and chanted to the person for whom the bard was reading.

Learning psychometry, or reading the vibrations of objects, is simply a matter of practice. Most people have no difficulty at all in learning this method. At one time or another all humans have picked up something or gotten into a car and immediately become uneasy.

"Something doesn't feel right," is the usual comment in such a situation. As soon as you distance yourself from the object causing your unease, you feel better. You were responding to vibrations.

To do psychometry, hold a small object belonging to someone else in both hands, one hand over the other. Relax and let the impressions surface in your thoughts. The impressions may come to you as colors, symbols, feelings, emotional impressions, or actual pictures. Do not try to analyze whether these are correct or not. Analyzing will bring the conscious mind into dominance and shut off the psychic impressions. Simply tell the listener what you are seeing and feeling. You may be surprised to learn that your impressions have deep meaning to the owner of the object.

Fith-fath (fee-faw) is a term heard in Scotland, particularly in the Highlands.[12] It is also given as fath-fith, which loosely translates as "the deer's cry." The *fith-fath* is the name for a spoken charm or incantation that is supposed to make the chanter invisible by changing the outward appearance. The usual form given by the *fith-fath* was that of a deer. However, other forms were used, such as a horse or a bull by men, or a cat or a hare by women.[13] This technique was primarily used by hunters, warriors, and travelers. The *fith-fath* is related to the Irish charm known as the lorica (breastplate charm). Celtic saints, including Patrick, are said to have used the *fith-fath*.[14]

In Ireland, the *féth fíada* is derived from *féth*, "mist, fog," and *fíada*, "master, possessor." Also known as *ceo draoidheachte* (Druid's fog), it described a magical fog or mist that covered the chanter and made her/him invisible. Legend says this power was given to the Tuatha Dé Danann by Manannán mac Lir after they were defeated by the Milesians. Later, it was believed that the gift was used by Celtic saints, such as Patrick, who wrapped himself and his companion Benén in the fog to escape enemies. Those waiting in ambush only saw a deer and fawn. The charm became known in these later times as Patrick's Breastplate.

The principal use of the *fith-fath* was for protection. However, it could be used in other ways. One of these ways, still used in Celtic countries, was to invoke a prayer that encompassed the home, family, and animals. *Airbe druad* was a protection cast by a Druid around a settlement or army.

According to folklore and legend, the *frith* of Brigit was an important form of divination. The seer, or *frithir*, walked around the household three times in bare feet at sunrise, ending at the threshold of the main door. With eyes closed, she/he placed one hand on the jamb and chanted a prayer to the goddess Brigit. Then she/he curled the hands into a "tube" through which the seer looked. This blocked out light and focused the seer's mind. Usually the seer interpreted what she/he saw as *rathadach* (lucky) or *rosadach* (unlucky). Sometimes the seer carried a small magical stone known as "the stone of quests," which was said to aid in the seeing.

Birds flying toward the house meant news; a duck meant a safe voyage for sailors. An animal lying down represented illness, while a raven signified death. Sometimes the color of animals, particularly horses, had special meanings: a bay horse for burial, a brown for sorrow.[15]

Another use of the tube made by the hands is mentioned in an eleventh-century text. In this manuscript it says that the *fili* were taught to recite spells, one of which was a spell to recover stolen cattle. The spell was chanted three times through the fist of the right hand while bending over the track of the thief or animal. The answer was said to come in a dream.

The hands were used in many Celtic spells. One such enchantment to tame a stallion was to recite the spell into the palm of the right hand, then rub the palm on the horse's rump.

Birds played a major part in the Celtic divination techniques that interpreted events through animals and their actions. The raven was always considered to be an evil omen of misfortune, primarily because of ravens' connections to goddesses of war and death. The Druids and diviners also watched wrens. The wren name of *drean* probably comes from *druí-én*, which means "druid bird." Wrens were considered sacred at one time because of their connection to the Druids. The later custom of hunting and killing wrens was probably initiated by the Christians as a method of destroying anything that was once sacred to a Pagan group.

A widely used method of the Druids was divination by weather watching. Cloud watching, or *néladóir*, is specifically mentioned in *The*

Siege of Druim Damgaire. We do not know if the Druids watched for symbolic shapes in the clouds or determined their prediction according to how the clouds moved. We do know that they gave each of the winds a specific name and color.[16]

Dreams and visions were an important part of Celtic life, as were their interpretations. Dreams were simply interpreted with no attempt made to change their meaning. On some occasions, however, the bard would attempt to make change by taking an Otherworld journey into fairyland. The story *The Adventures of Nera* has an example of such a journey.

Symbolic scenes, symbols, and actions in dreams have different meanings to different people; therefore no book on dream interpretation can be completely accurate. What may have negative connotations to one person will be a positive sign to another. Dream books frequently list cats as negative dream symbols. To a cat lover, this interpretation would not be accurate.

Some dreams are prophetic in nature. If you keep a dream journal for a time, you will soon recognize which dreams are prophetic and which are not, which symbols and symbolic actions repeat themselves. Prophetic dreams have an entirely different "feel" to them. You may understand where this will happen, the event, the emotions surrounding the event, and possibly the people involved, but will not know the date or time. These dreams rarely can be changed through creative dreaming.

Ancient legends also mention seers spending the night on certain mounds in order to access information. It seems that many ancient burial sites had guardian spirits that would converse with the seer in dreams. Either the burial sites were built deliberately over power spots, or the site itself created a power spot. In either case, it seems that the site opened a door into the Otherworld.

In ancient Scottish literature there is mention of spae-wives or seeresses who had a special connection with the Underworld and its beings. These women all bear names that contain the word *urlair* ("of the floor"). When they called upon the Lord of the Underworld for help in divination, they would strike the earth or floor three times to summon him.

Although interesting historically, most ancient methods in their original form are not practical today. However, one truth still holds: the power of the voice can bless or curse, not by the words, but by the intent.

Fairy Magic

The Celts had strong ties to fairies and Otherworld beings and recognized them as part of the land and all creation. They were aware of the differences between nature spirits, Otherworld beings, and fairies. Some they treated with caution, while others were warmly greeted and looked to for direct aid in life.

Fairies originally were viewed as full-sized beings, not the tiny, winged creatures of the Victorian Era. Since fairies tended to be insulted easily, the Celts referred to them by other names, such as the Gentry or the Good Folk. Most Celts were farmers, and as such had no wish for the fairies to cause sickness in their cattle, sour the butter in the churn, create sterility in themselves or their animals, or cause a bad harvest. To ward off unintentionally insulted Gentry, the Celts relied on oak wood stalls and doors, holy water, or the four-leafed clover. Most fairies were viewed as beautiful, magical beings who could be enticed into granting good fortune if they were treated properly. The fairies became associated with the *sídhe*, or mounds, which were said to be their dwelling places, and the mounds were eventually referred to as *sídhe*.

The Irish Celts knew the fairies as the *Sídhe*, or mound-spirits; sometimes they called them the *Feadh-Ree*, which is a form of the ancient Persian word *Peri*, that may be the origin of our word fairy and is pronounced similarly. However, the Celts thought it best to call the fairies the Gentry, Good People, or similar names to avoid insulting them. The country people of Ireland and Scotland still tell stories of fairies as great warriors, beguiling lovers, and the keepers of treasure and great wisdom. Old tales relate the helpful alliances that were often made between fairies and mortals.[17]

Brilliant Celtic musicians were said to get their special talents from the fairies. There are many stories of musicians encountering fairies and being taught songs that later made them famous in the mortal world. The music of "Londonderry Air" is credited to fairies. The Celts used several instruments for music, among them the bodhrán (drum), the lyre, the harp, the wooden pipes, the small bagpipes, and the timpani, all of which were known and used in the fairy realms.

The Otherworld of fairies does not ordinarily impinge on our mortal world strongly enough to produce physical sightings. However, certain cosmic tides of personal energy tend to thin the barrier between the two planes of existence, opening the world of the fairy and freeing it temporarily of the space-time walls that normally hide it from view. These cosmic tides break the continuity of time. This allows fairies freer access to the mortal world, even though they are able to come here any time they wish. This freedom of movement makes it more likely that humans will see and interact with these supernatural beings. The yearly energy tides that weaken the barrier between this world and the Otherworld occur at the times of the eight Celtic festivals, particularly Beltane, Summer Solstice, and Samhain. These traditional times when one may more frequently encounter fairies were recognized by the Celts.

Although fairies might interact daily with humans, the Celts knew that one courted retaliation if they were insulted or the earthly gateways to their homes disturbed or destroyed. In Ireland most country people still refuse to cut down a lone hawthorn tree or use the wood from one that has been cut. Lone trees, groups of stones, and certain hills have been known to be gateways for the fairies to pass between the worlds. These gates tend to coincide with power lines or power spots on the earth.

Secretive and retiring beings, fairies prefer not to be noticed all the time. Their bodies have a different vibrational rate than those of humans, which allows them to remain unseen if they wish. Most humans never see fairies. In most instances, a human will recognize the presence of fairies not by direct physical sight, but by briefly seeing a streak of movement off to one side or by simply "knowing" that they are not alone. When an empty room suddenly feels full, and the cats and dogs are alert and watching something you cannot see, perhaps you are being visited by fairies.

The fairies are attracted by friendliness, honesty, respect, and mutual interests, the same qualities that attract one human to another. Yet the fairies are not human; neither is their world the same as ours. We should not expect fairies to react as a human would or have the same ethics or laws. Things we consider immensely important have little meaning to fairies.

It is an amazing fact that those humans who spend much time in nature, such as gardening or walking, or those who use herbs for healing, are more apt to make contact with fairies than those who do not.

Fairies can assume any form they wish and have palaces of gold, silver, diamonds, and pearl deep in the heart of the hills. Their chiefs wear circlets of gold to mark their rank. These beautiful Otherworld beings love fine clothing and jewelry, music, song, dancing, and laughter.

Because of the fairy love for music, and their periodic kidnapping of young women, it was considered dangerous for any girl to sing beside a lake or near a fairy mound. If a girl was taken to be a fairy bride, she might on occasion be released in seven years. These girls were given the secret fairy knowledge of herbs, philters, and spells. They usually became known as fairy doctors, and cured people by using charms, herbs, and incantations. These doctors did not reveal their secrets until on their deathbeds. Then, the secrets were passed only to one chosen person. Some types of fairy knowledge were passed only from a man to a woman, or a woman to a man, but never passed to one of the same gender.

An ancient Irish belief says that if a person seeks entry into a fairy mound, she/he walks around it nine times under the full moon, after which the entrance flies open. If you happened to find yourself within a fairy palace, tradition said you should not eat the food or drink the wine. If you did, you were doomed to stay in fairyland. The same restriction applied if a man kissed a fairy woman.

Fairy chiefs often desired a pretty mortal woman as a wife. This did not mean the fairy would take the woman to fairyland; often the woman was simply enticed into a sexual union and became pregnant. These half-fairy offspring were beautiful and clever, but also wild and reckless. Frequently, they had the uncanny ability of music, singing, communication with animals, or healing.

"Taken by the fairies" was a phrase often used to explain a person's sudden bizarre behavior. The Irish say that someone is "touched by the fairies" when a person suddenly becomes depressed or acts oddly.

To be "taken" could happen in several ways. A person could make a wrong turn on a familiar path, "stepping on a stray sod" the Irish call it. One could be lured to follow a fairy or a white animal into a mound. The third method of entering fairyland was to fall into a deep sleep under the spell of enchanting birdsong or fairy music; when the sleeper awoke, she/he was inside fairyland.

Sometimes fairy queens tried to entice handsome young men into their dancing rings or into their palaces deep under the mounds. The Scottish story of Tam Lin is an example of a man taken by the fairies. Any man who went with the fairies and later escaped or was released would never again be satisfied with the mortal world.

The Celtic idea of fairies does not match the later ideas of Victorian times. Celtic fairies were full-sized, as large as humans. The tiny, flittering creatures with gossamer wings of Victorian times were actually nature spirits, distorted by Victorian romantics. Even though the term "Wee Folk" is sometimes used for fairies in Celtic areas, it does not describe their stature. Rather, it is a form of respect.

Even though fairies and humans are two very different species who live in different dimensional planes, the fairies have a deep need to share their secrets and knowledge with humans as do the deities and Otherworld creatures. There are many stories of communication between mortals and beings of the Otherworld, particularly fairies, that warn mortals to avoid disrespectful acts toward these Otherworld beings. For example, in some parts of Ireland and Scotland, women will not throw water out the door without calling a warning to any nearby fairies. Neglecting to do this could bring retaliation for the insult.

Several herbs were thought to have connections with fairies and Otherworld beings. The herb yarrow is widely known throughout the Celtic realms as a fairy herb. In Ireland it was called *lus na fola* (blood herb) and *lus na gcluas* (ear herb); both names are based on the healing uses of the herb. Another Irish name was *ahtair thalún* (earth creeper), which defines the way the herb grows. In Scottish Gaelic this herb is called *eárr thalmhuinn*, while in Wales it is known as *milddail* or *llysiau gwaedilif*. Yarrow is used for divination by holding a leaf against the eyelids; this enables the seer to locate and see a person, even at a distance.

In Ireland and Scotland few people are foolish enough to place a house or building in the middle of a known fairy track. If they do, they will have nothing but trouble until the offending building is removed. Although this track is used for earthly travel by fairies, particularly during certain times of the year, it also seems to be part of a time warp. The track not only allows fairies to travel along it, but it also enables ghosts or spirits of the dead to appear along its line in the human world.

Fairies were more plentiful during Samhain, Summer Solstice, and

Beltane, as they traveled the earth from one mound to another. To keep fairies out of a house, primrose petals were scattered on the threshold or a branch of rowan hung over the door. On May Eve, no doors were left open and young people were not allowed to go out into the hills alone. On Samhain when the veil or barrier was thinnest between the worlds, the fairies were out in force during the night. At Summer Solstice (Midsummer) in June, the fairies often tried to extinguish the bonfires and entice mortals into joining their revels.

The rowan, along with hawthorn and yew, was favored over oak by Irish Druids. Legend says that the Tuatha Dé Danann brought the first rowan tree to Ireland. Also called the quicken tree or mountain ash, the rowan was called *luis* in Old Irish, *caorunn* in Scottish Gaelic, *keirn* or *kern* in Manx, and *cerddinen* in Wales. It was said to give the best defense against fairy enchantments.

Fairies are said to appear during the "in-between" times and at "in-between" places. These times are twilight and dawn, when it is neither day nor night, and midnight, when it is neither one day nor another. One "in-between" place is the edge of a lake or ocean where the earth and water mingle but are not entirely either element. Other places are the traditional "doorways" where our world intermingles with the Otherworld, such as fairy rings in the grass, circles of stones, caves, mountaintops, and the magical circle.

"In-between" times are best for working magic. If one cannot work magic in any of the places in nature, a good substitute is a cast circle. The magical circle creates "a time that is not a time, in a place that is not a place, on a day that is not a day."[18]

A magical circle is very similar to the *frith* of Brigit. To create a magic circle, a person visualizes a stream of white or silver-blue light issuing from her/his forefinger, dagger, or sword. Beginning in the east and walking sunwise, she/he aims this stream of light at the ground or floor and defines the entire circumference of the circle. The ends are overlapped in the east to prevent any escape of energy, or the unwanted entrance of undesirable energy or entities.

The Celts had a variety of names for different Otherworld beings, particularly those they connected with the name "fairies." Although some of the names differed in Ireland, Scotland, or Wales, all three areas knew of basically the same types of fairies.

In Ireland during the nineteenth century, there still existed more than 30,000 ring forts, hill forts, and cashels (castles, or primitive forts built with low stone walls). The typical fairy fort is the ráth, or ring fort with an earthen ditch or wall. A frequent inhabitant of these ráths is the *amadawn* (Amadan), also called the fool or jester. He appears only in June to roam the countryside, driving people to irrational, mad behavior.

Tradition says that the hidden doors to the land of the fairies are frequently found in mounds (*sídhe*) and hills (Hollow Hills). At night many people have seen sparkling lights and heard laughing voices and beautiful music coming from these mounds. It was considered very foolish to be near these sites at dusk, midnight, or dawn, as well as on the traditional eight days (for example, Samhain of the "thin veil.")

The name banshee is derived from the Irish words *bean sídhe*, which means "fairy woman." Although the banshee was a death messenger, she did not bring death. She gave her sorrowing keen in sympathy for the doomed person and the family. Tradition says that if she is taunted by those who see her, she will leave the indelible five-fingered mark of her hand on the taunter's cheek.

Originally the leprechaun was not a little, cute character with whom humans bargained. In his original form, he was always male, unsociable, always by himself, bad-tempered, wizened, and given to drinking. Not only did he guard treasures and know where the hidden riches of the earth were, but he also cobbled shoes for the fairies. He usually wore green trousers, a red vest, and a small, conical hat.

The *púca* (pooka) was an evil, solitary fairy who was capable of assuming many shapes to attack people. Its favorite guise was that of a horse, but it could also assume the shape of a bat, bird, or calf. If an unwary traveler accepted a ride on a púca, it would take her/him on a furious, dangerous race through the countryside. The rider would be unable to dismount until sunrise. Púcas were most powerful when they appeared near a place connected with easy passage to the Otherworld, such as a crossroads, bridge, beach, or fence. Púcas are said to appear most frequently at Samhain (Halloween) and Beltane (May 1).

The mermaid was a supernatural being who lived in the sea and had a human upper body with the lower body of a fish. The selkie was a seal that could become human at times. Both could transform themselves into human bodies and associate with humans on the land if they wished. Many Celtic legends tell of marriages with humans and the birth of children. Some families trace certain physical characteristics to an ancient union of one of their family with a selkie or mermaid. These unions never lasted, as the sea creature would inevitably return to the ocean. Both mer-folk and selkies liked to sit on rocks along the coasts of Ireland and Scotland where they combed their long hair and enchanted humans.

The Irish said that high winds were raised by fairy hosts as they rode out through the countryside. Any small whirlwind was said to be the Gentry. When horses snorted during a windstorm, it was believed they blew the Good People out of the way.

Scotland had several supernatural creatures that were very different from those in Ireland. Among them are the *fríde*, the *gille dubh*, and the *glaistig*. The *fríde* is a Highlands fairy who lives under rocks; it comes out to devour crumbs and spilled milk. The *gille dubh*, or "dark boy," is a solitary fairy of the birch woods near Gairlock in the northwest Highlands. Generally benevolent, he dresses in leaves and mosses. The *glaistig* ("green maiden") is a malevolent female fairy who lives near lonely pools. A solitary fairy, she is half woman, half goat, but can take the form of any woman known to her male victim. She cuts her lovers' throats and sucks out their blood.

One particular supernatural fairy creature, called the *washer at the ford*, was known in Ireland, Scotland, and Wales. Sometimes this female spirit was beautiful, sometimes ugly, but she was always seen weeping and washing bloody clothes at a river ford. She was greatly feared as a death omen.

Another strange, fairy-like creature was said to inhabit the woodlands of Britain and Wales. Called the woodwose or wild man of the wood, this hairy, naked wild man is frequently mentioned in British and Welsh folklore. He was said to protect the trees. The Irish story of Suibne (*Buile Shuibhne*) is very similar to the Welsh stories of the woodwose.

Later beliefs connected the fairies with almost everything that went wrong. People had forgotten that fairies only created trouble when insulted or their nature areas damaged in some way. White cows were distrusted, as they were supposed to belong to the fairies and might lead the other cows away into fairyland. Oak stalls were built as protection against fairy influences. In May, farmers kept a close eye on the cows lest the fairies steal the milk.

The name "elves" was not used in the Irish Celtic tradition, although they may have known of it through their trading with the Scandinavians. In Scotland, however, the Celts were very aware of elves and considered them to be a type of full-sized fairy. Scottish tradition speaks of the Seelie (Blessed) and Unseelie (Evil) Courts who ruled over Elfame.

To work with fairies, first one must introduce one's self. This can be accomplished by a simple ritual. Set up a small altar in a place where it will not be disturbed. You can decorate this altar with flowers or small potted plants, crystals and other stones, seashells, pinecones, little statues of wild animals, and a special glass or metal bowl. Anything that reminds you of fairies and nature can be placed on this altar. Fill the bowl with fresh water, perhaps placing a floating candle in the water. The water should be changed daily. If you do not use a floating candle, put a regular candle on the altar. Each day, light the candle, and perhaps some incense, and meditate. Bid the fairies welcome to your home, and ask them for aid in solving any problems.

Never "play" at magic just to see if it works. Magic is serious business, and you can get your fingers burned in more ways than one if you misuse it. And never call up an Otherworld being or deity without a good reason.

Celtic Otherworlds

One of the strongest tenets of the early Celtic religions was a belief in reincarnation and continued life in the Otherworld after death. Unlike the Welsh who divided the Otherworld into three places, the Irish Celts believed in a more varied afterlife. All Celts believed that, since all things and all levels of dimension are interconnected, living humans could journey from our world into the Otherworld and back. Therefore, physical death held fewer terrors for them than for other early cultures.

Since human personality, the mind, and the soul are not bound up in the physical body, any human can learn to make the journey into the Otherworld. The only restrictions are that a person *should not* take these journeys if she/he has mental or emotional problems, is on medication for such illnesses, or is taking mind-altering drugs. This includes the drinking of alcohol.

The Otherworld is not an imaginary place, although it may seem so at first. It is another dimension of time and space and has as much reality as this world does. It has its own laws, conditions, and inhabitants. We can access and experience the Otherworld with all our five senses just as we do our own world. The traveler is fully awake and aware during journeys to the Otherworld. At any time she/he feels uncomfortable when encountering certain supernatural beings, she/he can tell them to go away. If this does not work, she/he can end the journey at once by simply willing it to be done.

There were a variety of names for sections of the Otherworld. Irish legends mention the names of Mag Mell (The Enticing or Pleasant Plain), Emain Abhlach (The Sacred Place of Apples), Mag Mór (The Great Plain), Mag Dá Cheó (Land of the Two Mists), Hy Brasil (Beautiful Island), Tír fo Thuinn or Thoinn (Land Under the Waves), Tír na mBan (Land of the Living), Tír Tairngire (Plain of Happiness), and Tír na nÓg (Land of the Forever Young). These were all pleasant places. The tale of Cú Chulainn and the Otherworld tells of palaces, fine horses, beautiful music, wonderful banquets of food and mead, trees bearing a constant supply of fruit, and all kinds of gold adornments. Although the Celts did not believe in hell, the Otherworld sites of Tech Duinn ("house of Donn" or the dead) and Dún Scáith ("fort of shadow/fear") were not portrayed as pleasant places.

A large number of surviving Irish texts tell of journeys (*Imrama*) to the Otherworld by mortals. These stories do not portray a misty, insubstantial place, but one of great beauty and marvelous beings.

Although ancient magicians and shamans often wore special costumes, had power amulets and talismans, and used numerous magical items in their work, it was never the costume or objects that projected magical power. The ritual items were only symbols to trigger action in the subconscious mind, from which comes the link to Otherworld power that creates magical manifestations.

Legends speak often of the Silver Branch, a kind of talisman given to certain humans by fairies. This branch always was adorned with silver bells or chiming fruit. Symbolic of the Tree of Life itself, the Silver Branch was a passport into the Otherworld, a talisman that gave the wielder safe passage on shamanic journeys as well as healing powers. When the Silver Branch was shaken, all who heard it were said to sleep and forget their sorrows. Its music also guided the shamanic traveler into the Otherworld. This was so powerful a symbol that it became a tool and hallmark of bards and poets. Master bards carried gold branches, while those of lesser rank carried silver ones.

Supernatural beings in the Otherworld, including what we call power animals, are usually willing to work with the traveler and offer guidance. If advice is sought for a problem, the answer may be in a riddle or some other cryptic phrase. This process is similar to the riddling "dark language" used by the Druids for teaching and prophecies. Sometimes, however, the answer may be shockingly direct. Over time the traveler learns to read between the lines when assessing any answers or advice given by inhabitants of the Otherworld. Frequently, the answer does not seem appropriate to the problem at all. However, with thought on the subject, the traveler will see that it does connect and offer a new way of looking at things.

Talking with inhabitants of the Otherworld is perfectly safe, although these beings are very different from mortals and operate under a different set of rules. They are very powerful and can cause changes and manifestations in the mortal world if they choose.

One cannot know one's power animals unless a journey is taken to the Otherworld to discover them. Establishing a deep relationship with your animal allies can be fulfilling as well as helpful in everyday life. A relationship with these creatures is vital to the shamanic practice of shapeshifting. For example, taking on mental characteristics of a fox or mouse may aid you in quietly leaving an unpleasant gathering without being noticed. These animal allies may remain with you for several months to a lifetime. The best way to discover them on an Otherworld journey is to seek out the Lord of Animals. He will call all the animals to him. Any animal that then approaches you could become an animal ally. The Lord of Animals was known to most Celts by the name Cernunnos. He appears in the story of "The Lady of the Fountain" in the Welsh *Mabinogion*.

The Lord of Animals

For instructions on setting up a meditation space and taping the meditation, please refer to meditations in Chapter Three.

The Lord of Animals

Close your eyes and visualize a brilliant white light over your head. As you inhale deeply, feel this light coursing through your body, from your head down to your toes. Feel your muscles relaxing, beginning with your feet. The deep sense of peacefulness moves up through your legs, into your body and arms. You feel the tenseness flow out of the muscles in your shoulders, neck, and head. You are completely relaxed.

Before you now is a well. Take all the problems in your life and throw them into the deep darkness of the well. The problems are quickly carried far away from you. Leave them there, turn and walk away. You will be constantly protected during this meditation. Absolutely nothing can harm you.

You find yourself walking on a path through a thick forest. Sunlight glimmers through the thick branches overhead, and you can see all varieties of trees around you. The air is warm and sweet. Birds sing in the trees as you walk along. Soon you reach a clearing. In the center of this clearing is a huge, ancient oak tree. Bright wildflowers dot the grass.

As you walk toward the oak, a tall man, crowned with antlers, steps from behind the tree. He is dressed in leather trousers and has a woven cloak thrown over his bare shoulders. He sits down near the tree, his legs crossed, and watches you as you approach. By the man's side, half-hidden in the grass, is a large drum.

"Greetings," he says in a deep voice. "I am the Lord of Animals. What do you wish of me?"

You sit down facing this Otherworld being and explain that you are seeking animal allies to help you along your spiritual path.

The Lord picks up the drum and strikes it with a wooden stick. The deep sound rolls out through the forest, echoing back from the thick groves of trees. Soon the clearing is full of a variety of wild creatures—animals, birds, insects—and aquatic creatures float in the air above you. As you look at this assembly of creatures, a few approach you.

"These will work with you," the Lord says. "They will teach you different ways of observing what is around you. Listen to them, and learn."

You spend time getting acquainted with these new helpers of the animal kingdom. If you have more questions, you may speak with the Lord of Animals. When you are ready to leave, your animal allies go with you into the forest along the path.

As the path once more exits into an open space, you think of your physical body and find yourself within it. The meditation is ended.

To gain help with visions of the past and future, the traveler must seek out the Seeress. This Otherworld being is sometimes found near a sacred well, deep in a cave, or near a circle of standing stones on a hilltop. She holds a golden rod with which she weaves and spins the threads of creation into a living web that creates the future. A great oracle, she has remarkably accurate powers of seeing the future and knowing the best action to take on any problem. The seeress Fedelm, whose story is in the *Tain Bó Cuailnge*, is symbolic of the Seeress in the Otherworld.

Visiting the Great Seeress

For instructions on setting up a meditation space and taping the meditation, please refer to meditations in Chapter Three.

Visiting the Great Seeress

Close your eyes and visualize a brilliant white light over your head. As you inhale deeply, feel this light coursing through your body, from your head down to your toes. Feel your muscles relaxing, beginning with your feet. The deep sense of peacefulness moves up through your legs, into your body and arms. You feel the tenseness flow out of the muscles in your shoulders, neck, and head. You are completely relaxed.

Before you now is a well. Take all the problems in your life and throw them into the deep darkness of the well. The problems are quickly carried far away from you. Leave them there, as you turn and walk away. You will be constantly protected during this meditation. Absolutely nothing can harm you.

You find yourself near a great circle of standing stones. The stones are on top of a hill. Far below you see woodlands with a sparkling river running through them.

As you walk toward the huge monoliths, you see a woman standing inside the circle with a golden weaving rod in her hands. She is dressed in a long white robe, and her dark hair falls loosely to her waist. She is weaving thin strands of a shiny substance between the great stones. As she moves, you see flashes of light from the golden torc about her neck and the gold and silver bracelets on her arms.

As you stand just outside the stone circle, the woman calls for you to enter and join her as she weaves. She explains that she is the Seeress, the one who weaves the life threads of all beings, all events, of the universe itself, into a living web. She lays aside her weaving rod and gestures for you to sit beside her on a large flat stone in the center of the circle. On the stone are a deck of tarot cards, a set of ogham sticks, a bag of runestones, and a crystal ball.

"Ask your question," the Seeress requests. "I will tell you what I can. However, you must hear the truth of actuality, not of wishes, if you would learn the answer to your question."

You ask the Seeress about some problem or goal in your life. She tells you what she can, then goes on to explain what divinatory device you should study at this time. She explains that, later, you may study another divinatory method if you wish.

You sit with the Seeress and ask any questions you may have about divination and the method she has suggested to you. You may also ask about any other event in your life that is troubling you.

Finally, she smiles and returns to her weaving. You step outside the circle of standing stones. You think of your physical body and find yourself within it. The meditation is ended.

Communicating with the ancestors while on an Otherworld journey can be very important. "Ancestors" may be people in your immediate family who have died or those from ancient times from any cultural group—the elders and wisdom-keepers of any clan or race. They can instruct you on ancient knowledge or help to awaken a sense of cultural and self-identity. The ancestors are usually found in the section of the Otherworld known as the Underworld.

Celtic stories repeatedly mention music signaling an encounter with fairies, Otherworld beings, and their land. Mircea Eliade wrote that in many cultures the words for magic and song are identical. For example, the English word "enchantment" is derived from "chant."

The Otherworld, particularly the Underworld where the ancestors live, can be entered through an ocean voyage, the *sídhe* mounds ("hollow hills"), a well, lake, or cave. Another way to enter the various levels is to enter the Tree of Life. Climbing the branches to the top will take you to the Upperworld; going down through the roots will bring you to the Underworld. Going through the trunk of the Tree, from one side to the other, will take you into the Middleworld. The deities are usually found in the Upperworld or the Underworld, while the Middleworld seems to be an alternate universe to our own. Other points of entry can be between two tall standing stones, two hawthorn bushes, or two tall trees.

The Otherworld landscape consists of natural settings, such as valleys, deserts, moors, enchanted forests, and mountains. Castles, forts, and dwellings are scattered throughout. Everything is brighter or darker, more splendid, more alluring to the senses than our world.

When entering the Otherworld, the human traveler will encounter certain consistent aspects. In Irish lore the Otherworld is frequently described as a series of islands, especially if the voyager began the journey by sea. The roofs of houses are often thatched with feathers or gold. Crystal windows are common. The birds sing sweeter here, and the music is beyond human understanding. Travelers are given all they want to eat or drink. The Otherworld beings and fairies are very beautiful and wise. Time passes differently than it does in our world.

One of the features of the Otherworld, whatever Celtic culture wrote of it, was the special Otherworld Cauldron. This huge, supernatural vessel represented the womb of the Goddess, who created everything. From its depths the shaman could bring back healing, replenishment, rebirth, and inspiration. A plunge into this cauldron signified initiation.

The Celtic shamans and spiritual leaders made journeys into the Otherworld for specific reasons, which are still valid today. They always came back with a heightened sense of reality, visions of the future, a new power to use to help people, the ability to discern a lie, or the burning need to pursue and reveal the truth. The journeys were not frivolously undertaken.

A deeply spiritual people, the Celts believed that, although the deities and spirits lived in the Otherworld, this other plane of existence was part of this life as well. Deities could live anywhere in nature, from a grove of trees, a solitary tree, river, lake, or spring to a mountaintop. Some of these natural features were such a strong focus of worship and pilgrimages that the Christian Church could not stop the people from visiting them. In an effort to control this impulse, the Christians rededicated these spots to "saints."

The Celtic cultures believed in life after death, but not in hell. To the Irish Celts, the Otherworld was a multilayered plane of existence that included a multitude of spiritual islands. Each soul passed from incarnation to incarnation until it reached a state of perfection that allowed it to enter the Land of the Blessed.

The Celts always honored their dead by expressing their grief without shame. Originally, the Irish wakes were attended only by the men, who smoked their pipes, drank whisky, and listened to the *fili* tell of the deceased's family history and lineage. Legend says that the first *caoineadh* (keening) heard in Ireland was cried by Bríg when her son was killed during the Second Battle of Mag Tuired. Until recently, an Irish wake included the keening women (*mná caointe*) who cried out their sorrow as the dead person's life story was recited.

True journeys into the Otherworld bring about subtle changes in the traveler. They will either stop making journeys to the Otherworld and claim that the entire idea is a hoax, or decide that they will develop all their potentials to the fullest, and seek out knowledge and wisdom. The gifts of the Otherworld are always artistic in some manner: singing, music, poetry, writing, or healing.

The Celtic culture in Wales had a more orderly design of the Otherworld. They believed the Otherworld consisted of three concentric circles, which the *Barddas* explain in a series of questions and answers.[19] However, it appears that there are actually four circles, if Ceugant is counted as a circle of the Otherworld, but is beyond the reach of anyone, mortal or immortal.

Abred was the innermost circle, our world, which is a place of struggle and evolution for human souls. This is the Middleworld, the alternate world to the mortal world, and is inhabited by nature spirits, fairies, and other supernatural beings and animals. It was here that the Scotsman Thomas the Rhymer gained his skills of prophecy. The famous Irish and Welsh physicians and several great Celtic musicians also received their fantastic skills here. If the traveler follows a white deer or other white animal, the creature will lead you to this plane of existence. People have been known to stumble into this land by accident, not realizing they have gone astray on their path until they find that they do not recognize the landmarks.

The next circle is that of Annwn (the Underworld) and Gwynfyd. The Underworld realm is ruled over by Arawn, Pwyll, and the Irish god Donn. The Underworld (Annwn) is more dimly lit than the other worlds and is haunted in some parts by shadows and deep dreams. A rich place of many wonders, this world has stars within the earth, a phrase frequently used in Celtic literature to describe a specific phenomenon that occurs in the Underworld, or Annwn. The souls of the dead stay in Annwn until they reincarnate. This astral plane is a place of continued initiation into earthly experiences until the soul makes the necessary changes in attitude and goals and moves beyond the sensual, physical realm. Annwn also contains a fiery abyss, or the cauldron of Annwn, from which comes all earthly creation.

The Celts did not look upon the ghosts or spirits of returning dead as hauntings. They knew the walls between the worlds were thin at times, particularly at Samhain. Celtic mythology never mentions ghosts attacking or terrorizing the living without a good reason. One of the reasons for returning might be a warrior or murder victim seeking revenge or justice.

The traveler cannot enter certain areas of Annwn unless she/he can pass the guardian of the threshold. However, the journey is well worth the effort, for here one can access the most ancient teachings of the ancestors, and often surprising information about the future. This is a place of unpredictability and change where the supernatural rulers rectify imbalances and demand that the truth be revealed. Descending into Annwn is not an action to be taken lightly, for it can be a shattering experience in which the traveler is forced to face all the facets of her/his soul. However, the journey into Annwn is a liberating experience for those who face the truth.

Journey to Annwn and the Ancestors

For instructions on setting up a meditation space and taping the meditation, please refer to meditations in Chapter Three.

Journey to Annwn and the Ancestors

Close your eyes and visualize a brilliant white light over your head. As you inhale deeply, feel this light coursing through your body, from your head down to your toes. Feel your muscles relaxing, beginning with your feet. The deep sense of peacefulness moves up through your legs, into your body and arms. You feel the tenseness flow out of the muscles in your shoulders, neck, and head. You are completely relaxed.

Before you now is a well. Take all the problems in your life and throw them into the deep darkness of the well. The problems are quickly carried far away from you. Leave them there, turn and walk away. You will be constantly protected during this meditation. Absolutely nothing can harm you.

You are standing beside one of the ancient burial mounds. It is midnight and the dark sky above is dotted with bright stars. A full moon hangs overhead, illuminating the landscape around you. Strains of music come from the mound—music of bagpipes, flute, violin, bodhrán, and harp. Slowly, a door opens in the side of the mound and you go inside and find yourself in the Underworld.

Although it is also night in the Underworld, you can see castles, forts, and dwellings scattered about this strange place. As you walk along a road that leads you farther into this landscape, you are aware that everything is brighter or darker, more splendid, more alluring to the senses than in our world.

Again you hear the beautiful music and follow the sound to a castle, with torches burning brightly at the gates. As you get closer, you notice what look like stars within the earth beneath your feet. The gates open before you. Music and laughter flow out through the open door to the castle hall. As you stand at the door and look into the bright hall, you notice many people dressed in a variety of costumes representing different time periods of history. Some are sitting at long tables, while others dance to the fairy music.

"They wait for you," someone says. You turn and find a fairy standing close beside you. He smiles as he bows in welcome. "Come inside, and join us. Your ancestors are celebrating your visit to the Underworld."

The fairy man escorts you into the hall and calls out your name to the crowd of people. Many of them hurry forward to greet you, all introducing themselves as your ancestors. One woman gives you a mug of cider, then finds a place for you at a table.

"What do you wish to know?" asks a man beside you. "We are all related to you, from many previous generations." He indicates the room with a sweep of his hand.

You can talk to any of the people you wish, finding out more about your family's ancient history and bloodlines. You may even see a loved one from this time who has passed on to the Otherworld. If you need advice on some problem in your life, many of these ancestors will be happy to share their insight and experiences.

When you are ready to return to this time, think of the door in the mound, and you will instantly return there. You look back as you step through the door and out into the night. As you think of your physical body, you will find yourself within it. The meditation is ended.

The third circle is called Gwynfyd, known also as the Blessed Realm (Isles of the Blest or Avalon) or the Upperworld. The ruler of Gwynfyd is the goddess Rhiannon. Celtic cosmogony speaks of the Upperworld as a place occupied by the gods and animal allies. The wisdom found here includes astrology, the workings of the stars and planets, and the purest form of inspiration. An ancient Welsh poem says that the Rainbow River flows into the entrance of Gwynfyd. This entrance is guarded on one side by a holly tree and on the other by an oak. The two trees form the pillars of a bridge that crossed this river. It was the goal of all spiritual seekers in the Celtic world to advance from Abred, the arena of reincarnation, to Gwynfyd, a place of the developed spirit.

Journey into the Upperworld

For instructions on setting up a meditation space and taping the meditation, please refer to meditations in Chapter Three.

Journey into the Upperworld

Close your eyes and visualize a brilliant white light over your head. As you inhale deeply, feel this light coursing through your body, from your head down to your toes. Feel your muscles relaxing, beginning with your feet. The deep sense of peacefulness moves up through your legs, into your body and arms. You feel the tenseness flow out of the muscles in your shoulders, neck, and head. You are completely relaxed.

Before you now is a well. Take all the problems in your life and throw them into the deep darkness of the well. The problems are quickly carried far away from you. Leave them there, turn and walk away. You will be constantly protected during this meditation. Absolutely nothing can harm you.

You are standing on the banks of a gently flowing river. The rain has just stopped, the grass and trees still sparkling with wet drops. You notice a great holly tree on one side of the river, with a great oak tree on the opposite bank. This is the Rainbow River that flows upward into the entrance of the Upperworld. The two trees form the pillars of a bridge that crosses this river.

As you walk toward this mystical bridge, you notice that the center span seems to wink in and out of sight in a mist that hangs there, as if this center span is half in this world, half in the Otherworld. You begin to cross the bridge, the great wooden planks creaking under your feet. When you finally step into the mist, you see brilliant flashes of color and hear mysterious chords of music. As you step out of the mist, you notice that you did not cross the river, but are now in a very beautiful place. Throughout the fairy-tale landscape are golden castles with crystal windows and roofs of colorful bird feathers. You are standing on the dirt road that leads down into a lush valley with a shining river through the center.

This is the Upperworld, the abode of gods and goddesses, heroes and heroines, ancient seekers and mystics. The wisdom found here is of a more advanced nature; it includes astrology, the workings of the stars and planets, advanced healing, and the purest form of inspiration. This is the place to seek guidance for your spiritual and artistic goals in life.

A chariot, pulled by white horses and driven by a Celtic warrior, races up the road to meet you. The warrior shouts a greeting, and you realize the warrior is a woman. You climb into the chariot with her, and she drives the chariot down the dusty road to one of the golden castles.

The goddess Brigit meets you as you step down from the chariot. She takes your arm and walks with you into the magnificent structure. In the great hall you find many of the Celtic deities waiting to talk with you. Lugh, light shining around his golden hair, sits beside the giant Ogma, while the goddesses Bóann, Dana, and Mórrígán sit nearby. The hero Cú Chulainn stands with a group of Druids and bards, talking with the Welsh bard Taliesin. The healer Dian Cécht and his daughter Airmid are passing around tankards of an herbal drink. Many other people are clustered within this hall. All greet you as Brigit leads you to a chair.

"The Upperworld is a place to seek spiritual guidance and the higher knowledges," Brigit says as Airmid hands you a tankard. "Trivial pursuits have no place here. Ask what you will of any here, but ask only about the greater needs in your life."

You drink from the tankard and find the herbal brew has a pleasant taste. Small groups of the people move toward you, one by one, and speak with you. If you have spiritual goals, they may offer advice. If you do not have any specific goals at this time, they may suggest a pursuit that would be fulfilling to you.

If you wish to ask questions about a certain subject that interests you, these people will be happy to talk with you about astrology, healing, and any number of advanced studies.

When you are ready to leave, thank those gathered here for

their help. Go to the door of the great hall. The mist is gathered around this door. You step into the mist, think of your physical body and find yourself within it. The meditation is ended.

The last circle, and outermost, was called Ceugant; it was a place of infinity that is never entered, even by the most experienced spiritual traveler. Ceugant is the residence of the Great Creating Spirit, the power behind the gods and goddesses. This Creating Spirit is beyond the comprehension of even the initiate and is never seen by humans. Tradition says that from Ceugant shine three rays of light that stir up creation. The surviving written material about these light rays is sketchy and incomplete. However, one ray of this light seems to shine into each of the three circles of the Otherworld: Abred, Gwynfyd, and Annwn.[20]

The Welsh idea of the Otherworld is further complicated by the listing of mysterious, spiritual castles or caers, such as those given in *The Spoils of Annwn*, or the *Preiddeu Annwn*. Caer Wydyr, or the Glass Castle, was said to be a joyful resting place of the dead. It was found in Annwn, along with several other castles. These eight castles were: Caer Sidi (Revolving Castle), Caer Pedryvan (Four-Cornered Castle), Caer Vedwyd (Castle of Revelry), Caer Rigor (Kingly Castle), Caer Wydyr (Glass Castle), Caer Vandwy (Castle on High), and Caer Ochren (Castle of the Sloping Sides).

It is possible that these castles were metaphors both for areas in the Welsh Otherworld and the eight chakras of the human astral body. Caer Pedryvan, known as the Four-Cornered Castle, may be symbolic of the four elements and the four earthly seasons. Caer Sidi, or Caer Arianrhod, symbolizes the entrance to the *Sídhe* or the fairy world, a kind of time warp through which mortals or supernatural beings can pass.

This threefold idea of the Otherworld is consistent with the Celtic idea of the importance of the trinity. Many of their teachings and laws were in triads, as in the *Druidic Triads*.[21] The trinity, the cornerstone of Celtic religious belief, was expressed in the beautiful, intertwining designs, such as the three-pointed knots and the three-leafed shamrock.

Although the Celts thought of the Otherworld as a separate plane of existence, they also believed that these supernatural realms were intertwined with our mortal world. The ancestors, deities, and Otherworld beings could associate with humans. The gifted people who knew how to walk between these worlds were called the *áes dana*. The *áes dana* not only included the trained Druids, poets, and seers, but also the individuals and families who received the skills through blood inheritance.

These "Walkers Between the Worlds" were interpreters of the spirit realms. They deliberately journeyed into the Otherworlds where they communicated with the ancestors and supernatural beings. From these journeys they returned with knowledge, healing advice, and predictions for the future.

Many beings and guardians in the Otherworld have some animal features. Antlers are common. Some of these beings who guard secrets or initiatory thresholds may even appear as monsters to the mortal traveler. The secret will not be revealed or entrance allowed unless the traveler faces the guardian without fear and with respect. Some myths tell of a traveler who is asked to be guardian for a period of time. The Welsh tale of Pwyll, Prince of Dyfed, relates that Pwyll met Arawn, Lord of the Underworld, while hunting. Because of a breach of hunting etiquette, Pwyll served in Arawn's place for a year.

The Otherworld realms frequently intermingle with our world. Seekers on the path of Celtic spirituality acknowledge the existence of these realms and the beings who inhabit them. Much wisdom and enlightenment comes through these Otherworld beings.

Power of the Voice and Sound

The Celtic Druids understood well the power of the voice to heal or maim, bless or kill. According to the myths, all Druidic poetry fitted into *moladh agus aoir* ("praise and satire").

The praise or blessing consisted of positive words calling upon a deity or deities to bring good fortune to a person, house, or clan. A few of these Irish blessings remain, although rephrased to call upon the Christian god or a saint. "May good luck be with you wherever you go, and blessings outnumber the shamrocks that grow." "May the road rise with you, the wind be also at your back, and may the Lord hold you in the hollow of His hand." "May God be with you and bless you. May you live to see your children's children. May you be poor in misfortune and rich in blessings, from this day forward and in the days to come." In one example in Irish mythology, the hero Cú Chulainn used a blessing to heal the goddess Mórrígán when she was wounded.

It was common for visitors to bless the house and family when entering a home. This practice not only revealed the visitor's intent, but also thanked the family for being hospitable to strangers.

It is not the words that constitute a curse or a blessing, but the intonation of the voice and the intent behind it that decides whether the words bless or curse. The great Welsh bard Taliesin knew that the tone of an incantation was able to stun his enemies' senses, thus disarming them physically and mentally.

Irish Celtic mythology is full of examples of satires and curses. Satires were similar to mild curses since they were usually said as a reprimand for breaking laws or engaging in unsociable behavior. Neither satires nor curses were to be spoken unless they were justified. When satires or curses were spoken, the object of the spell might fall ill, develop red blemishes on the face and body, or even die in extreme circumstances.

The *glám dícenn* was a special curse given by a poet and was a potent weapon. To speak the glám dícenn, a Druid had to stand on one leg, close one eye, and hold out one hand while he chanting the blighting spell. Another method of cursing involved holding a stone in one hand while the curse was said; a pile of cursing stones was built and then scattered in all directions at the end so that the curse could not be reversed.

The Old Irish word for "curse" is *cúrsachadh*, which means "abuse." The Irish Travelers, who are like gypsies, use *shorknesing*, or "withering," to describe a curse. The Celts feared the curse of the bard most of all, but were also leery of the curses of widows.[22] The most dreaded of Druidic powers was *dásacht*, which produced madness. The Druidic orders were also skilled in brewing a drink of forgetfulness called *deog dermaid*.

Records from the Highlands of Scotland reveal the uncanny accuracy of Gaelic curses. To the Scots the art of cursing required courage, for it had to be done face to face with the person being cursed. There could be no midnight muttering over a candle or angry whispers in the dark. Cursing was eye to eye. Curses in the Highlands were primarily made by the victims of injustice who had nothing left to lose or gain. Once said, Scottish curses tended to stick to the victim and her/his family for years, if not generations.

The bard should be very careful about the use of curses. Unjustified curses return with devastating effects. Curses require clear judgment and unfortunately can be affected by personal emotions. It is safer to forego the use of curses and satires entirely, unless you are quite positive about the identity and motives of the offender, such as child molesters, abusers, rapists, and murderers.

Ancient records sometimes refer to the bard as the "vision singer." When bards recited clan histories, genealogies, or legends, they used music, singing, or chanting as part of the performance. Bards knew the power of the voice to create or make changes. The most famous of all "vision singers" was the Welsh bard Taliesin. His surviving poetry tells of his initiation within the cauldron of the goddess Cerridwen. The brew from this magical cauldron gave Taliesin the inspiration, knowledge, and power to become a great bard.

Many ancient cultures studied the power and effect of certain sounds when intoned with intent. Although they did not have the modern scientific words to explain the effects of sounds on the human body and the environment around it, they knew that certain sonics could alter life. These sounds could bless, heal, or hurt. Sounds are "words" with universal meaning.

Sounds, whether words or musical tones, have been used as part of rituals and magic for thousands of years. To the uninitiated, they are meaningless noises. To the trained magician or spiritual disciple, they hold great power. Words and magic are inseparable when used with directed intent, because they work within the scope of universal laws that apply to all worlds. Without directed intent, the words and sounds will accomplish nothing. There are several different theories about the use of the voice in toning, and not all of them agree, except on one point: only toning with intent will balance and heal.

To learn how to intone either vowels or consonants, the student must first learn to control the breath. To learn this, you should practice the yogic method of slowly breathing in to the count of five, holding the breath for the count of five, and then exhaling slowly to the count of five. Increase the count very slowly, as this method will cause dizziness at first.

Proper breathing during toning is also important. Take a deep breath and do diaphragmatic breathing, which means that the stomach must expand when you breathe in. The sounds should be made in your ordinary natural voice.

In Tibet, the voice is considered to be the perfect instrument to perform magic or increase spirituality. At one point, the Tibetan priests and shamans were trained to use sound to create and manifest.

When striving to improve your voice, do not make the mistake of changing your natural tone to an artificial one. Every person has a unique voice pattern of pitch and level that is as distinct as a fingerprint. This pitch and level will automatically rise when you are frightened or angry. In the Western world, men in the fields of business, radio and television, and sports often adopt an artificially deep voice, one that is usually against their nature. Women, on the other hand, are convinced that a higher pitch makes them sound more feminine. The practice of changing the voice pitch is not desirable, unless you habitually imitate someone else's voice. Then, it is desirable to change the pitch and return to your normal voice.

The best way to know what you normally sound like is to read something into a tape recorder in your ordinary voice. When you play this back, you will be surprised at what you hear. When a person listens to her/his voice when speaking, hearing is affected by the vibration of the sound through the bones of the head; thus, we do not hear ourselves as we actually sound.

If you have ever listened to a room full of people sounding the "Om" together, each at their own pitch, you will realize that the sounds blend together in a harmonious, beautiful song. No one is attempting to sound like anyone else or to intone the "Om" at the same pitch or key, yet the blending is perfect. Each voice is individual, as it should be.

The practice of humming or toning is beneficial to all levels of the body, and it affects the surrounding people and environment. Humming or toning should not be done in public, however. Like other spiritual practices, this method should remain private to avoid negative thoughts interfering with the positive intent behind it. Certain vowels and consonants historically have been linked to certain results. Some of these effects will help in magic, while others aid in healing. Singing or humming certain tones, particularly the vowels, also sets up a resonance that can open a door to the Otherworld.

Most consonants are rather explosive in sound, while vowels are softer and soothing. Some ancient cultures considered consonants to be connected with God and the vowels with the Goddess. These were called Father sonics and Mother sonics.

The following sounds can aid with healing when intoned, either by a healer for a patient or by the patient alone.

The "a" sound in "ahh" can help with depression. This sound helps the blood assimilate more oxygen, which causes the brain to release endorphins. These endorphins provide a lift in mood. This "ahh" sound attracts attention and can be used as a signal for the conscious mind to focus on a definite goal. A Goddess sound, "ahh" is considered to be one of the Matrix or Mother sonics.

The "e" sound in "emit" or "feel" stimulates the pineal gland and boosts your alertness. This is a God sound and arouses the body's energies.

The short "e" sound in "echo" can affect the thyroid gland, increasing the secretions of hormones and the metabolism.

To control sugar cravings, intone the long "o" sound as in "ocean." This sound stimulates the pancreas, which controls the level of blood sugar. The "ohh" sound, more neutral than most others, also can create connections between the person who sounds it and the environment immediately around her/him.

If you have trouble with your immune system and seem to catch every virus that makes the rounds, intone the "oo" sound as in "tool." This has a beneficial effect on the spleen, which controls the white blood cells. This "oo" sound also can bridge the conscious and subconscious minds.

A "mm" tone has long been connected with the Goddess. It helps to establish balance. Repeating this closed mouth sound builds up a vibration within the physical body, then begins to vibrate within the astral body. A Goddess sound, "mm" is another of the Matrix or Mother sonics.

Mothers frequently use the "shh" sound, another Matrix sonic, as a signal for children to be quiet. This sound actually restores harmony and brings peace. If repeated constantly, at the same tone and speed, it can be almost hypnotic.

The Celts were very familiar with many Hindu concepts of religion, healing, and martial arts. It is very probable that they knew of the chakras and mantras.

The chakras are "wheels of fire" that exist in the astral body, but affect the physical if they are out of balance. The major chakras are: the first at the base of the spine; the second halfway between the pubic bone and navel; the third at the navel; the fourth in the center of the chest; the fifth at the base of the throat; the sixth in the center of the forehead; and the seventh at the top of the head. There are also two other major chakras, such as the ones below the feet and above the head, and minor ones in the palm of each hand and the sole of each foot. The chakras are related to the endocrine system, or ductless glands, of the physical body.

Mantra is a Sanskrit word that means "the thought that frees and protects." These chanted words or groups of words were used to rebalance the chakras, unite with a deity energy, and connect with certain psychic powers. There are thousands of Hindu mantras, each with a different purpose.

To rebalance and energize the chakras, the following sounds should be intoned five to seven times each. Intoning will not overload or unbalance any chakra. Use the "uh" sound, as in "huh," for the root chakra at the base of the spine. An "ooo" sound, as in "fool," affects the spleen chakra. "Oh," as in "low," will vibrate the navel chakra, while "ah," as in "hah," will benefit the heart chakra. "Eye" is used for the throat. "Aye," as in "hay," will balance the brow chakra, also known as the Third Eye, while "eee," as in "feel," will benefit the crown chakra at the top of the head.

The bard or healer can intone these sounds to balance her/his own chakras. If working on another for balance or healing, she/he must concentrate deeply while mentally projecting the sound at the appropriate chakra.

Sounds can also be used to empower magical spells by intoning the sound appropriate to the desired manifestation. Spells for love and relationships are affected by "ahh eh," a combination of Mother and Father sonics. "Shoo maa" helps with the manifestation of material goals. "Paa maa eye oh" can aid in protective spells.

Music also falls into this category of sounds, as the musical tones produced by some instruments have the same effects as the voice. The most effective instruments seem to be those of the stringed or small woodwind families, such as the harp, lyre, piano, zither, guitar, flute, recorder, tin whistle, panpipes, and chimes. One does not have to be an expert to pick out pleasing tones. Picking out musical notes on an instrument also aids those who are determined they do not have a singing voice. You do not have to read music, have taken lessons, or even play a known tune to benefit from playing individual notes on an instrument. No matter how it is created, this music can raise the energy, calm the emotions, inspire, or heal.

The flute, tin whistle, and wooden recorder are all based on the oldest of musical instruments—the panpipes. A small keyboard or synthesizer, as well as the harpsichord, organ, piano, zither, and guitar are based on the older string instruments—the harp and lyre. Another good "instrument" is the chimes or metal bars played by tapping with a small mallet.

The harp and lyre are found in wall paintings as far back as ancient Egypt. Along with the drum and panpipes, the harp and lyre are the oldest instruments used in temples and gatherings. Although historical evidence does not confirm the use of the harp until the Middle Ages in Ireland, it is quite possible that this instrument was used long before that era. The damp environment of the Celtic realms is not conducive to preserving relics fashioned of wood. We do know from the Celtic histories and legends that the Druids frequently dedicated their harps to an Earth goddess or a goddess of inspiration, such as Brigit or Cerridwen.

The advantage to plucking out sounds on a harp or other stringed instrument is that the bard can recite a spell, prayer, or story at the same time. She/he should choose a key or tone that reflects the mood she/he wishes to impart to the audience. Sounds in a minor key can reflect sadness, regret, anger, or intrigue. The rhythm also should be calculated to fit the emotion of the spoken word.

Celtic spells or prayers were often composed in sets of three lines, or three sets of lines, using the ancient knowledge that three is a very powerful number. You may not consider yourself a poet or capable of writing poetry, but that should not stop you. Remember, it is the intent behind the words and music that produce the desired effect.

For example, you are in need of a prayer to Brigit for healing. You could use three lines that rhyme, three lines of which only two lines rhyme, or three lines that do not rhyme. "Brigit, hear my earnest plea. Bring your healing, I do ask thee. Let this person be pain free." "Brigit, bring your healing water. Give it to your ailing daughter. Bless her, goddess of the well." "Goddess of the sacred well, Brigit of light and healing, restore your child to good health."

The same rhythm and rhyming can be applied to spells for protection, good fortune, or any other goal you desire to manifest. Rather than a curse, do some creative thinking, and investigate your own inner motives. It is better to use magic to catch a criminal by her/his own words and deeds than to involve yourself in a fatal curse that could be reflected back upon you.

Symbols

As we discussed in an earlier chapter, symbols are a very important form of communication with the subconscious mind. The following symbols represent concepts found along the path of the Bard. They may be used in jewelry or embroidery on clothing, or as drawings placed near the area where you meditate.

Butterfly: This insect was used as a Celtic symbol of the immortal soul. It also became a symbol of the belief in fairies and ancestral spirits. People wore butterfly badges or brooches both as a way to identify those of like mind and as a show of respect for the fairies and ancestors.

Eagle: Associated with the deities of the sun, this bird also symbolized ancient wisdom.

Harp: This instrument represented the bridge created by sound, a bridge between this world and the Otherworld. Along with the pipes and flute, the harp was said to create a link with inhabitants of the Otherworld, particularly fairies.

Hazel Tree: Connected with great wisdom, the hazel as a tree was a symbol of the Celtic Tree of Life, the great mythological tree that reached into all of the Otherworlds and connected them with the mortal world.

Raven: A bird associated with the war goddesses, the raven also symbolized prophecy and omens.

Spear: A symbol of magical power and defense, the spear is similar to the staff and wand of the magicians and wizards.

Triskele: This triple symbol consists of three spirals that come together at a center point. The Celts understood that the triskele represented the sun, the moon, and the earth. It also represents the human aspects of body, mind, and spirit, and the three shamanic worlds.

Wand: A symbol of the magician's willpower and ability to make changes, the wand acts as a conduit to concentrate magical energy to bring about a desired result.

All Welsh Bards considered experiences at Cerridwen's Cauldron to be the high point of their career and studies. A Bard who had not undergone an initiation in the Cauldron of Cerridwen was not considered to be a true Bard.

The Cauldron of Cerridwen Meditation

Learning and practicing meditation is an absolute must for anyone on the Celtic spiritual paths. Regular meditation, not less than once a week, keeps you balanced and more able to cope with unexpected happenings. It also opens you to true messages from the ancestors, guides, and others from the Otherworld. These messages may come during meditation itself or through dreams.

For instructions on setting up a meditation space and taping the meditation, please refer to meditations in Chapter Three.

The Cauldron of Cerridwen Meditation

Close your eyes and visualize a brilliant white light over your head. As you inhale deeply, feel this light coursing through your body, from your head down to your toes. Feel your muscles relaxing, beginning with your feet. The deep sense of peacefulness moves up through your legs, into your body and arms. You feel the tenseness flow out of the muscles in your shoulders, neck, and head. You are completely relaxed.

Before you now is a well. Take all the problems in your life and throw them into the deep darkness of the well. The problems are quickly carried far away from you. Leave them there, turn and walk away. You will be constantly protected during this meditation. Absolutely nothing can harm you.

You are standing on the pebble-strewn shores of a wide lake with beautiful mountains around you. Thick stands of trees cover the slopes, their boughs and leaves rustling in a small breeze. You hear the songs of birds as they flit from tree to tree. The sun is sinking behind the distant mountains and casting a brilliant red and gold glow across the waters of the lake. As the last rays of the sun leave the lake, the birds of the forests around you fall silent. You watch a white stag and doe come down to the lake to drink. A night chorus of frogs calls to each other from the reeds along the bank, while overhead the moon begins to rise in the sky.

When the deer leave, you walk to where they drank and watch as the moonlight lays down a silvery path across the lake. As the light touches your feet, the waters of the lake gently pull back, opening a path from the shore to the center of the lake bed. At the end of this path you see the bright, firelit opening of a cave mouth. Strange, enthralling music drifts to you from the cave, and you feel compelled to see what lies within this hidden place.

You quickly follow the path until you stand at the entrance to the underwater cave. As you peer within, you see a huge cauldron hung over a blazing fire in the center of the smooth cave floor. Sitting in a chair behind the cauldron is a figure shrouded in a dark cloak, the hood pulled low over the face, concealing the facial features. By the chair sits a beautiful fairy woman playing a harp. The fairy beckons you to enter.

As you pass the cauldron to sit beside the fairy, you notice the dark liquid roiling within the great cast-iron vessel and catch glimpses of strange pictures as they quickly come and go from sight. When you reach the fairy, the dark, silent figure in the cloak moves, thrusting back the hood with one wrinkled hand. A strong, aged woman stares at you intently. Her dark eyes are like mirrors, reflecting the firelight.

"Welcome," the old woman says. "Why do you come to the cave of Cerridwen? Do you seek initiation and inspiration?"

If you answer "no," the woman will not speak to you again, although you may converse with the fairy woman.

If you answer "yes," the old woman takes up a cup and dips a little of the cauldron water into it.

"Drink this, and prepare for initiation," she says. "I am Cerridwen, the great initiator, the opener of the way, the guardian of the door to the past."

You swallow the liquid and immediately feel different. Your sight is clearer, and you can see the energy running through the rocks of the cave walls. You feel the harp music against your skin and taste it on your tongue. You hear the sounds of colors around you, and smell scents drifting from the

Otherworld. You explore these new dimensions of your senses for a time.

At last, Cerridwen takes your hand and leads you to stand beside the cauldron. She suddenly plunges your hand into the dark liquid. To your surprise, it is cool to the touch, even though it bubbles and boils over the fire.

"This is the gate to the past," Cerridwen says. "The past history of this world. The past lives and history of yourself. Do you wish to see who you were before and what lessons you have carried with you into this life to learn?"

If you answer "no," you leave the cave and return to the lakeshore.

If you answer "yes," Cerridwen suddenly plunges you into the dark cauldron. You sink deep into the cauldron but are not afraid. You see brilliant colored pictures floating around you. To see more of a past life, you focus on a picture and find yourself in that time and place, observing all that takes place. You may explore several past lives before you once more find yourself standing beside Cerridwen.

"Always search for the truth as it is," she admonishes you. "Not as you wish the truth to be. Truth is the key to the great spiritual mysteries. Without seeking and recognizing truth, you cannot progress and learn."

You spend a few more minutes talking with Cerridwen and the fairy harper. When you are ready to leave, you look out the mouth of the cave to see the strange path of moonlight illuminating the waters of the lake. The waters open, leaving a clear path out of the underwater cave. You follow the moonlit path until you once again reach the lakeshore. You think of your physical body and find yourself within it. The meditation is ended.

Dress

Ancient texts portray the bards, or Druid poets, wearing very colorful clothing. A manuscript from the eighth century describes one bard as wearing a purple robe with a gold color on the top and a speckling of bronze particles on the lower part. Brightly colored bird feathers were sewn in a pattern down the middle of the robe. To complete the outfit, the bard wore gold and silver jewelry.[23]

I doubt that all bards were quite so flamboyant. Most of them probably dressed in the customary tunic and trousers with a cloak pinned about their shoulders. The colors of these articles may have been bright, with several colors worn together. However, the bird feathers would have been inconvenient unless a bard stayed exclusively at a clan chieftain's hall. Besides, the feathered cloak or trim was allowed only to an *ollam,* the highest rank of bards. Because a bard often journeyed about the country, he would have worn laced, leather boots.

The bard's leather bag contains magical symbols of his professional rank, along with certain stones, leaves, fossils, bones, twigs, and other talismans that have spiritual meaning to her/him.

I have chosen green as the basic color for bards. Green is a color associated with the trees and the ancestral connections. Green is also a color of growth and renewal and one of the favorite colors of the fairies.

1. Dallán Forgaill was a fabled poet of sixth-century Ireland.
2. The word *dryas* may be connected with the word "dryad." Dryads were said to be Otherworld beings who dwelt in trees or groves of trees.
3. Some translators list the co-walker, or *coimimeadh*, as a guardian spirit, while others consider it the astral double.
4. Much of what we know of the ogham alphabet comes from the *Book of Ballymote*, which was compiled in the fourteenth century from much older material.
5. Since the grapevine is not native to Ireland, Scotland, or Wales, this may refer to the blackberry.
6. This crane was actually the woman Aífe, who had been transformed into the bird by a jealous rival. She spent two hundred years in the house of Manannán mac Lir before she died.
7. Michael Howard, *The Magic of the Runes*. The word *coel* or *cole* means "an omen" or "a prophet, magician, diviner." *Coel bren* was "wood used for casting lots," while *coel fain* meant "omen stones." In Welsh *coel y beirdd* meant "alphabet of the bards."
8. The superconscious, or genetic mind, was called the Collective Unconscious by Carl Jung. The mind is connected to all the knowledge known by one's ancestors.
9. See the section on astrology for more information on this mystical planet.
10. The Akashic records are astral records on the past lives of all people.
11. Caitlin and John Matthews, *Encyclopaedia of Celtic Wisdom*.
12. D. A. Mackenzie, *Scottish Folk-Lore and Folk Life*.
13. A. Carmichael, *Carmina Gadelica*.
14. This practice is very similar to the shamanic shapeshifting, which is more fully explained in Chapter Six.
15. A. Carmichael, ibid.
16. The references to cloud-divining are rather vague and may refer to astrology.
17. Robert Kirk. Editor, Stewart Sanderson. *The Secret Commonwealth*.
18. This phrase is frequently used in Pagan rituals after the circle is cast.
19. The *Barddas* was published by the Welsh Manuscript Society at Llandovery in 1862.
20. This information comes from the *Barddas*, a collection of ancient Welsh knowledge compiled by Iolo Morganwy.
21. W. Faraday, *Druidic Triads*.
22. This idea of the widow's curse may be another version of the mother's curse so feared in the Middle East.
23. Dáithí Ó hÓgáin, *The Sacred Isle: Belief and Religion in Pre-Christian Ireland*.

CHAPTER 4

THE WAY OF THE WARRIOR

The Celts are usually portrayed in history as a culture of warriors. Their histories and legends are full of great battles and brave and cunning warriors. One of the Druid admonitions for good living was to be brave. However, they also were spiritual seekers and the legends of many famous Celtic warriors tell of their spiritual and magical disciplines that took place off the battlefield. Celtic warriors tried to live a balanced life.

The Celts seem to have acquired a wide range of weaponry as they journeyed from their original homeland to their final settlements. The most frequently mentioned weapons were swords and spears. However, they also used slings and battleaxes.

The swords were usually forged of iron and kept in bronze scabbards. These swords were the huge two-handed blades called the *spathae* by the Romans. The Irish straight swords were called *cliabh* and *claidheamh dorn chrann*, while the slightly curved blades were called *airben*, which comes from *airbe*, meaning "a rib." These long weapons were carried in a baldric slung from one shoulder and crossing the chest.

The metal heads of the long spears were leaf-shaped, a distinct Celtic feature. The rectangular shields were made primarily of alder and covered with leather.

Chariots are mentioned in the myths and legends. A warrior was considered to be especially skilled if he could run up and down the shaft between the horses while the charioteer drove the team full speed into the battle. Although no chariot remains have been found in Ireland, these vehicles are mentioned in such epics as *The Cattle Raid of Cooley*. Finding no buried chariots is not unusual as the wet climate would not be conducive to preserving wooden remains.

Many battles were decided by single combat between the heroes of the opposing armies. To best an opponent in single combat required more than physical strength. Quick wits, confidence, and physical and mental agility were also necessary. It was not uncommon for these combatants to trade eloquent verbal exchanges as well as sword blows.

Not only men were heroes and great warriors. Some women followed the martial example of Celtic queens and war goddesses and were as skilled with weapons as men. Queen Medb drove her own chariot into battle. Aífe of the martial arts school on the Isle of Skye was known as the hardest woman in the world. This school on Skye was run by the greatest warrior woman of all, Scáthach. Warrior queens such as Cartimandua of the Brigantes and Boadicea of the Iceni in Britain are mentioned in history. Creidne was a champion of the Fianna, as was Erc. Eis Enchenn was an adversary of Cú Chulainn. In fact, the great hero Cú Chulainn was trained by two women: Scáthach and Aífe. As late as the sixteenth century, Gháinne Ní Mháille (Grace O'Malley) was a successful pirate who raided the English fleets. A Celtic warrior woman held a high status, even above the liberated Irish woman who had many rights and protections under the law, among them the right to own and inherit property.

In later traditions, particularly the Arthurian sagas, Druids are mentioned as physically taking part in battles. However, laws before this time mention that all members of the Druidic order were exempt from military service but could participate if they desired. Since the Celts were well acquainted with Eastern techniques, it is likely that the Druids knew of and taught Eastern martial arts to their members. A description in the *Book of Invasions* lists the type of weapons that the Tuatha Dé Danann Nuada carried into battle in his chariot. These weapons are identical to those attributed to Ninja warriors in the Orient.

The modern Celtic warrior is primarily a warrior of the spiritual and magical realms. She/he uses esoteric and Otherworld knowledge to protect the self, family and friends, and those unable to protect themselves. The modern warrior works for peace and stability through the use of magic and Otherworld journeys, and does not allow personal emotions and desires to interfere. She/he knows that peace must first be established within the self before tackling larger problems. She/he also is vigilant to preserve religious freedom for everyone.

Warrior Traits

Traits of the modern Celtic warrior are courage, a willingness to see the truth, self-discipline, defense, responsibility, and keeping physically and mentally fit.

The ancient Celts understood courage not only as being brave in the face of danger, but also as having no fear of death. They believed strongly in life in the Otherworld after death in this world. They taught that there was a constant exchange of souls between this world and the Otherworld. When someone died in this world, the soul traveled to the Otherworld and a new life. At the same time a soul traveled from the Otherworld to this world and was reborn as mortal again.

A modern Celtic warrior must always be willing to see the truth in every situation, regardless of any personal desire for things to be different. Sometimes the truth is not what we want it to be, in accordance with our narrow perception, conditioning, or personal thoughts on the subject. Facing the truth often means we must accept that we were wrong and make changes.

Responsibility is often a misunderstood and uncomfortable concept because it requires each individual to be responsible for their words and actions, good or bad. Each individual must make choices on every aspect of life, without trying to lay blame on another.

Cultivating self-discipline is a lifelong process. It requires effort to step back in any given situation, view the problem with balance and without emotion, and then make a decision. Humans tend to react out of emotions rather than reason, a response that is learned from childhood. However, we cannot simply find a place or event to blame for our condition and be free of responsibility.

In general, we are not taught how to defend ourselves properly and so we may find ourselves believing that we should never physically defend ourselves when necessary. If we accept a "doormat" attitude, we will only attract trouble. Rather than react with physical force to the small attacks in life, however, the warrior should learn to create defensive astral armor. This invisible protection will aid in deflecting most negative people and events, thus removing the problem before it ever arises. The warrior also should learn how to work defensive magic as a means of protection for both the self and others.

Keeping yourself physically and mentally fit does not mean you have to engage in strenuous exercise every day or keep an unnaturally positive attitude. Humans experience swings in moods, which are affected by astrological influences, illnesses, and whatever life throws at them on any given day. Tai chi or yoga practiced daily is of greater benefit to both the body and mind than strenuous exercises you do not enjoy and will inevitably stop doing. Both tai chi and yoga build better balance, flexibility, and mental harmony, all essential to the modern Celtic warrior.

Mythic Warriors

Celtic legends are full of stories of great warrior men and women. The Celts respected courage and cunning. The average Celt, however, was just as brave and fierce when necessary as the great heroes of legend. The mighty legions of Rome feared the Celts because of their ferocity and bravery. One Roman writer related that fighting the average Celtic man was trouble enough, but when his wife entered the fray, things got considerably worse. In early Celtic history, it was not unusual for women to fight alongside their men.

The goddess Mórrígán was a terrifying warrioress. Once, during a great battle between the men of Ulster, with the hero Cú Chulainn, and with the men of Connacht, Mórrígán with Badb and Nemain appeared in the midst of the battle. Their screams of battle fury caused one hundred men of Connacht to drop dead of fright. Mórrígán then turned into her favorite guise as a great raven and prophesied victory for the hero and his men.

Scáthach was an Amazonian warrior woman who taught martial arts on the Isle of Skye. Her pupils included the hero Cú Chulainn, to whom she taught the aggressive leap known as the *torannchless* ("thunder"). For Cú Chulainn's aid against her enemy, Aífe, Scáthach gave the warrior his famous spear, the Gáe Bulga. A tough, relentless woman, Scáthach did not make it easy to get in the gate of her school. The bridge to the gate would rise and fall under the feet of those trying to enter. If they could not master the bridge, she refused to teach them.

Cú Chulainn is considered to be the greatest hero of early Irish legends, and one of the three great heroes. Said to be the son of Lugh by the mortal woman Dechtire, he was originally named Sétanta and fostered by Conchobar at Emain Macha. When only seven years old, he went with Conchobar to the smith Culann at Cuailnge, where he killed the smith's great guard dog when it attacked him. The smith was upset by this, so the boy promised to serve as his guard dog until a new pup could be raised. Thus, he obtained the name Cú Chulainn, "Hound of Culann." Before he could marry Emer, he had to concede to her father's wishes and first train with Scáthach. Before going into any battle, Cú Chulainn underwent a transformation into the *ríastrad*, or battle fury. His famous Salmon Leap has been compared to the jump of a modern soccer player.[1] One of his best-known exploits is detailed in the *Táin Bó Cuailnge* (Cattle Raid of Cooley), where he single-handedly defended Ulster against Queen Medb and King Ailill.

Fionn mac Cumhaill, anglicized into Finn MacCool, was an Irish warrior and seer who led the famous Fianna Éireann. His story is part of the Fenian Cycle of Irish literature. He was courageous and generous, admitting only strong, brave men and women to his warrior band. At age seven, Fionn became a pupil of the Druid Finnéces and ate the Salmon of Wisdom; this gave him great knowledge and prophetic abilities. He trained under the warrior woman Búanann and the warrior Cethern mac Fintain. A stanch defender of Ireland and justice, Fionn and his Fianna are said to be sleeping in some hidden place and will return when Ireland needs him.

Conn Cétchathach, also known as Conn of the Hundred Battles, is said, in some ancient annals, to have lived in the second century C.E. The province Connacht is named after him. Conn was the first of the Irish kings to hear the groan of acceptance from the Lia Fáil, when he stepped on it. He was still a very young man when he seized Tara from Catháir Mór and began his long reign. The epithet of "Hundred Battles" was bestowed upon him because of his constant warfare against his rival, the king of Munster. Fionn and the Fianna were among his most faithful allies.

Boadicea, sometimes spelled Boudicca, was queen of the British Iceni. A tall woman with hip-length red hair, she expected to rule her clan when her husband died. However, the Romans who ruled most of Britain at that time seized her territory, as they did not honor the Celtic right of inheritance. When Boadicea objected, the Romans scourged her and raped her two daughters. Infuriated at this treatment, Boadicea raised an army of several Celtic tribes in 64 C.E. and swept through southern Britain like a whirlwind. She put all of London to the sword and fire, killing 20,000 people, before turning her armies north. General Suetonius was at the Isle of Mona at the time, exterminating all the gathered Druids. Only his swift return, to meet Boadicea on the march, saved what remained of his legions. Defiant to the end, the Queen managed to drink poison she had hidden in her clothing rather than be taken to Rome and put to death.

Cináed mac Alpín was the first king of Scotland, or of Dál Riada. Legend says he ruled from 844 until 858 C.E. He united the Irish invaders in Argyll[2] with the Picts of his mother's family, thus consolidating the first substantial kingdom in Scotland. His name is anglicized as Kenneth MacAlpin.

Brian Bórama[3] (Boru) was the victorious High King (Ard Rí) of the Battle of Clontarf in 1014, where the Irish Celts defeated the Vikings. In the *Book of Armagh*, Brian is called the emperor of the Irish, although he never created a national monarchy. He began his rule at Kincora on the Shannon, where he first fought the Danes of Limerick. He was seventy-four years old when he led forces from all over Ireland against the Norsemen at Clontarf. This battle was not to expel the Norsemen, but to break their control so all could live in peace.

The Four Mystical Tools

Irish legends in the *Book of Conquests*, the *Lebor Gabála Érenn*, say that the Tuatha Dé Danann came to Ireland from four mysterious cities that are described as located in the sky. The four cities were Falias, Murias, Findias, and Gorias. Along with the Sacred Isle (in Wales called the Glass Castle), they marked the five points of a circle—the four cardinal directions and the center. The cities corresponded to the elements of Earth, Air, Fire, and Water, with the Sacred Isle in the center representing Spirit. These elements can also be laid out on an upright pentagram, or five-point star, with Spirit at the top point. This concept was used in Ireland to lay out the five provinces, with Uisneach marking the spiritual center.

When the Tuatha Dé Danann left these mystical cities, they brought with them four magical tools or weapons. These were the spear of Lugh from Gorias ("burning fort"), the cauldron of the Dagda from Murias ("fort of the sea"), the sword of Nuada from Findias ("bright-white fort"), and the coronation stone called the Lia Fáil from Falias. There were four *fisidh*, "seers," who lived in these cities: Morfessa in Falias, Esras in Gorias, Uscias in Findias, and Semias in Murias.[4]

The spear of Lugh gave the wielder the power to win any battle. When the sword of Nuada was unsheathed, no one could escape. The cauldron of the Dagda always contained enough food to satisfy everyone.

The Lia Fáil, or Stone of Fál, is the most intriguing of the four Irish treasures as it was said to shout or cry out whenever the true king stepped upon it or touched it. Originally, this stone was said to rest on a platform within a structure later called "Cormac's House." The goddess of Tara was called *Medb Temrach*, "she who intoxicates."

These four magical tools are important to the modern Celtic magician for the practice of magic, aids on Otherworld journeys, meditations, and as symbols of progress on the path of life and spiritual growth. Each tool can be placed on the Year Wheel for rituals and on the magic circle for spellwork to represent each of the Celtic paths. These tools also may be used as actual objects, as suggested in the rituals at the end of this section.

The Lia Fáil, symbolized by a flat stone, is placed at the north and belongs to the path of the mystic; it represents the element of Earth.

The spear of Lugh (a modern staff or wand) belongs in the east, where it represents the bard and the element of Air. The mighty sword of Nuada is placed in the south for the warrior path; its modern equivalent is a sword and is connected with the element of Fire. The healing cauldron of the Dagda belongs in the west, where it represents the healer and the element of Water.

The Thirteen Treasures of Britain[5] are mentioned in Welsh tradition. These treasures may have referred to the thirteen consonants in the ogham alphabet or they could represent thirteen magical and sacred objects used by the Welsh Druidic orders. According to the Welsh *Triads*, the Thirteen Treasures of Britain are:

1. Drynwyn, the sword of Rhydderch the Generous
2. the Hamper of Gwyddno Garanhir
3. the Horn of Bran
4. the Chariot of Morgan the Wealthy
5. the Halter of Clydno Eiddyn
6. the Knife of Llawfronedd the Horseman
7. the Cauldron of Dyrnwch the Giant
8. the Whetstone of Tudwal Tydglyd
9. the Coat of Padaen Red-Coat

10 & 11. the Crock and Dish of Rhygenydd the Cleric

12. the Chessboard of Gwenddolau ap Ceidio
13. the Mantle of Arthur of Cornwall

Mirror Magic

There have been a number of beautiful mirrors found in Celtic graves. They are decorated with swirling Celtic designs and are in excellent condition, suggesting that they were not used entirely for cosmetic purposes. Smiths made these beaten and polished copper mirrors, just as they did the elaborate jewelry favored by the Celtic clans.

The mirror can be used for scrying. The goddess Brigit was sometimes portrayed holding a mirror in her aspect as prophet. Water and wells, also used in much the same way as mirrors, are connected with other goddesses of inspiration and divination, such as Bóann.

To scry with a mirror, place it in an upright position with a candle behind it. Turn off any lights, and gaze into the mirror. Blink your eyes when necessary. Let your gaze go slightly out of focus. Watch for changes in your reflected image or strange scenes to appear.

Depending upon your intent, you can use this procedure for glimpses into the future, seeing yourself as you looked in past lives, or discovering your personal spiritual teachers and guides.

Two mirrors also can be used with a candle spell. By placing each mirror to reflect the burning candle and its image in the other mirror, you intensify the power put forth by the spell.

If you have a poor self-image and are very critical of yourself, gaze into a mirror while reciting all the good qualities you have. Continue to look at yourself, even though you may be embarrassed to do this at first. Vocalize all the nice things you do. This procedure will influence your subconscious mind where the poor self-image is kept, eventually reversing it so that you feel better about yourself. This is not a one-time effort but must be repeated until you stop associating yourself with negative personal images. This method can also help you to change bad habits, if you recite such positive phrases as "I will live a healthy lifestyle," "I can find the perfect job and stick with it," or "I will keep better control of my spending."

Gestures and Exercises

Certain hand gestures are mentioned in Celtic legends as well as being represented in Celtic art, such as the Gundestrup Cauldron. On this famous cauldron are portrayals of men and women with their hands and arms in various positions, which are known to be sacred in other cultures.[6]

When both arms are raised and the fists are clenched, with palms forward, the figure is performing an invoking ceremony. Arms crossed on the chest with the hands open is praising. When the hands are raised to the chest with the left hand open above the right hand, it symbolizes a blessing.

For a shaman or magician to accomplish a desired goal, the intention of a new perception of reality must exist. This requires unbending purpose. To help achieve unbending purpose, the spiritual warrior can use passes with the hands to reach into the astral planes of the Otherworld and bring back the right type of energy.

Cleansing: The first pass to use, whether working magic, performing a healing, or preparing for a journey into the Otherworld is to clean your personal aura. The aura is the invisible energy field that surrounds your physical body. It acts as a giant psychic filter to strain out most of the negative thought forms that bombard us each day. If not removed, this leaves a psychic sludge that can eventually filter into the physical body as disease or imbalance.

To do a cleansing pass, stand straight with your hands palms up close to the chest and close your eyes. As you breathe in, visualize your hands filled with brilliant white light. As you exhale, sweep the arms down to the sides, then up above the head. End with the palms together above the head. Inhale again, and draw the hands down over the outline of the body. Do not touch the body itself, but keep the hands about two to four inches away. Continue the sweep down to the feet. Finish by shaking the hands sharply to dislodge any contaminating particles.

This pass may be used before a healing, meditation, ritual, or at any time during the day when you feel stress creeping up on you.

Gathering: Rub the palms of the hands together until they begin to feel warm. Inhale as you stretch your arms out to each side and slowly bring the hands close together in front of you. The closer your hands get, the more you will feel a slight tingling and/or a pushing against the palms. This is psychic energy between your hands. Exhale slowly, and then breathe normally. This gathering can be repeated until you feel you have gathered as much energy as you can at this time. This energy can be molded into a tight ball, as described in the next hand pass.

Molding: When you feel as if you have gathered enough energy between your hands, begin to move your hands back and forth in a slight rocking motion. Visualize yourself molding the energy as you would a ball of clay, smoothing the sides and making it more compact. As the energy becomes more compact, it will produce a stronger tingling or pushing feeling against your hands. This energy can be placed directly on the diseased part of a patient's body for healing, on a candle to be used in spellwork, or in the center of your ritual or meditation space as a working aid or protector. It also can be directly on top of the head or on the shoulder for protection. This ball of energy will last from a few minutes for a beginner to several hours or days for an advanced student.

Defense: We all come under attack at one time or another, perhaps not physically, but certainly mentally, emotionally, and psychically. When this happens, quickly gather the astral energy with your hands. Do this by making a scooping motion with your hands, followed by bringing your hands close together as if holding a ball. Holding the energy ball in your right hand (left hand if you use that hand), turn your hand, palm inward toward your throat. Then, making a sharp "pah" sound, throw your arm straight in front of you and release the ball. You do not have to be facing the responsible person for the energy ball to find her/him. Simply keep the person's name in mind as you do this magical pass.

It is also possible that the Celtic priests were familiar with the positions of yoga. The horned, male figure on the Gundestrup Cauldron is seated in a semi-lotus position; both legs are drawn up, with the right foot tucked under the left thigh like an Eastern Buddha. Both arms are raised, and he holds a torc (a symbol of divine nobility) in his right hand. In the left hand, he holds a serpent, which is a worldwide symbol of spiritual power.

There is no clear definition given in the myths of Cú Chulainn's famous Salmon Leap. However, it was an extremely effective and aggressive combat strategy. What we do know of it is reminiscent of the leap used in soccer, or perhaps the kick moves in tai chi or other martial arts techniques.

Yoga exercises, as well as tai chi, are mild but highly effective exercises for anyone at any age and promote suppleness, balance, and breath control, especially when you get older. If done properly, there is no danger of pulled muscles, overexertion, or the aggravation of existing health problems. However, if you are suffering from heart or lung disease or hypertension, check with your doctor first.

Calming Breath: Sit with your feet cross-legged, your head up, and your shoulders relaxed. Let your arms hang down by your sides. As you raise your arms slowly straight over your head, inhale deeply. Exhale as you return your arms to the down position. Repeat this five times.

The Twist: Still sitting cross-legged, place your left hand on your right knee as you inhale and twist the body slowly to the right. Let your right arm hang loosely for balance. Exhale as you return to center. Repeat by twisting to the left with the right hand on the left knee. Repeat four times, going as far as possible, without straining.

The Cobra: Lie face down on the floor with your hands beside your shoulders. Slowly inhale and push your upper body upward with your hands, at the same time raising your head as far back as you can but keeping your lower body and feet on the floor. Exhale as you slowly return to the face down position. Repeat three times.

Forward Bend: Sit on the floor with your legs straight out in front of you. Bend the right leg and place the sole of the right foot against the left leg at the knee, if possible. Inhale and raise your arms over your head; then exhale and bend forward as far as you can without strain. Return to the upright position. Straighten the right leg out. Bend the left leg and place the sole of the left foot against the right knee. Repeat the movements. Do the exercise five times with each leg.

The Mountain and the Moon: Stand up straight with your shoulders relaxed and your weight evenly distributed on both feet. Clasp your hands together straight over your head. Inhale as you bend slowly to the right; exhale as you move slowly back to the starting position. Repeat by inhaling and bending to the left, then returning to the upright stance. Do this five times to each side.

The Warrior: Begin by standing in the upright position. Step forward with your right foot. Inhale and clasp your hands over your head. Keep your clasped hands over your head during the entire exercise. Exhale as you bend your right knee, keeping your left leg straight behind you. Do not bend the right knee to extend over the foot, but keep the thigh parallel to the floor. Return to the upright position, and repeat with the other leg. Repeat five times with each leg.

The Triangle: Stand straight with your feet apart. Inhale as you lift both arms straight out from the shoulders. Exhale while bending down to place your right hand on your right shin or ankle. If you cannot reach the shin, go as far down as you can. Inhale as you return to the center. Repeat on the other side. Do five times on each side.

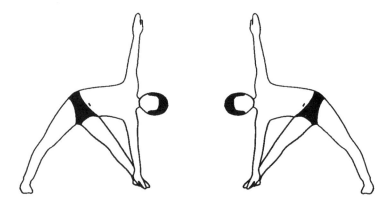

At One With the World: Lie on your back with your legs straight and your arms beside your body. Relax all your muscles until you feel as if you are sinking into the floor. Breathe slowly in a regular pattern as you let your mind blend naturally with your environment. Continue relaxing until you feel calm and centered. Sometimes you may feel as if you are floating on a cloud.

The Eight-Spoked Sacred Circle

The Celtic symbol of the eight-spoked wheel or circle was actually a diagram representing the Celtic year according to the eight religious festivals. The festivals were counted from the top spoke moving sunwise, or to the right, around the wheel. Each festival was usually celebrated for a period of three days, beginning on the eve before the festival.

Although any ritual can be done at any time if it is necessary, you will have more success if you time your rituals and projects to coincide with specific seasonal holy days. There are distinct flows of energy during these times that can be tapped into. The following list of energies begins with Samhain, the beginning and ending of the Celtic year.

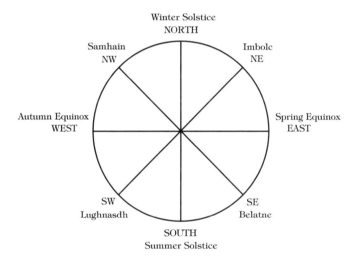

Samhain: The earth energies are winding down into a deeper, slower rhythm. This is a time for making peace with the past, taking stock of the year's accomplishments, and getting rid of negative things in your life.

Winter Solstice: The sun's energies are once more awakening. Although still weak, they can aid in thinking about new goals for the coming year.

Imbolc: The earth's energies are beginning to awaken. This is a good time for initiations, planting thought-seeds for specific desires, and doing spring cleaning as a symbolic gesture of making way for the new.

Spring Equinox: The earth's energies have moved into a creation mode, as seen in all nature at this time. It is a time for renewing your relationship with nature spirits and all deities of the earth.

Beltane: A fertility festival, this is a ripe time for moving ahead with plans for changes in your life. You may need to rethink goals. This is an excellent time to make a "wish book" of things you would like to see happen.

Summer Solstice: Both the sun's and the earth's energies are at their peak now. This is an excellent time for strengthening your connections to the Otherworld and its inhabitants, particularly with the fairies.

Lughnasadh: A harvest festival, this is a time of preparing oneself for the coming winter. Decide which events, goals, or relationships are actually "dead" issues and make preparations to remove them from your life.

Autumn Equinox: The sun's energy is beginning to fade and grow weaker. This is a time to think conscientiously about new goals or rewriting existing ones. Plan rituals to give thanks for all your desires that have manifested during the year.

It is also profitable to learn to work with the energy flows of the moon as it changes each month from full moon to new moon and back again. In a simplified form, the full moon energies are for drawing things to you, while the new moon energies are for moving things away from you.

The Druids were acquainted with astronomy and astrology, as well as having the ability to calculate a lunar-solar calendar. They recognized and used the current of energy created by the changing moon and the solar seasons. The energies of the moon change four times a month, with the full moon tides being strongest. The full moon directly after the Winter Solstice is the strongest of the year. The solar energies change only four times a year, and have longer lasting influences.

Samhain, Calan Gaeaf in Wales: Celebrated on October 31, the last day of the Celtic year, this festival was placed at the top spoke of the wheel. It was a time when the veil between this world and the Otherworld thinned so much that communications with the ancestors were easily accomplished. It was also a time for settling old grudges and debts before the start of the new year on November 1, not by physical force, but by negotiation and compromise.

Winter Solstice, Alban Arthuan in Wales: The shortest day and the darkest part of the year, this midwinter festival on approximately December 21 celebrated the returning sun.

Imbolc, Bwyl Mair Dechrau'r Gwanwyn in Wales: This festival of returning life to the earth was celebrated on February 1. It was dedicated to the triple Brigit, whose birth in a flaming house of the sun was said to usher in fertility and new life for the dead. The name may be connected to the Irish word *imb-fholc*, which means "washing oneself." The Celts considered this a festival of purification. Brigit's colors were often shown as black, red, and white.

Spring Equinox, Alban Eiler in Wales: Celebrated on about March 21, this festival celebrated the time when night and day stood equal and the sun was growing stronger.

Beltane, Calan Mai in Wales: This festival on May 1 was the spiritual balance for Samhain. Although a fertility celebration, it was not considered an auspicious time for marriages. This festival of purification and contact with the Otherworld ushered in the summer season. The Old Irish name for this festival was *Belo-tenia*, "bonfires of Belos, the Bright," or the god of the sun, healing, and cattle. The medieval Irish name was *Cétshamain*, which was derived from the Old Irish *Kentu-saminos*, "first of summer," or *cét-sam-sin*, "first of summer weather." The Scots Gaelic name for the month of May is *Céitein*.

Summer Solstice, Alban Heruin in Wales: Celebrated on approximately June 21, this festival celebrated the high point of the sun before it began to decline. The Old Celtic name was *Medio-saminos*, "midsummer." Modern names for the month of June are *Meitheamh* in Irish, *Mehefin* in Welsh, and *Metheven* in Cornwall. In Welsh tradition, Summer Solstice was considered one of the *tair ysbrydnos*, "three spirit-nights," of the year. The other two were Calan Gaeaf (Samhain) and Calan Mai (Beltane). At one time in Munster, Ireland, people picked mallow leaves on Summer's Eve and touched all in the family with them before throwing the leaves into the bonfires.

Lughnasadh, Calan Awst in Wales: Celebrated on August 1, this was the first of two harvest festivals. The name means "Lugh-assembly." Legend says that the god Lugh instituted this festival in memory of his foster mother Tailtiu. Many marriages took place then.

Autumn Equinox, Alban Elved in Wales: On about September 21, the day and night again stood equal, but this time in a period of the waning sun. In the Celtic areas, the last of the harvest would be gathered by the end of September, with the last sheaf of grain plaited into a "corn dolly." In Wales this was called the *caseg fedi*, "harvest mare." In Scotland a good harvest was recognized by calling the sheaf the Harvest Queen; a bad harvest was recognized by calling it the Cailleach. This sheaf was kept and burned at the end of the next year's harvest.

The wheel of eight spokes also served as a diagram for the ritual area used for working magic. The vertical divider from top to bottom signified the north-south delineation, with north at the top and south at the bottom. Or if facing north, north before you, south behind you. The horizontal divider represented east and west; if one stood in the center of the circle facing north, west would be on the left hand and east on the right. See illustration on page 131.

North: Winter Solstice
Northeast: Imbolc
East: Spring Equinox
Southeast: Beltane
South: Summer Solstice
Southwest: Lughnasadh
West: Autumn Equinox
Northwest: Samhain

Each sacred circle, whether cast for magic or a ritual, is traditionally divided into four quarters. The Irish text called the *Suidigud Tellaig Temra* (The Settling of the Manor at Tara) reveals the traditional meanings of the quarters to the Celts. These quarters were based on the functions of the typical Celtic clan. The north corresponded to *cath*, "battle"—the protection of the clan and its members. The east represented *bláth*, "plenty"—an adequate supply of food, shelter, and clothing. The south corresponded to *séis*, "song" or "inborn artistic talents"—music, storytelling, art, and singing are necessary ingredients for the development of the soul. The west represented *fios*, "knowledge"—knowledge and learning are essential for the development of both the body and soul. (See page 135.)

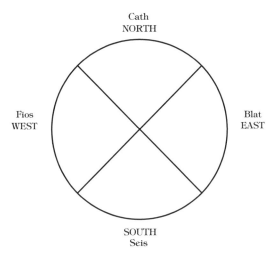

There was an old Celtic custom of passing things to the right, rather than to the left. This probably emerged from the ritual turnings in religious celebrations. The Irish called the sunwise movement *cor deiseil*, or "the auspicious right-hand turn." This phrase and movement is distinctly different from *cor tuathal*, "the mundane left-hand turn." The only time the widdershins, or left-hand turn, was made during ritual was to "unmake" or "unravel" something.

In Wales the same custom of sunwise turn is found. The Welsh Druids believed that one should face east toward the rising sun when praying. This accounts for the Welsh word *gogledd*, "under the left hand," or north, as opposed to *deheu*, "under the right hand," or south.

Originally, Ireland was divided into four provinces and a sacred center. The hill of Uisneach, which lies between Mullingar and Athlone, marked this center. On the Celtic holy days, the priests lit ritual fires on the hill of Uisneach. These fires symbolized the spiritual fire of enlightenment, not the physical light or the sun as they are often interpreted. All light represented enlightenment. For this reason, the hearth fire in homes was never allowed to go out except at Beltane. During this festival, families from each province went to the hill of Uisneach and carried back torches lit from the central sacred fire to rekindle the hearths of their clans.

The four paths of the Celtic spiritual seeker also can be placed on the Wheel. The bard corresponds to the east, the area of mental work;

the warrior in the south in the field of action; the healer in the west where emotional and psychic issues come into play; and the mystic in the north, the area of deep earth and cosmic wisdom.

The directions themselves represented certain aspects of life. These aspects were used in both magical workings and divination. In order to protect and defend, warriors need to know how to travel forward and backward in time to find the causes of problems or the possible outcomes of actions. By aligning themselves mentally with a certain direction and its symbolic meanings, they can time-travel more accurately.

The east symbolizes spring, new beginnings, skill and fortune, inspiration, renewal, the dawn, mental activities, and the element of Air. The south represents summer, light, growth, dreams, changes, getting rid of old ideas, noon, physical actions, and the element of Fire. The west stands for autumn, creativity, fertility, love and the emotions, inner purpose and dreams, twilight, and the element of Water. The north symbolizes winter, strength, wisdom, clarity of thought, minerals, darkness, rebirth, and the element of Earth.

Casting a Circle

Place all your ritual items inside the area in which you plan to work. Unless it is an emergency, you should not leave the circle until you are finished.

Stand before your altar and take deep breaths to calm and center yourself. Using your forefinger, dagger, or sword, begin in the east and move sunwise around the circle. Visualize a stream of white light pouring from the end of your finger or tool and marking out the sacred area. Finish by overlapping the ends of the circle in the east. This invisible circle will contain the power you raise by your work there, and then disperse it in one blast when you are finished.

After you have completed your ritual or spellwork, break the circle by a backward movement of your finger or tool over the boundary. The circle is now cut and open.

Rituals

You can, and should, write your own rituals for each occasion or seasonal celebration. This also applies to the chants for candle burning magic. However, if you feel uncomfortable doing this, there are several books with appropriate rituals. Even using these, feel free to change any parts you wish. Carefully plan out your ritual before attempting it. Chaos and indecision will kill all your efforts.

It is important to gain the subconscious mind's cooperation during a ritual. This is accomplished by providing appropriate visual symbols, such as colors and objects. Without the cooperation of the subconscious mind, which makes the vital connection with the Otherworld and its beings, you will not have success.

Intoning specific sounds or playing pleasant music on an instrument can be valuable in calling up the power and/or deities you wish to help you. This also applies to chanting a verse to a particular deity. These actions attract the attention of the deity, thus making it easier for you to ask her/his aid.

After you have finished the basic ritual, remember to thank all who helped you: deities, nature spirits, fairies, and animal allies.

You will become more comfortable and confident as you continue to do rituals within your sacred area.

Universal Shamanic Principles

There are certain universal principles that must be understood before one can be successful in magic, shamanism, or simply extending one's spirituality.

1. *Everything in the universe is mentally created.* Therefore, it is affected by concentrated mental processes.
2. *As above, so below.* There are corresponding existences, rules, and events in any plane of existence. What exists in the Otherworld has its reflections in this world, and vice versa. These may not be identical, but there are similarities. Everything that manifests in the physical world must first be created in the Otherworld. This is accomplished through magic and intent.
3. *Everything moves.* There is no rest in any object, even inanimate. Everything vibrates to its own frequency, which allows it to exist and have form and substance.
4. *There is always duality, polarity, and pairs of opposites.* Without polarity, there would be imbalance. The universe does not tolerate imbalance, but reconciles every paradox. When the pendulum of events, reactions, or thoughts swings too far in one direction, it will compensate by swinging in the other direction.
5. *The rhythms and tides of the universe compensate for every pendulum swing.* Nothing stays static. Change is constant.
6. *Every action provokes a reaction.* Every cause produces an effect.
7. *Everything in the universe has positive or negative attributes, feminine or masculine aspects.* Nothing is neutral. Even within humans, there are both masculine and feminine attributes and hormones.
8. *The only thing truly hidden is that which cannot be understood.*
9. *There is only one thing that cannot be understood: the Great Creating Spirit.*

Anyone who seeks to become a shaman or warrior, or who seeks to progress spiritually, must acknowledge and understand why she/he is taking such a path. Shamanism is a practice that is a way of life. It teaches you how to take mental control of your life and attain your goals through altered states of consciousness and contact with the Otherworld. It also makes you face the truth of your own actions and thoughts.

1. Understand who you really are and love yourself anyway.
2. Decide what you want to do with your life. If it will better your life in a positive way, set appropriate goals to achieve this.
3. Cultivate a sense of connectedness with all things, animate or inanimate.
4. Develop self-confidence and self-esteem by accomplishing small shamanic tasks at first.
5. Take control of your life by balancing your energy. Balance your responsibilities of self, family, work, and spiritual pursuits. This will help you to be less stressed and more relaxed, thus increasing your self-control.
6. Get in touch with your inner self, the "you" that you hide behind your public personality mask.
7. Develop a strong communication with your Otherworld guides and your ancestors. This will help to build peace and serenity.

Symbols

The path of the warrior requires new symbols, an expansion of the language the Celtic shaman uses to reach the subconscious mind. Meditating upon drawings of these symbols will aid in the shaman's reaching a deeper understanding of their meanings.

Boar: A symbol of cunning, strength, and courage, the boar was considered to be a magical, mythical creature by the Celts, an animal who had connections with the Otherworld, particularly the Underworld.

Eternal knot: Used as a protective device in everyday ornamentation, the eternal knot also was used by the Celts to represent the labyrinth path that led into the very center of the Otherworld, the path that led to the cauldron of Cerridwen.

Hawthorn: This tree was both loved and feared by the Celts, as it was connected with fairies and the Otherworld. Frequently, it was either the abode of fairies or marked a gateway into the Otherworld.

Hound: Hounds were frequent companions to Otherworld beings. Guardians of the innocent and hunters of those who break spiritual and ethical laws, hounds were believed able to carry blessings or curses sent by others.

Shield: Although shields were primarily used for defense, they also had another important purpose. The design on a shield was a method of identification:

Sun: The Celts recognized both goddesses and gods of the sun. As a symbol of light and enlightenment, the sun represents both creative and destructive power.

Sword: This weapon has dual purposes. It can defend and liberate, or it can attack and wound. These purposes extend to the magical level.

Isle of Skye Meditation

For instructions on setting up a meditation space and taping the meditation, please refer to The Well of Slane Meditation in Chapter Three.

Isle of Skye Meditation

Close your eyes and visualize a brilliant white light over your head. As you inhale deeply, feel this light coursing through your body, from your head down to your toes. Feel your muscles relaxing, beginning with your feet. The deep sense of peacefulness moves up through your legs, into your body and arms. You feel the tenseness flow out of the muscles in your shoulders, neck, and head. You are completely relaxed.

Before you now is a river. Take all the problems in your life and throw them into the swiftly moving water. The problems are quickly carried far away from you. Leave them there, turn and walk away. You will be constantly protected during this meditation. Absolutely nothing can harm you.

You are in a small boat approaching an island. Huge rocky hill masses rise into the blue sky, clawing at the fleecy white clouds sailing overhead. As the boat bumps up onto the beach, you see a group of warriors, both men and women, waiting for you. As you join them, they lead the way along a path that passes thatched stone cottages, with fishing nets hung on racks.

You go beyond the village toward higher ground. There, with the rugged mountains as a backdrop, you see clusters of rough stone buildings surrounding a leveled field. On this field are warriors practicing their leaps and lunges, swords in hand.

As you watch, a tall woman wearing a concealing helmet walks toward you. Her long black hair is pulled through the top of the helmet and falls in a thick braid down her muscled back. As she takes off the helmet, she looks at you with penetrating dark eyes.

"Welcome to my school," she says. "I am Scáthach. I have been waiting for you. Come with me."

You follow her into a long stone building with a steep thatched roof. The interior is brightly lit with torches; a round stone hearth with a low-burning fire marks the center of the room. Tapestries hang on the walls with wooden benches beneath them. Scáthach walks to a high-backed chair and sits down, gesturing you to sit on the bench near her right hand.

"Do you understand what makes a spiritual warrior?" Scáthach asks. "It requires courage and dedication, determination and discretion. A spiritual warrior does not rely on physical weapons, but on weapons of the heart and mind. You must dedicate yourself to fight evil wherever you find it. However, the fight takes place only in the astral planes of the Otherworld." Her dark eyes hold yours as she looks deep within your soul. "Personal desires, likes and dislikes, have little to do with fulfilling your task as a spiritual warrior. You will always recognize evil when you see it. Evil is your only enemy, whether the evil is done by a personal foe or by a friend against someone you dislike. Will you accept this challenge?"

You answer truthfully, asking any questions you may have.

"Why do you want to walk the path of the spiritual warrior?" she asks.

Answer her as best you can with truthfulness and sincerity. Scáthach will answer other questions you may have about your life and goals. Listen closely to what you need to hear, not what you want to hear.

"Come," she says as she rises and goes to the outer door.

You follow and find that a dense fog has rolled in off the sea and is so thick over the practice field that you cannot see halfway down its length. The silent warriors are now lined up on both sides of a path of glowing coals, a path that stretches off into the blinding fog.

"To be initiated into the path of the warrior, you must walk this path of coals." Scáthach points to the bright ribbon that leads from just before you off into the fog. Heat waves rising from the coals make ripples in the air. "If you do not walk the path now, you cannot return for four moons."

The warriors lining the path of coals begin beating their swords against their shields. You take a deep breath and begin walking down the glowing path, your eyes locked on the end in the fog ahead. The warriors shout wild cries of encouragement.

You do not look down, although you can hear the crunch of coals under your feet. You feel no heat or burning as you stride confidently toward the end. You walk on and on, determined to succeed. When you reach the end of the path of coals, you find Scáthach waiting for you.

"You have done well," she says and smiles. "As a warrior, you must believe in yourself and what you can do, even when others do not believe in you."

She hands you a silver armband in a symbolic design that will have meaning to your life. Look at it closely. This symbol will remain with you in an astral form even after you return to the physical world.

"You may return at any time for further instruction," Scáthach says. "If you need help, call upon me, and I will come."

You may now talk further with Scáthach and her warriors if you wish.

When you are ready to leave, you look up to see a white stag waiting at the edge of the bank of fog. You follow the stag until you once again reach the ocean. You think of your physical body and find yourself within it. The meditation is ended.

Dress

Most of the time warriors dressed like most other people, except for times of battle. In battle, they may have worn a shorter tunic-shirt than they did for everyday use. The *brat*, or long cloak, was fastened with bronze brooches; sometimes it was wound around the body several times against the weather.[7] The *brat* may have been dyed or woven in special colors or a tartan plaid to distinguish warriors of different clans. They tied their long hair or wound it up on the top of their heads to keep it out of their eyes.

Warriors often wore torcs around their necks and wide, bronze wrist cuffs. Iron was considered to have magical properties for the warrior, and was frequently made into torcs and other ornaments to wear into battle. It is unlikely that Celtic warriors wore rings into conflicts as the rings would have impeded a secure grip on weapons. Laced leather boots were worn to protect the feet from stones and thistles.

There are many women warriors listed in Celtic legends. They held equal status with male warriors and would have dressed in a similar fashion.

I have chosen the color red as the predominant color for the warrior. Red symbolized the color of blood and life itself.

Although ancient warriors carried swords, daggers, and spears, this is no longer necessary. The modern Celtic warrior fights with magical weapons instead. The actual weapons would be used only within a magical circle when performing protection rituals.

The warrior's leather bag would contain amulets and talismans, plus representations of chosen symbols. Perhaps she/he would include objects that symbolize the four mystic weapons of the Tuatha Dé Danann.

1. James MacKillop, *Dictionary of Celtic Mythology.*
2. Argyll has been called Strathclyde since 1974.
3. This king also bore the patronymic name of mac Ceinnéidigh. The name Bórama comes from Béal Bórama, "The Pass of the Tributes," which was an earthen fort near Killaloe.
4. John & Caitlin Matthews, *The Aquarian Guide to British and Irish Mythology.*
5. Ibid.
6. In India, these gestures are known as Mudras. In many magical traditions, they are called magical passes.
7. Originally, the Irish cloak did not have sleeves or a hood. The length of the cloak denoted the social status of the wearer with kings and chiefs wearing theirs with five folds and warriors with three folds. Sometimes the cloak had bright, colorful braid or fringes attached.

CHAPTER 5

THE WAY OF THE MYSTIC

Although members of the Celtic religious order were known basically by their degrees of study, collectively they were known as Druids. Unlike some modern institutions of study, no Druid was admitted to a higher rank without passing stringent tests given by elder Druids. Technically speaking, the Druids were the highest rank of the Celtic religious order and were the mystics and most proficient shamans.

The mystics fully understood that humans are part of the entire natural world, in fact, part of the entire universe and everything in it. This philosophy was the foundation of Celtic traditions and spiritual belief. They realized that to be able to create and use the supernatural power of shamanism they had to raise their spiritual thinking until it met and meshed with the powers of the Otherworld, which are of a different vibration.

Although this spiritual journey may appear to be an outward one, it is actually an inward process. Everything necessary for advanced spirituality and magic is found deep within each person. Like the mystical Celtic spiral, each person must work to reach the core of her/his being. However, the journey does not end there. The traveler must pass the threshold of the genetic mind, or collective unconscious that was discussed earlier, then begin the spiral again, this time into the Otherworld realm of deities, creatures, spirits, and spirituality.

The ancient Celtic Druids were renowned for their knowledge of a wide range of subjects. They were very familiar with the principles and practices of astronomy and astrology. Their healing skills were superb. Repeatedly in Celtic legends there is mention of Druids who could control the elements. They used their mental powers to start fires, call down lightning, and cause storms. They were able to shapeshift into animals, they were said to be able to fly, they could communicate with birds, and they had the ability to create the Druid's fog, or *ceo druidechta*. Their ceremonies incorporated the shamanic practices of ritual drumming and dancing.

The Druids, like all shamans, had one major function, to mediate between this world and the Otherworld for the Celtic clans. There are frequent mentions of a "divine language" used to communicate with Otherworld beings. This may refer to the ogham code by which they passed messages from one Druid to another. However, they also used a system of riddles and dark sayings that could be interpreted as a secret or divine language. The obscure phrases used in these sayings were known as *bélra na filed*, or "language of the poets." This poetic language was said to have *duibhe* ("obscure blackness"), *dorchatu* ("mysterious darkness"), and *dlúithe* ("compactness" or "succinctness").

Although not much is known about the ceremony of baptism (*baisteadh geinntlídhe*), the Druids used it long before the Christians arrived in the Celtic world. This ceremony may have been performed for two reasons. First, the Druids may have baptized a very young child with water from a sacred well to protect it. Second, they also may have used the ceremony to symbolize the birth to a higher state of members of the order when they passed from one degree to another.

The Druidic order contained both men and women. We know from ancient records that Ireland had Druidesses, called *ban-druí* (woman-Druid). The goddess Brigit was called both a *ban-druí* and a *ban-fili* (poetess). Druids were the professional educators of their time and were employed to teach the children of kings and clan chiefs.

Mystic Traits

Desirable traits for the mystic to cultivate are balance, faith, discernment, patience, persistence, continual curiosity for truth and the seeking of knowledge, concentration, and continual practice in entering the Otherworld.

Mystics must strive for balance in all things, particularly in their individual lives. Without balance, there can be no harmony or positive progression toward goals. Balance is also needed for spiritual growth and positive interaction with other people.

The requirements of the Celtic faith are not the same as those of orthodox religions. Faith to the Celts meant believing in the deities and in one's own abilities, and understanding that all events happened in the proper time.

Every person following the Celtic paths to greater spirituality must practice the art of discernment, a word that seems to have fallen out of favor with people today. Mystics must train themselves to listen to their intuition regarding other people and events and not be gullible. Not everyone is positive in thoughts and actions. The mystic must weed out those students or friends who are not sincere. My grandmother had an appropriate saying to describe such people: "If you lie down with dogs, you get up with fleas." Bad habits and negative vibrations can be catching if you spend enough time with the wrong people.

Patience must be the hardest lesson faced by all humans, particularly today. People want shortcuts to instant wealth and success without the work that goes along with securing it. They desire a pill that will immediately reverse any health problems caused by intemperate living, but will not change their habits. They want good grades in school without studying for them, advances on the job without working for them, love without taking the time to build a lasting relationship. However, nothing lasting is gained instantaneously. We need to cultivate patience and not fret when universal timing does not coincide with our desires and goals.

Being persistent is necessary when working toward any goal, physical, material, or spiritual. If we want something bad enough, we should be prepared to work at that goal, no matter how long it takes.

Continual curiosity for truth and the seeking of knowledge is one of the prime characteristics of anyone on the Celtic paths, but particularly the path of a mystic. An insatiable curiosity about all things fills life with surprises and wonder. No one person will ever learn all there is to know about this world or the Otherworld, but the journey to knowledge can be an endless, delightful quest.

To accomplish anything through Otherworld journeys or magic, the mystic must be able to hone her/his concentration to a fine point when journeying or working spells. She/he must be so absorbed in what is taking place that few, if any, outside distractions are noted. The deeper the concentration, the quicker the manifestation will appear.

Although frequent travel to the Otherworld is an activity of all the Celtic paths, it is particularly important to the mystic. She/he needs these journeys to clarify new knowledge learned, search for ancient information, look into personal past lives, and gain vital guidance for life goals. Nothing in life remains static. Otherworld journeys help to keep life balanced, and warn of future events that may cause problems. To stay balanced, the mystic must journey to the Otherworld on a regular basis.

Mythic Mystics

The celebrated Druid-mystic Mog Ruith who wore a special costume of a bull's hide and a winged, feathered headdress, called an encennach, is mentioned in The Siege of Knocklong. His patroness was the goddess Anu, but his teacher was Ban Buanann, the Long-Living Lady, who lived within a sídhe. Thus, Mog Ruith was trained in the Otherworld or the land of the fairies. Legend says he built a flying machine, roth rámach (Irish, "rowing wheel" or "wheel of circling light"), which he displayed at the fair at Tlachtga. He could make animals and plants speak and was highly attuned to the elements of Air, Earth, Fire, and Water. In a poem about the saint Colum Cille (Columba), the roth rámach is again mentioned as a huge vessel that could sail over both land and sea.

Morann was an advisor and counselor to the Irish king Conchobar mac Nessa. He foretold the birth of Cú Chulainn and the troubles that would follow him.

Figol was a powerful Druid of the Tuatha Dé Danann. During their battle with the Fomorians, Figol made fire rain down on the enemy and killed nearly two-thirds of them.

According to the *Book of Invasions*, the Druid Mide, a Nemedian, was the first to light a fire at Uisneach. This fire burned for seven years. All other fires in Ireland had to be lit from this blaze, for which Mide charged each house a pig and a sack of grain.

Sithchenn was the Druid at the court of Eochaid Mugmedón. Through his cunning contests, he arranged for Niall of the Nine Hostages to become his father's successor.

Menw fab Teirgwaedd was a Welsh wizard who used his power of invisibility to shield him from sight at the court of Ysbaddaden Bencawr. He also was able to take the form of a bird.

Myrddin, whose anglicized name is Merlin, was a Welsh Druid and prophet who was later associated with the Arthurian sagas. When he became traumatized by the death and violence of the battle of Arfderydd in 573 C.E., he fled to the Caledonian forests where he lived as a wild man for nearly fifty years. He had the power of prophecy and could communicate with animals.

Several Druidesses also are mentioned in Celtic literature. Birog helped Cian find and enter Balor's tower where he seduced Eithne,

Balor's daughter. Birog later saved their son Lugh from drowning. Bodhmall was a Druidess and the aunt to Fionn mac Cumhaill; she cared for him as a child. The Druidess Dornoll trained heroes in the martial arts and taught Cú Chulainn. Duibhlinn was a Druidess who gave her name to Dublin.

The mystics of legend and myth could prophesy, shapeshift, raise winds or fog, cause hills to flatten, and make lakes and rivers go dry. Along with the bards, they arbitrate in disputes or in war, at times even stopping battles. Trained to be "living books," they studied law, medicine, clan lore, nature, the deities, the Otherworld, astrology, astronomy, divination, and magic.

Sacred Spots and Circles

Although the Druids did not build any of the ancient stone circles or erect any of the monoliths, they clearly understood their importance and how to use them.

The Celtic peoples believed that the land remembers everything. Their myths and legends portray this earth-awareness in sacred tales of warring dragons and goddesses of sovereignty. A goddess of sovereignty was a deity of a specific clan area or a country. Without her favor and support, no man was lawfully or in actuality a true king. To be a true king, their leaders were required to marry the goddess of the land. This sacred marriage was consummated by the joining of the king and a priestess representing the goddess of sovereignty. To be exiled from their country was one of the greatest punishments that could be given to those who broke certain laws. This exile is usually referred to in old legends as "retiring beyond the ninth wave." Being spiritually severed from their land was a greater punishment than death, for this exile was a refutation of the person's existence and membership in the Celtic clan.

Their spiritual leaders were said to be so connected with the land and everything in it that they were consciously aware of any imbalance that occurred. They could also use this connectedness to draw upon the energy that runs through the earth. When Ireland was being invaded by the Milesians led by Amairgin, the Tuatha Dé Danann used magic to drive them beyond the ninth wave. Amairgin, however, was a powerful Druid. He recited a chant, with one line for each wave, that drew power up from the land itself and gave the Milesians the magical force to land once more on the shore.

The isle of Iona off southwestern Mull in the Hebrides of Scotland was sacred long before St. Columba (the Irish Colum Cille) landed there. Ancient bardic groves had been established on this island soon after the arrival of the Celts to the region. If it were not for a clerical copying error in a fifth-century manuscript, we would call the island by its correct Celtic name today—Ioho or Ioha. This name is connected with the Celtic ogham alphabet letter of Yew, which symbolizes rebirth and everlasting life. In this burial place of ancient Scottish kings and queens, the Scottish Celts believed there was a door to the Underworld.

In the northern part of Iona is the Hill of Eternal Youth (Dún I). From here one can see the Bay at the Back of the Ocean, a bay that faces the setting sun and other islands of the outer Hebrides. The island, this hill, and the bay symbolize the Celtic concept of entering the "Great Deep" or the Underworld. The Irish Celts placed this door on the west coast of Ireland.

Although ancient Welsh writings refer to St. David's Head, the westernmost point in Wales as a door into Annwn, earlier legends say that this door is on the Isle of Man and guarded by the sea god Manannán mac Lir.

Groves of trees were especially sacred to the Celts, particularly to those of the Druidic orders. On the Continent, these sacred groves were called *nemetons*, and in Ireland they were named *neimheadh*. Considered to be power spots, certain rites and ceremonies were held in these places. Uisneach in County Westmeath was not only the divine center of Ireland, it was also the focus of Druidic ceremonies, especially the celebration of Beltane in May. The Druids also held judicial court at Uisneach where they settled disputes and passed judgment on cases.

Another famous site was that of the divine and royal hill of Tara (*Teamhair*) in County Meath. There is some dispute as to the meaning of the name Tara. However, it is possible that it means "spectacle." The age of this site has been dated by archaeologists to 4,000 B.C.E. The Celts frequently used poetic names for places, and Tara was no exception. It also was known as *Liathdruim*, or the Grey Ridge.

The ley lines of Britain have been the subject of much discussion for many years. These lines of earth energy have been meticulously mapped out and studied. These ley lines exist in Britain and circle the entire surface of the Earth, from north to south and from east to west. Since there is a bulge around the equator in relationship to the more flattened poles, the grid made by these lines has diamond shapes, not squares. Where these energy lines cross, vortices or spirals of energy frequently form. Some of these vortices are quite strong while others are barely detectable.

Because of natural shifts in the earth's crust and plates, minor lines of power can fracture off from the main lines and appear almost anywhere.

Frequently they follow underground streams of water or fractures caused by earthquakes. These minor lines often do not flow in a straight line.

The energy of these lines also ebbs and flows during the day, with the power strongest at dawn and dusk. There also is a distinct change in the rhythm of these ley line tides at the full moon, the Equinoxes, and the Solstices.

Power spots and lines, even minor ones, can easily be detected through the use of a pendulum or divining rods. To see if your property has these minor lines, all you need is a pendulum or divining rods and a supply of markers, such as small wooden stakes or rocks. Using your pendulum, walk slowly along the width of the area you are testing. If the pendulum swings steadily from side to side, front to back, or in a circle, place a marker at that spot. Continue walking until you have covered the length and the width of the property. If your markers form a line, straight or crooked, you have a minor power line on your property.

Usually, minor power lines can be found by two passes along the length and two more along the width. The detection of power spots, however, may require that you perform a more meticulous coverage of the land, since a power spot is in one place only. Power spots will show up in the placement of one marker only. A power spot can be detected with a pendulum or divining rods by their positive reaction over just one area of ground. In other words, you will not be able to trace any extending lines from this spot as you would when detecting and marking a power line.

Power spots and lines make a wonderful place for outdoor rituals, if it is possible for you to conduct rituals without interference from your neighbors. Otherwise, you can use this power place by situating a bench or chairs over it and retreating there for brief meditations and a recharge of energy.

If you do not find an outdoor power spot, or cannot use freely the one you find, you can create an indoor power area. An indoor power area should be one that is used for ritual and meditation, and nothing else. If you have set aside a certain corner of a room, or have a separate cabinet or shelf, and do not allow anything of a mundane nature to overflow into this area, you can still create a power place. You cannot build up power in a ritual area if you perform your rituals in the living room where other activities frequently occur. By doing meditations or working rituals and spells in this special area on a regular basis, you will build up a continuous flow of power that will remain. This power will aid in any magical spells you perform there.

The Elements

The Celts called the four elements the four winds. They believed that the keys to the Underworld and control of the four winds belonged only to the Great Goddess. In Scotland the four winds are called Airts. The Irish poem *Saltair Na Ran* tells of four chief winds and eight subordinate winds. Each of these is listed with the colors that identify them. There is also a vague reference to a large number of elements in the writings of the Welsh bard Taliesin. Obviously, the colors of these "winds" are not seen by the physical eyes, so they are identified for the trained person who uses magic or who journeys to the Otherworld. A tenth-century Irish poem also tells how to use these winds for divination purposes.

The four chief winds correspond to the four cardinal directions. According to an ancient list of winds, in the North the color is black, the east purple, the south white, and the west "pale." Of the eight other winds, the next four prominent ones fall between these cardinal directions. The northeast is speckled and "dark"; the southeast red and yellow; the southwest gray-green and green; and the northwest dark brown and gray.

These "winds" can easily be placed on the eight-spoke Celtic Year Wheel. This placement helps the magician or spiritual seeker learn more about the nature of the Otherworld and the universe. It also enables her/him to know the correct powers to call upon during magical work.

In many cultures the World Tree is considered to be the center or axis pole of the world. The Celts knew of the World Tree, calling it the Tree of Life. In Wales it symbolized the *awen* or fiery inspiration necessary to make a true bard or spiritual seeker. Sometimes this Tree is portrayed as burning but not being consumed, an apt description of spiritual inspiration. With the Tree defining the center of the mortal world, the Celtic mystics were able to understand the boundaries between their physical world and the Otherworld. These boundaries, including edges of the sea or lakes and twilight or dawn, marked potential gateways through which the mystic could pass from one world to the other.

Studying all the corresponding parts of the following tables will help you with rituals, spells, and spiritual understanding. By incorporating into any ritual or spell as many symbols as you feel are necessary, you will increase the strength of your contact with elemental powers. Simply visualizing these symbols will strengthen the contacts and better enable you to produce a desired manifestation.

For example, if you are working on a ritual to balance earth energy in your home or are using a candle-burning spell to produce something material in your life, you can decorate your altar or special area with a black or dark green candle, several crystals and stones to surround the candle, and pictures or statues of the appropriate animals. Then call upon the influencing deity to aid you.

For an Otherworld journey or deep meditation, you either can use the same objects or visualize them to make the bridge stronger. In this manner you will be able to experience more detailed meetings with deities and Otherworld beings. Also look for the symbols during meditation and dreams so you will know what Otherworld messages are being sent to you.

North (South in Southern Hemisphere)

Element: Earth

Description: Solid or dense matter; anything having solid form

Welsh Description: Calas, every*thing hard or firm in structure

Celtic Celebration: Winter Solstice, approximately December 21

Irish Mythological Tool: Stone (Lia Fáil, or Stone of Destiny) from Falias

Magical Tool: Pentacle, stone altar, crystals and other stones

Time: Midnight

Celtic Month: Luis — Rowan

Color: Scottish Airt, black; traditional, dark green

Irish Province: Ulster

Zodiac: Sagittarius, Capricorn

Planet: Moon

Otherworld:

Ireland: Sídhe of Dana, Holy mountain of Aíne

Wales: Caer Hydry (Arianrhod and Arawn), Carreg Cennen
Scotland: Ednam

Celtic Deities:

Ireland: Aíne, Anu, Banba, Dana, Bel, Cailleach, Cernunnos, Don, Ériu, Flidais, Macha, Mórrígán, Niamh
Wales: Arawn , Arianrhod, Cerridwen, Donn, Herne the Hunter, Myrddin, Rhiannon

Ritual Work: Wealth, prosperity, treasures, surrendering self-will, touch, enhancing empathy, incorporation, business, employment, stability, success, natural fertility, birth, money, healing mental and physical illnesses.

Power Animal of Light: Bear, turtle

Power Animal of Dark: Wolf, lynx

Personality Traits:

Positive: Responsibility, stability, thoroughness, purpose in life, endurance and persistence, respectfulness
Negative: Rigidity, unwillingness to change or see another side to a problem, stubbornness, lack of conscience, vacillation

Tail of the Dragon: Subconscious action in response to magical and spiritual beliefs

Northeast

Element: Earth-Air

Description: Solid matter mixed with vaporous gases; anything having solid material combined with an invisible gaseous form

Celtic Celebration: Imbolc, February 1

Magical Tool: Incense

Time: 3 A.M.

Celtic Month: Fearn — Alder; Saille — Willow

Color: Golden-brown

Zodiac: Aquarius

Planet: Jupiter

Otherworld:

Ireland: Sídhe of Angus mac Óg, Enchanted cave of Keshcorran
Wales: Circle of Gwynyvd, Caer Pedryfan (Four-Cornered Castle),
where nine maidens or goddesses guard a cauldron, Cader Idris
Scotland: Inverness

Celtic Deities:

Ireland: Angus mac Óg, Brigit, Cernunnos
Wales: Arianrhod, Blodeuwedd, Cerridwen, Gwynr ap Nudd,
Myrddin, Rhiannon

Ritual Work: Any psychic work that calls for direct contact with spirits;
inspiration for improving life on a material basis; centering oneself;
organized material and spiritual manifestations; healing plants and
animals; achieving equilibrium; divine inspiration for creativity.

Power Animal of Light: Swan, butterfly

Power Animal of Dark: Cat, bat

Personality Traits:

Positive: Leadership, bringing out the best in others, tolerant of
different spiritual paths
Negative: Unscrupulous when dealing with matters of competi-
tion; grasping for material things; vicious belittling of others and
their contributions

Feet of the Dragon: The basic foundation of spiritual and magical
beliefs

East

Element: Air

Description: Gaseous, vaporous matter; anything having an invisible,
gaseous form

Welsh Description: Breath, every wind, breeze, respiration, air

Celtic Celebration: Spring Equinox, approximately March 21

Irish Mythological Tool: Spear of Lugh from Findias

Magical Tool: Wand, staff

Time: Dawn, or 6 A.M.

Celtic Month: Nuin — Ash

Color: Scottish Airt, red; traditional, yellow

Irish Province: Leinster

Zodiac: Pisces, Aries

Planet: Mercury

Otherworld:

> Ireland: Sídhe of Ogma, Tory Island.
> Wales: Caer Rigor.
> Scotland: Isle of the Cave.

Celtic Deities:

> Ireland: The Dagda, Dian Cécht, Lugh, Ogma
> Wales: Arianrhod, Cerridwen, Gwethyr , Gwydion, Math
> Mathonwy, Taliesin

Ritual Work: Business, legal problems, travel, information and knowl edge, inspiration, logic, writing, controlling runaway emotions, lo cating the proper teachers, memory, science, creativity, divination, healing nervous disorders, speech, harmony, plant growth, ideas, mental and spiritual freedom, revealing the truth, finding lost things.

Power Animal of Light: Falcon, griffin

Power Animal of Dark: Raven, bees

Personality Traits:

> Positive: Optimism, joy, intelligence, mental quickness
> Negative: Frivolity, gossip, fickleness, inattention, bragging, forget-fulness, lying

Body of the Dragon: The physical procedures of magical and spiritual practices

Southeast

Element: Air-Fire

Description: Gaseous matter mixed with hot, burning material; any thing of invisible gaseous form mixed with hot material

Celtic Celebration: Beltane, May 1

Magical Tool: Candles, lamps

Time: 9 A.M.

Celtic Month: Huathe—Hawthorn; Duir—Oak

Color: Spring-green

Zodiac: Taurus

Planet: Venus

Otherworld:

> Ireland: Sídhe of Nuada, Holy mountain of Grían (sun goddess)
> Wales: Circle of Abred, Caer Feddwyd, Ogof Arthur
> Scotland: Iona

Celtic Deities:

> Ireland: Badb, Lugh, Macha, Mórrígán, Niamh, Nuada, Scáthach
> Wales: Bran, the White Lady

Ritual Work: Honor, friendship, the heart's desires, luck, accomplishments, religions, trade and employment, justice in legal matters

Power Animal of Light: Hound, hare

Power Animal of Dark: Fox, mouse

Personality Traits:

> Positive: Friendly, positive in thought, sets goals, believes in justice and honor for all
> Negative: Dishonest, friends only if something is to be gained, critical of different life paths, negative in speech

Wings of the Dragon: Astral travel that reveals new knowledge, and the faith in the beliefs

South (North in the Southern Hemisphere)

Element: Fire

Description: Brilliant, burning matter; heated or hot material

Welsh Description: Uvel, heat, fire, light

Celtic Celebration: Summer Solstice, approximately June 21

Irish Mythological Tool: Sword of Nuada from Gorias

Magical Tool: Sword, dagger

Time: Noon

Celtic Month: Tinne — Holly

Color: Scottish Airt, white; traditional, red

Irish Province: Munster

Zodiac: Gemini, Cancer

Planet: Sun, Mars

Otherworld:

> Ireland: Sídhe of Lugh, Fire shrine of Brigit
> Wales: Caer Goludd, Craig-y-Dinas

Celtic Deities:

> Ireland: Banba, Bel, Brigit, Cernunnos, Goibniu, Lugh
> Wales: Arawn

Ritual Work: Power, physical freedom, change, passion, sexuality, energy, authority, confidence, destruction of negatives, success, personal fulfillment.

Power Animal of Light: Horse, unicorn

Power Animal of Dark: Bull, crow, raven

Personality Traits:

> Positive: Enthusiasm, activity, courage, daring, willpower, leadership
> Negative: Hate, jealousy, fear, anger, ego, contentiousness

Head of the Dragon: Conscious commitment to studying the basic knowledge and lore of the beliefs

Southwest

Element: Fire-Water

Description: Hot or fiery matter mixed with liquids. The Celts said that dew was an element of the divine, a magical substance since it was an essence of the earth's spiritual nature distilled by the fire of the sun.

Celtic Celebration: Lughnasadh, August 1

Magical Tool: Headband, magical jewelry

Time: 3 P.M.

Celtic Month: Coll — Hazel; Muin — Vine

Color: Orange

Zodiac: Leo

Planet: Jupiter

Otherworld:

Ireland: Sídhe of Don, Holy mountain of Grían (sun goddess)
Wales: Circle of Annwn (Underworld), Ogof Myrddin
Scotland: Durness

Celtic Deities:

Ireland: Angus mac Óg, Mórrígán, Nuada
Wales: Cerridwen

Ritual Work: Courage, defense, willpower, self-discipline, ridding yourself of negatives in order to attain higher aspirations, bringing rhythms and stability into life.

Power Animal of Light: Otter, deer

Power Animal of Dark: Badger, hawk

Personality Traits:

Positive: Disciplined, always striving for improvement, open to new ideas
Negative: Undisciplined, chaotic lifestyle, self-indulgent, always on the defensive

Eyes of the Dragon: Opening of the Third Eye, and seeing the truth behind illusions and misconceptions

West

Element: Water

Description: Liquid matter

Welsh Description: Fluidity, moisture, flux

Celtic Celebration: Autumn Equinox, approximately September 21

Irish Mythological Tool: Cauldron of the Dagda from Murias

Magical Tool: Cauldron, chalice

Time: Sunset, or 6 P.M.

Celtic Month: Gort — Ivy

Color: Scottish Airt, gray; traditional, blue

Irish Province: Connacht

Zodiac: Virgo, Libra

Planet: Neptune

Otherworld:

Ireland: Sídhe of Lir, Isle of Manannán mac Lir
Wales: Caer Manawyddan, Llyn Dywarchen
Scotland: Loch Uaine

Celtic Deities:

Ireland: Bóann, the Dagda, Dana, Dian Cécht, Don, Nuada
Wales: Blodeuwedd, Branwen, Donn, Lir, Manawyddan

Ritual Work: Change, divination, magic, love, medicine, plants, healing emotions, intuition, communion with the spiritual, purification, the subconscious mind, pleasure, friendships, marriage, difficult fertility, happiness, sleep, dreams, the psychic

Power Animal of Light: Salmon, dolphin

Power Animal of Dark: Sow, boar

Personality Traits:

Positive: Compassion, peacefulness, forgiveness, love
Negative: Laziness, indifference, instability, lack of emotional control

Breath of the Dragon: Speaking and living the beliefs

Northwest

Element: Water-Earth

Description: Liquids mixed with solid matter

Celtic Celebration: Samhain, October 31

Magical Tool: Crystal ball, runestones, tarot cards, all divination tools

Time: 9 P.M.

Celtic Month: NgEtal — Reed; Ruis — Elder

Color: Dark purple

Zodiac: Scorpio

Planet: Saturn, Pluto

Otherworld:

Ireland: Sídhe of Mórrígán, Cave of Cruachan (Mórrígán)
Wales: Caer Ochren (Cerridwen), Pentre Ifan
Scotland: Isle of Skye

Celtic Deities:

Ireland: The Dagda, Ogma, Scáthach
Wales: Arianrhod, Cerridwen, Epona, Herne the Hunter, the White Lady

Ritual Work: Stabilization of thought and life, help with groups, comfort when in sorrow, contact with the Goddess power, developing the power of faith

Power Animal of Light: Crane, eagle

Power Animal of Dark: Owl, snake

Personality Traits:

Positive: Positive spiritual seeking, understanding the problems of others, open to psychic experiences
Negative: Little or no spiritual seeking, no tolerance for the problems of others, not open to psychic experiences, does not work well with other people

Blood of the Dragon: Believing in your right to practice the magical and spiritual powers

Center

Element: Spirit

Description: Primal Matter; vital, creating, ethereal energy having no form; Balances and blends together all other elements

Welsh Description: Nwyvre, every life, every spirit, every soul, and from its union with the other elements, other living beings. This element was known as nyu to the Druids. In modern Welsh, Nwyf means "energy," Nwyfriant, "vigor and vivacity," while Nwyfre means "the sky or firmament."

Celtic Celebration: None

Irish Mythological Tool: The Silver Branch

Magical Tool: The magical circle

Time: Time that is not a time

Celtic Month: None

Color: Traditional, white and black

Irish Province: The hill of Uisneach and the hill of Tara

Celestial Body: The Milky Way

Otherworld:

> Ireland: Sídhe of the Dagda, Hill of Uisneach, the Lios at Lough Gur
> Wales: Cauldron of Life, Circle of Ceugant — above the center, Mount Snowdon
> Scotland: Dunadd in former Dal Ríada
> England: Stonehenge

Celtic Deities:

> Ireland: The Dagda, Dana
> Wales: Arianrhod, Rhiannon

Ritual Work: Divine consciousness, illumination, enlightenment, spiritual development and attainment, finding the karmic purpose in life, connection with the entire cosmos and the Supreme Power behind the gods, achieving a state of perfect balance to blend all the other elements

Power Animal of Light: White dragon

Power Animal of Dark: Black dragon

Personality Traits: None

Wisdom of the Dragon: Completely understanding that the melding of the totality of the beliefs will lead you to the Heart of the Dragon, which is the ultimate goal. The Heart of the Dragon allows you to connect and communicate with everything in the universe.

Numbers

The Celts considered numbers very important, even sacred in some instances. There is evidence that the Druids used numbers to represent certain ideas. For example, religious significance was strongly attached to the numbers three and five.

The number one represents the Great Creating Power, or the creating spirit behind the deities. It also represents independence, strength of will, and the art of discrimination.

Two represents the alliance of opposites, such as male and female, positive and negative, hot and cold, inner and outer, this world and the Otherworld. Two symbolizes the cooperation needed to keep this universe balanced and in existence.

From earliest times, the Celts considered the number three the greatest of all numbers. Three represents seeing in all directions at the same time. Tripling any number or image intensifies the energy of that number or image. The triple spiral is found in such places as Newgrange, a very sacred place to the Irish Celts.

In Ireland, legends tell of triple deities. The Sovereignty goddesses who intermarried with the Tuatha Dé Danann were Ériu, Banba, and Fódla; these women married three sons of the Dagda. One text refers to the Tuatha Dé Danann as "men of the three goddesses or gods," *fir Trí nDéa*. In a later medieval manuscript there is mention of the three gods of Danu, *trí dée Tuath*. Even civil laws were in sets of threes. The Welsh tradition speaks of the Otherworld as consisting of three concentric circles. They also had bardic laws called the Welsh Triads.

The number three represents male, female, and progeny; past, present, and future; sky, earth, and the Otherworld; farmers, warriors, and clergy. The basic foundation of the bardic teachings consisted of sound, music, and speech. The Celtic depiction of a head with three faces represented not only seeing into the past and the future, but also into the Otherworld. Three is also a number of inspiration and creativity, the arts in all their forms, and the ability to express inner feelings.

The number four represented the stability of the social order in Celtic society. Tara was considered to be the polar opposite and complement of Uisneach, the religious hill of the Druids. As the spiritual site of the king and communal judgment, Tara had four sides. However, within the boundaries of Tara was the Stone of Boundaries, which had five sides. Four is also a number of the four directions, the four winds, the four elements, and balance and harmony with nature.

The number five has great spiritual significance as it represents the four elements plus spirit, and the four directions plus the center. When the Irish King Cormac visited the god Manannán mac Lir in the Otherworld, he found a fountain with five streams in the sea god's palace. The five streams symbolized the five senses, both physical and psychic, of both mortals and Otherworld beings, the senses through which true knowledge can be obtained.

In both Irish Celtic myth and history, the number five is frequently mentioned. Ireland was divided into five provinces[1] and had five great roads. There were five paths of law by which the Celts lived and five prohibitions that governed provincial kings. Legends say that the hero Fionn mac Cumhaill counted in fives, as did the inhabitants of the *sídhe*. Each craft or art was allowed to have five masters. The hero Cú Chulainn painted five wheels on his shield. A medieval text on languages mentions that five words are said to be the breath of the poet. The pentacle, or five-pointed star, was a symbol of Earth with its five elements—Air, Earth, Fire, Water, and Spirit. Five Celtic deities corresponded to these five elements: Ogma (Spirit), Dana (Air), Manannán mac Lir (Water), Ana (Earth), and Brigit (Fire).

In the Druidic belief system the sixth night of the waxing (growing) moon after the new moon was particularly sacred. Called the Druid Moon, or "the moon between the halves," this phase of the moon was considered to be extremely powerful for magic.

The number seven is frequently mentioned in Celtic myths. When the bard Amairgin sings his magical chant, he says that he has been a stag with seven tines, or points on the antlers. The stag is frequently associated with forest deities, such as Cernunnos and Flidais. This number may have symbolized a seven-month reign of the sun or solar deities. In the myth of the Welsh deities Bran and Branwen, seven survivors are mentioned; these "survivors" symbolize the seven major planets known to the ancient world.

The number eight, a doubling of the number four, raises balance into the higher realms, where it represents true judgment, confidence, and the unification of the rhythms of the physical world with the rhythms of the Otherworld.

Nine was another sacred, powerful number as it is the number three times itself (a triple triad). Nine is a completion number, ripe with the power for change. Tradition says that certain actions or words repeated nine times or special objects placed in groups of nine can create an opening or gateway to the Otherworld. In the Welsh tale *Culhwch and Olwen*, the malevolent giant called Ysbaddaden Bencawr (the father of Olwen) lived in a castle guarded by nine watchdogs and nine guards.

Irish legends mention the number nine frequently. Queen Medb rode to battle against Ulster with nine chariots. Cú Chulainn carried nine weapons. The famous curse of labor pains was laid on the Ulstermen (for forcing Macha to run while pregnant for nine times nine generations.) Noidhiu gave nine judgments, and the famous king who founded the Uí Néill clan was called Niall of the Nine Hostages. Bricriu's Hall was said to have nine rooms. The triple Sovereignty goddesses of Ireland (Ériu, Fódla, and Banba) married three sons of the Dagda; a three multiplied by itself into a power number.

In Scotland the Beltane fires were traditionally built by nine men using nine different woods. Lit at dawn, these Beltane fires were used for purification and protection. Cattle were driven between two fires. This is very likely the origin of the Irish phrase *idir dhá thine Bealtaine*, which translated can mean "between a rock and a hard place."

Welsh legend speaks of the Nine Maidens who blow on the fire under Cerridwen's Cauldron of Inspiration. Ancient Welsh law stated that the ninth day of each month marked the end of the beginning of a period of time.

The number thirteen was not considered an evil number, but one of potential fate. This idea of the relationship between thirteen and potential fate probably arose from the way Celtic chiefs rode into battle. The chief rode with a warrior on each side and three more behind. When the number of chariot bearers and himself were added, the immediate number of men surrounding the chief equaled twelve. The thirteenth rider was the invisible specter of Death, who was a constant companion of all Celtic warriors. Since the Celts did not particularly fear inevitable death, this acknowledgment of Death was merely recognition of the fate of every human.

Thirteen is also strongly connected with ancient lunar goddesses and the thirteen-month lunar calendar. Some sources believe that the thirteen lunar signs represent the universal feminine energy, while the twelve solar signs represent the masculine.

The giant Ysbaddaden Bencawr, in the Welsh tale of *Culhwch and Olwen*, demanded thirteen treasures from Culhwch before he would give his permission for Culhwch to marry his daughter Olwen.

The number seventeen also frequently appears in Celtic legends, particularly in Ireland. A youth was recognized as a man when he celebrated his seventeenth birthday. Significant events were often said to take place after seventeen days or seventeen years. The Druid who instructed Mael Dúin to take an *imram*, or spiritual voyage, told him to take seventeen men with him. While on the Island of Women, Mael Dúin and his men were greeted by seventeen maidens.

Magical spells work best when repeated for three, five, seven, nine, or thirteen consecutive times. Old magical records from many cultures around the world refer to this custom. Repeating a magical spell increases its power by incrementally building upon that power. Also, when the magician concentrates repeatedly on the same desired result, the manifestation will occur more quickly and with greater strength.

Understanding the meanings of numbers can aid in interpreting dream symbols, for example, having the same dream three times, or seeing three of any thing in a dream. This information also helps when one experiences a recurring event that makes a deep impression or sights certain creatures more than once.

You also can use the science of numbers to determine your Destiny, or life goal, according to your given birth name: first, middle, and last. However, if you have rejected your birth name in favor of another name, both names should be considered as forces that shape you and your life. This also applies if you take a magical name to be used only in ritual work.

The Destiny number is determined by assigning a numerical value to each letter, adding the numbers together, and then reducing them to a single number. Numbers eleven and twenty-two, however, are not reduced, as they have special significance of their own.

A, J, S	1
B, K, T	2
C, L, U	3
D, M, V	4
E, N, W	5
F, O, X	6
G, P, Y	7
H, Q, Z	8
I, R	9

An example would be the numerical value of the name Thomas John Hancock, which totals the number seven.

Destiny Number One: You are a natural leader, independent and ambitious. Limitations frustrate you as you need freedom to make your own decisions.

Destiny Number Two: With tact, refinement, and strong intuition, you are good at avoiding problems and working well with others. You need partnership for your abilities to surface. Sensitivity, however, can make you vulnerable.

Destiny Number Three: A charming, expressive person with lots of creative talent, you could excel in writing, the theater, art, or music. Discipline and order, however, may be lacking.

Destiny Number Four: You are a grounded person who always approaches life in a methodical manner. You never make spur of the moment decisions and always see a project through to the end.

Destiny Number Five: You must have freedom, change, adventure, and excitement in your life. Being an adaptable person, you work well under these conditions.

Destiny Number Six: A responsible person who has justice and honesty high on your list of necessary life traits, your duties sometimes feel like heavy burdens. However, these traits also help you with creative talents, parenting, counseling, and negotiating problems.

Destiny Number Seven: This number expresses great curiosity for the truth in all things, clarity of thought, and persistence of purpose. It also causes you stress if you engage in too much social activity.

Destiny Number Eight: A highly competitive person, you enjoy challenges in your struggle to be the best of your field or overcome obstacles. Your natural talents could fit you for several careers in management or negotiating.

Destiny Number Nine: A born humanitarian, you are extremely idealistic, sometimes to the point of being naïve. Your friends and acquaintances come from all walks of life.

Destiny Number Eleven: Your ideas, intuition, and psychic abilities can make you a powerful presence if you learn to control the energy. Because of a sense of separateness that developed in childhood, you may be very cautious about sharing your ideas.

Destiny Number Twenty-Two: This number is often referred to as the Master Builder. You are capable of making your mark on history in either a positive or a negative way, depending upon how you interact with others, the ethics you embrace, and the goals you set.

For more in-depth information on the study of numerology, you should consult a number of books on the subject.

Astrology

The word "astrology" is derived from the Greek word *astrologos*, which means "star-knowledge." The Irish word *astralaíoch* (astrologer) was borrowed from the Greek and the Celts were well acquainted with the art. The closest term in Irish Gaelic might be *néladóir*, "cloud diviner." From its use in legends, *néladóir* appears also to mean the "study of the stars."

Although rarely mentioned in legend, the Celts' knowledge of astronomy and astrology equaled that of the Romans and Greeks. Both the Romans and Greeks learned this knowledge from ancient cultures in the Middle East. Irish legends mention the casting of birth charts to determine a person's future, such as the time the Druid Cathbad cast a horoscope at the birth of the beautiful Deirdre. Another historical figure, St. Colum Cille (Columba) created a horoscope to find out the best time for his foster son to start his education.

We also find confirmation of the Celtic knowledge of the stars in the writings of ancient Romans and Greeks. Pomponius Mela, who lived around 43 C.E., said that the Druids were highly regarded for their knowledge of astronomy and astrology. Flavius Magnus Aurelius Cassidorus (c. 490–583 C.E.) wrote that the Druids knew the zodiacs and planets well. Herodotus mentioned that the Celtic religion was strongly connected with the Corona Borealis and that the bright star Alpheta was considered to be a gateway into the Otherworld. Alpheta is connected with the Cretan moon goddess Ariadne, who was known to the Celts as Arianrhod. The Greek goddess Persephone is also associated with Arianrhod.

It also is recorded in the *Hanes Taliesin* that the great bard Taliesin was an acclaimed astrologer. In the tenth century in Ireland, the *Saltair na Rann* (Psalter of Quatrains) relates that every educated person must be able to recite the signs of the zodiac.

The Celts knew the Earth as "the bovine enclosure." The Earth sometimes was symbolized by a white cow. It was also associated with goddesses and spoken of as female.

The Celtic culture viewed the moon as a symbol of the feminine principle of creation and of the primordial matter from which everything is formed. They associated it with the Goddess and recognized its influence upon the Earth, the seas, and human emotions. In the deep lunar mysteries of the Druids, the moon's shadow was said to guard a secret source of hidden wisdom.

Although a lunar eclipse is far less spectacular visually than a solar eclipse, the Celts felt that the lunar eclipse was more significant. They associated it with both birth and death.

The Druids watched several planets, stars, and constellations very closely. Among these were the sun, the moon, the Pleiades, Orion, Auriga, Arcturus, Castor, and Deneb. Arcturus, close to the tail of Ursa Major, and Orion were the two main navigational aids for all Celtic travelers.

Stars and Constellations

We do not know all of the Celtic names given to the constellations, although the myths may hold clues, as yet unidentified.

Andromeda — the Princess: This princess of ancient Mediterranean legend was known as the King of Egypt's daughter Sabrina to the British Mummers. The early British Celts knew Sabrina as the "fir tree queen." In the Celtic Tree Calendar, the silver fir tree (Ailim) was the tree of the Winter Solstice.

Antares: The Druids called the red star Antares the "Watcher in the West." They watched the rising of Antares closely, for its rise could signal the election of a prince or the proper time for passing a decree.

Aquila — the Hawk: The Hawk of Welsh legend was actually thought to be the soul of Lleu Llaw Gyffes. His uncle Gwydion searched through the Milky Way until he found Lleu and restored him to life after Lleu was murdered by Blodeuwedd's lover. After that Lleu was known as Gwalchmai, or the Hawk of May.

Auriga: In Celtic legend this star grouping represented the yoked oxen that Hu Gadarn used to drag the Afanc, a water monster, from the Welsh Lake Llion Lyon.

Bellatrix: Another Druidic star, Bellatrix was believed to foretell military victories.

Capella: The northern star of Capella, which is in the Auriga constellation, was closely observed by the Druids. It was associated with the moon, the lunar mysteries, and the goddess Arianrhod, who controlled Fate.

Cassiopeia: This is known in Wales as the Llys Don, or the Palace of Don. Legend also calls it the chair of Cerridwen.

Castor and Pollux: In the deeper mysteries of Celtic mythology, frequently one can find references to deities being born as twins, thus representing the duality of all life and universal laws. The stars Castor and Pollux were a heavenly representation of this idea, as are Pollux and Procyon. The Druids associated Pollux with the immortality of the soul and Procyon with healing.

Corona Borealis: This was said to belong to the moon goddess, with the stars representing a crescent. Llys Arianrhod or Caer Arianrhod also symbolized the Silver Wheel of death and rebirth, aspects ruled by the goddess Arianrhod. Arianrhod's Gate in Caer Arianrhod was said to be the astral entrance to Annwn, an Otherworld dimension known to the Welsh Celts. In one section of Annwn was a fiery abyss, the cauldron of rebirth from which came all earthly life. Annwn was also referred to as the Great Deep.

Cygnus: The Celts believed that the Gray Lag Goose carried the souls of the dead to the heavens behind the north wind. The Welsh said that this constellation represented the magician Gwydion who flew along the Milky Way, looking for his nephew Lleu.

Deneb: Deneb is part of the constellation of Cygnus the Swan. The Milky Way flows through Cygnus. In Irish lore, the White Swan was a symbol of the divinity of the Tuatha Dé Danann.

Draco: To the Celts these stars represented the dragon that was ridden by Cerridwen or the Cailleach every night.

Lyra: Telyn Idris is the Welsh name for this constellation. It symbolized the fabulous oak harp of the Dagda.

The Milky Way: Known as Sarn Gwydion to the Welsh Celts, the Milky Way symbolized the circle of Ceugant to the Welsh Druids. The other Celtic name for the Milky Way was the Great Star-Serpent.

Orion: The Druids of Ireland associated the constellation of Orion with their great warrior Cú Chulainn, the Hound of Ulster.

Pegasus: Sometimes called the Horse of Llyr, the sea god, these stars also represented the horse goddesses Epona and Rhiannon.

Perseus: This represented Lugh of Ireland or Lleu Llaw of Wales.

Pleiades: When the Pleiades rises in the eastern sky in September, it is aligned with the Heel Stone at Stonehenge.

Pluto: Although Pluto was not verified by astronomers until 1930, the Celts knew about its existence. This planet symbolized the bringing forth of hidden wisdom. The Welsh referred to this wisdom as awen, an intelligence that was imbibed only from the Cauldron of Cerridwen.

Sirius: The Druids closely observed Sirius and gathered many sacred plants when it rose.

Spica: The Druids associated the star Spica with riches and fame.

Ursa Major: The Welsh knew this as Plough Y Saith Seren, the Seven Stars. They also knew it as Uthr Medelwr, the Terrible and Wonderful Reaper.

Ursa Minor — The Little Plow Tail: This was Caer Pedryvan, the Four-Cornered Castle, that belonged to the King of the High Place.

Vega: Vega, the blue star, was an important aid to travelers and navigators. The Celts believed it controlled the seas. When Vega moved to a position in the north, and Sirius to a position in the south, the Druids knew it marked the turning of the solar year. In July Vega is directly overhead, a position occupied in winter by Capella, another star closely observed by the Druids.

Venus: The Welsh Druids knew the planet Venus as Gwena, the "fair one."

Zodiac: Known as Caer Siddi, or the Revolving Castle, by the Celts. The Celts are believed to have had twenty-seven constellations in their zodiac.

The constellations of Auriga, Cygnus, Sagittarius, and Carina mark the four directions of the galactic plane. Auriga locates the very rim of the galaxy, while the cusp of Sagittarius and Capricorn mark the center. Cygnus was associated with the mystical home of the Great Creating Spirit.

The spiritual leaders of the Celts were well aware of the constellations that were prominent in the heavens during each of the four sacred days. At Imbolc, the sun rises in the constellation of Aquarius. At Beltane, the prominent constellation is Taurus, the Bull, while above the ecliptic lies Perseus. On Lughnasadh, the major constellation in the sky is Ursa Major, the Bear, and on Samhain, the constellation of Cygnus, the Swan, is high in the sky.

The planet Vulcan is a controversial planet, not accepted by modern astronomers. However, the Celts knew of it, as did astrologers and astronomers in other ancient cultures. Vulcan is a hypothetical, intra-Mercurial planet, one whose existence has yet to be proved. Ancient astronomers believed that Vulcan's orbit lay between Mercury and the sun. There may well have been ancient records about this planet that were lost.[2] Pythagoras mentioned several such "invisible" planets. Alice Bailey[3] called Vulcan a sacred planet, one that is a custodian of divine will. With its combustible, fiery, explosive, and ethereal nature, Vulcan will nullify the effects of any planets in conjunction with it, except for the sun and Mercury.[4] This planet symbolizes the struggle toward spiritual light, a process that involves every soul to one degree or another. It represents the endurance of the will to hold out against the dark night of the soul and continue to seek the Light.

Various ancient Welsh manuscripts describe the constellations that Myrddin and Taliesin frequently observed in the sky. We do not have enough information to adequately translate some of the Celtic names, but others pose no problems. Caer Sidi, also called the Revolving Castle, probably referred to the entire zodiac.[5]

- Caer Arianrhod — Corona Borealis
- The White Throne — the star Spica in Virgo
- Telyn Idris — Lyra
- Caer Gwydion — the Milky Way
- Arthur's Plow Tail — Ursa Major
- The Little Plow Tail — Ursa Minor
- The Wain — Orion
- Twr Tewdws — the Pleiades
- Llys Don — Cassiopeia
- Soldier's Bow — Sagittarius
- Winds' Wing — Cygnus
- Horned Oxen — Gemini

- The White Fork — the Pole Star
- Woodland Boar — Leo
- The Hawk — Aquila
- Horse of Llyr — Pegasus

Nodes of the Moon

Knowing about certain placements and aspects of a natal chart will help the mystic discover various characteristics of past lives that are still affecting the present life, whether the mystic is looking at her/his own chart or working with another person. In their present life, every person is working out past life problems to a greater or lesser degree. Astrological clues will not tell us where a person lived or who they were. They will, however, help reveal characteristics and attitudes.

The North and South Nodes of the moon are always directly opposite each other in an astrological chart. They are only one method of using astrology to help uncover personality problems established in other lifetimes so that a person can make positive changes. The South Node is not symbolic of one incarnation, but of the effects from several incarnations. Those people who are actively working on their lives are less influenced by the Nodes than those who are simply coasting through life.

Since positive influences from past lives do not create problems now, the following list only details negative influences. Once aware of causes, most people are able to consciously break the pattern.

Aries North Node, Libra South: You have been indecisive in past lives and were highly sensitive to disharmony. Because you judged your happiness by what you considered success in those around you, you suffered from bouts of depression when things did not go the way you thought they should.

Taurus North Node, Scorpio South: Because several of your past lives were full of tragedies and disappointments, you let yourself become immoderate in behavior and emotions. Relationships were usually destructive in nature, causing inner turmoil.

Gemini North Node, Sagittarius South: In past lives you refused to accept responsibility for your selfish, unfaithful behavior and did not care if you lacked social finesse or tact. Your get-rich-quick schemes and shortcuts always got you nowhere, which increased your selfishness and excesses.

Cancer North Node, Capricorn South: In this life you cannot tolerate failure and may even be a perfectionist because in past lives you never made an effort to meet obligations and responsibilities. You were self-righteous and an opportunist who may have married only to achieve a higher social position. Cold and calculating, you used others to get whatever you wanted.

Leo North Node, Aquarius South: You did not care for rules and dissipated your energy on worthless goals. When things went wrong, you felt sorry for yourself, drove away friends by your martyrdom and exposed yourself to long periods of loneliness.

Virgo North Node, Pisces South: A daydreamer who never achieved much, you were deep into self-pity. Subconsciously, you constantly created an atmosphere of confusion that would draw sympathy and make you dependent on others.

Libra North Node, Aries South: At one time you were highly competitive, uncooperative, and selfish. Your restless and opinionated attitude caused disharmony in relationships. Not being in the least subtle, your favorite topic for discussion was you.

Scorpio North Node, Taurus South: There was serious damage to your ego in past lives where you carried heavy burdens without much sense of security. This left you with a need to acquire the material things you never had and to suffer depression.

Sagittarius North Node, Gemini South: Through several lives you liked to play both sides of any situation with no commitments or discrimination. You thrived on gossip and constant conflicts. A restless person, if you did not find conflicts in a situation, you created them.

Capricorn North Node, Cancer South: An irresponsible person who would not face the truth, you tended to hang on to people and things. You became a hypochondriac, fearful of rejection and clinging to others to provide what you wanted.

Aquarius North Node, Leo South: Past lives saw you as a domineering, ego-centered person who deserved a higher social level. You had trouble with relationships, but would take up useless causes at the drop of a hat.

Pisces North Node, Virgo South: In other lives you were a person who demanded strict order in your life. You found fault with everything, an attitude that caused you to develop nervous irritability, sexual problems, and a loss of friends.

Planetary Influences

Several of the planets—Mercury, Mars, Saturn, and Pluto—also can give clues that can help you determine your soul mission in this life. All soul missions are not highly spiritual, but frequently are undertaken to provide a balance from past life influences.

Mercury

The placement of Mercury in a natal chart explains how you deal with communication in this life and the way you see the world around you.

Mercury in Aries: You see the world as a place to be explored and experienced. You believe that self-awareness and creativity will aid you in making any goal possible.

Mercury in Taurus: Material security is your prime goal in life. A cautious, conservative person, you have the patience to finish projects.

Mercury in Gemini: You flit from one subject to another, like a butterfly around flowers. Although you are clever and curious, you have difficulty with patience to finish classes or projects.

Mercury in Cancer: Your favorite astral apparel is a pair of rose-colored glasses. If the world and those around you do not provide emotional support and security, you pretend that they do.

Mercury in Leo: To you, applause and happiness go hand in hand. There is nothing low-key about your life; you tend to dramatize everything.

Mercury in Virgo: A perfectionist, you think the world needs structure and order. Since you cannot influence the entire world, you settle for exacting order from your immediate environment and those closest to you.

Mercury in Libra: You desire balance and harmony in your environment. However, you subconsciously create the opposite by spending too much time looking at both sides of an issue and being unwilling to make a decision.

Mercury in Scorpio: Although you see potential for transformation in everything, you frequently create the opposite effect by seeking emotional chaos.

Mercury in Sagittarius: You are a person who likes to see the best in everyone. Your goals are primarily idealistic and full of opportunities.

Mercury in Capricorn: As one who wants everything organized logically, you try to impose this on all around you.

Mercury in Aquarius: Your life slogan is: "All things happen for a reason." You believe that the world can operate with equality and reform.

Mercury in Pisces: You are not a very practical person as your ideals are colored by your emotions.

Mars

The planet Mars reveals possible past lives dealing with emotions and subconscious karmic fears in the present.

Mars in Aries: Possible past lives: An adventurer or traveler who died alone; a bout of anger led to your death; someone who died of a fever or was killed by a sharp object; a person in command who died after losing all of her/his supporters.

Karmic fears: Any form of violence; sharp objects; dying alone; open anger in any form.

Mars in Taurus: Possible past lives: Someone whose property or possessions were taken away; one with wealth who was greedy; a person who resisted new ideas on principles and who unwittingly created a conflict.

Karmic fears: Loss of the security provided by land and possessions; denial of success by others.

Mars in Gemini: Possible past lives: A writer, journalist, lecturer, teacher, or one in a position of power who used effect rather than truth to accomplish a goal; one who habitually used lies for gain; a person who was unfaithful in relationships.

Karmic fears: Fear of gossip or being forced to speak out; a strong dislike and distrust of those who wield power; refusal to lie even if it hurts someone.

Mars in Cancer: Possible past lives: A parent who drove away her/his children by creating guilt; a healer or spiritual leader who intentionally created codependent followers; a person whose clinging to the past destroyed opportunities; a moody person who made the lives of family miserable.

Karmic fears: An abhorrence of uncontrolled emotions; reluctance to let go of children; a dislike for becoming a parent; refusal to commit to a relationship.

Mars in Leo: Possible past lives: One in power, such as royalty or head of a powerful business, who disregarded those under her/him; an adult who refused to grow up and always demanded to be the center of attention; an actor, singer, or courtesan who raged at getting old; one who was assassinated.

Karmic fears: Uncomfortable with attention from others; a paranoia about secret enemies; a deep-seated fear of being murdered.

Mars in Virgo: Possible past lives: One in the healing field who developed a martyr complex; a healer whose carelessness caused the death of a patient; a hypochondriac; a workaholic.

Karmic fears: Terrified of making mistakes; a deep dislike of doctors and nurses; obsession with the perfect body; overly self-critical.

Mars in Libra: Possible past lives: A person who was obsessive in a relationship; an unjust person who sat in judgment of others; one whose entire life revolved around social status.

Karmic fears: A dislike of social climbers and braggarts; fear of being unjustly accused; a need for peace, whatever the cost.

Mars in Scorpio: Possible past lives: A vengeful person who stalked others; one who was manipulative and unyielding in their demands; a jealous person who brooded on imaginary slights; one who would use any avenue, such as black magic, to gain a goal.

Karmic fears: Control by others; the showing of any emotion; a dislike of displaying anger.

Mars in Sagittarius: Possible past lives: A religious fanatic who delighted in creating fear in others; a loner who refused to make a commitment in relationships; one whose claustrophobic fears led to constant travel.

Karmic fears: A deep dislike of open spaces or traveling long distances; aversion to established religions; fear of being abandoned in a relationship.

Mars in Capricorn: Possible past lives: A harsh, dictatorial parent (usually a father) who alienated the family; one who had total disregard for those working under her/him; a miser; a person whose entire life revolved around self-righteous anger.

Karmic fears: A dislike of authority figures and rules; tendency to be oversensitive and/or lenient with children.

Mars in Aquarius: Possible past lives: A revolutionary; a nonconformist who caused others to be hurt; a radical scientist or philosopher; one who was so inflexible that she/he could not get close to others.

Karmic fears: A fear of standing alone in any disagreement; a refusal to become dedicated to any cause.

Mars in Pisces: Possible past lives: An alcoholic or drug addict; a martyr for religion; one who was impulsive without thinking things through.

Karmic fears: An aversion to drugs in any form; a distrust of intuition and anyone who takes a martyr attitude.

Saturn

The planet Saturn symbolizes the karmic teacher and connector.

Saturn in Aries: Possible past lives: A warrior, adventurer, pioneer, one from a primitive culture.

Karmic needs: To be motivated, assured, or self-aware.

Saturn in Taurus: Possible past lives: Farmer or one who lived close to the land; one in finance; an architect.

Karmic needs: Security; a need to cultivate creative talents; happiness.

Saturn in Gemini: Possible past lives: A writer or storyteller; a teacher; one who sold goods.

Karmic needs: Trust; strength of self; ability to communicate.

Saturn in Cancer: Possible past lives: An abandoned child;

an emotional parent left to care for children alone; a servant who constantly served others.

Karmic needs: Development of sensitivity and nurturing toward others; the ability to express emotions without feeling foolish.

Saturn in Leo: Possible past lives: A gambler; an adult who refused to grow up; a person whose job or talents put her/him in the center of attention, such as an actor or priest/priestess; a person in a high position of authority.

Karmic needs: Opening to connections with others; love; developing leadership ability.

Saturn in Virgo: Possible past lives: A radical leader; a healer; one who tended animals with devotion; a servant to one in authority.

Karmic needs: Not to be too organized; releasing the need for perfection and not making mistakes; a fear of getting sick.

Saturn in Libra: Possible past lives: A social climber; an artist or interior designer; a person of power in the judicial system.

Karmic needs: Building balance and harmony with others; sharing ideas.

Saturn in Scorpio: Possible past lives: An undertaker or mortician; a government spy; one who handled high finance; a magician.

Karmic needs: To become comfortable with money and success; understanding the values and importance of others; death.

Saturn in Sagittarius: Possible past lives: A lawyer; teacher; wandering religious teacher; philosopher; one involved in travel and a job that went into uncivilized and/or dangerous areas.

Karmic needs: To express thoughts without preaching; to find a spiritual path of personal comfort; to commit in relationships without fear.

Saturn in Capricorn: Possible past lives: A business owner or land baron; a strict parent; one who made and enforced laws.

Karmic needs: Discipline; responsibility.

Saturn in Aquarius: Possible past lives: Astrologer; inventor; rebel or revolutionary.

Karmic needs: To establish a balance of body, mind, and spirit.

Saturn in Pisces: Possible past lives: A dancer or musician; an addict or alcoholic; a martyr who sought out destruction; a healer who used unorthodox methods, such as the psychic.

Karmic needs: An understanding of the emotions of yourself and others; using psychic and creative talents for positive ends.

Pluto

The placement of the planet Pluto shows how we may express past life fears in our present existence. Since Pluto moves extremely slow, the following list will not cover all the astrological signs.

Pluto in Cancer: Past lives of financial and emotional insecurity; loss possibly of the family; a life with little power for change; no home for any length of time.

Pluto in Leo: Past lives of ruling over others; a self-centered attitude toward life; a dictatorial person who saw those under her/him as slaves.

Pluto in Virgo: Past lives of judging others harshly; holding a position of God-like power; structuring the lives of all around you.

Pluto in Libra: Past lives of codependency in relationships; indecisiveness; an overwhelming need to climb the social ladder; someone who liked to destroy relationships.

Pluto in Scorpio: Past lives of chaos created by extremes; a ruthless person who had control over many people; one who sexually misused others; a person filled with paranoia, distrust, and secretiveness.

Pluto in Sagittarius: Past lives of no commitments in relationships; a dislike of cities and civilization; one who was restless and always sought adventure; a person who spoke her/his mind with little thought to diplomacy.

The best use of astrological knowledge is to improve the self, not to criticize others. If we become aware of past life tendencies that still influence us, we can make changes. These changes will create a better life and eventually bring harmony and balance into the world.

Shapeshifting

Shapeshifting is one of the basic practices of a true shaman. The ancient Druids believed that true shapeshifting was the mark of an initiation into the deeper spiritual mysteries.

Many people are fascinated by the concept of shapeshifting. However, people make the mistaken assumption that shapeshifting means a person transforms her/his physical body into that of another creature. Physical shape is not changed, only some of the personal characteristics. Not only can one assume the character of an animal, one can also shapeshift into inanimate objects. However, at no time does a shaman physically become something besides the human that she/he is. Shapeshifting is the process of shifting the consciousness and taking on the character of an animal or an object so completely that astrally the shaman becomes that animal or object. Then the shaman's personality becomes flooded with the character of the other creature and emanates aspects of that creature's nature. She/he *appears* to become other than what she/he is.

This process is possible only if the shaman or mystic fully understands the interconnectedness of everything in the universe. The Celts sometimes referred to this connectedness as the Web of Life. This connectedness is a series of interwoven strands of energy that link every bit of creation, from the smallest speck of dust to mortals of this world to the gods themselves.

Whether a mystic is journeying to the Otherworld or shapeshifting, she/he must become adept at stepping out of the mind and body into the timeless, no-place of the Web. Everything begins in the mind of the traveler. Some people derisively call this "imagination," but it is far more than that. However, daydreaming is one way to begin to loosen the restrictive bonds of the analytical left brain. When the traveler or shifter has sunk into deep relaxation and shifted to the right brain mode of intuition and imagination, she/he can "emerge" from the body-mind matrix and step into an alternate universe.

For a true shaman to perform great magic, she/he has to be able to identify with the land and every creature on it. This identification at its most powerful involves the assuming of the animal personality. There are several reasons to use this magical ability. The shaman can acquire a stronger connection with nature from shapeshifting, thus gaining a greater appreciation for nature. She/he can discover information, stalk an enemy, hide from someone, or survive in dangerous times. Sometimes she/he can also help beings in the Otherworld by becoming a temporary guardian there.

Although the shapeshifting shaman does not take on the physical appearance of an animal in this world, the assumed animal's spirit can be seen by those who are psychic, known as having *da shealladh*, or "two sights," in Gaelic.

Several Celtic deities and heroic figures were known as shapeshifters, including Angus mac Óg, Arawn, Cáer, Mórrígán, Pwyll, Cú Chulainn, Myrddin, and Taliesin.

This total emergence into the nature of the Otherworld began to be denied and fell out of use during the Middle Ages. However, certain Celtic families still hold an inherited memory of this craft. They find themselves able to communicate with animals and, on stressful occasions, to assume an animal's characteristics.

Every tale of shapeshifting speaks of learning the craft in the Otherworld or from Otherworld beings. An example is the "Compert Mongain," which is found in the *Book of Fermoy*. The god Manannán mac Lir was noted for his love affairs with mortal women. His son Mongan was the result of one of these affairs. Manannán took his son to the Otherworld to teach him shapeshifting and the art of magic, believing that this would prepare Mongan for a better life in the Middleworld. However, Mongan instead used his craft to become a resourceful trickster when he returned to his mortal family.

The power of shapeshifting was well known in Ireland, Scotland, and Wales. It is mentioned many times in the myths and legends. In the physical world, this ability manifests itself primarily in assumed characteristics. However, in the Otherworld, shapeshifting becomes more powerful, and the shaman looks like the chosen animal, as well as behaves like it.

Shapeshifting cannot occur without an exchange of power between the shapeshifter and the Otherworld equivalent of the animal form. This exchange can happen only if there is mutual respect between the human and the animal. If a shapeshifter is fortunate enough to receive sacred secrets during her/his Otherworld journeys, she/he can transfer power from the Otherworld to this world.

Shapeshifters must be able to bridge different times and dimensions in order to be successful, which puts them in direct contact with Otherworld beings. Because of this association, Celtic shapeshifters were believed to have direct access to tradition, ancient memory, and knowledge. In a sense, they were spiritual leaders from whom the clans could learn and find guidance.

In Gaelic, the word for Picts is *cruitni*. The Picts painted pictures or representations of animals on their skin with blue woad. The word *cruth* actually means "shape, form, appearance." A similar Welsh word, *pryd*, means "form, aspect." The underlying meaning of both words is "shapeshifter" or "one who shapes."

Animal allies are an important part of a shaman's spiritual world, for they guide and protect the shaman on Otherworld journeys and lend them the power to shift into their "shapes" or characters when necessary. Animal allies also aid in healing and magical spells, as well as in divination.

To shapeshift, one concentrates deeply on a creature, visualizing all its characteristics and abilities as a part of oneself. For example, you may find yourself in a gathering and suddenly see someone you absolutely do not want to be around. If you visualize the fox or the cat, you can use its cunning and ability to exit the gathering unseen. Or, you may decide not to leave but want to feel protected. You could assume the abilities of the badger or ferocious hound to send signals of "don't dare bother me."

The ability to shapeshift requires much practice and patience for the user to convince the mind that this can and will take place. The ability also is valuable to use if you want to visit the Otherworld in a disguised form. This sometimes makes a Walker Between Worlds more comfortable during the first few visits. However, this disguise will not fool the deities and fairies, who can see through it. Shapeshifting is also useful when sitting in nature. If you choose a nonthreatening creature, you will be able to observe the natural actions of wild creatures without them being afraid of you.

Badger (*Brocc* in Old Irish; *broc* in Scottish Gaelic; *broch* in Wales): Badgers represented great strength, courage, tenacity, and ferocity to the Celts. In the Welsh story of Rhiannon's wooing by Pwyll, the former suitor Gwawl, who had the power of a badger, enters the party and threatens everyone. The only way he could be defeated was to trap him in a magical bag. The Scottish Highlanders wore *sporrans* made of a badger's head to keep their money and small valuables safe.

Bear (Arth): Although the Welsh god Math exhibited bear-like qualities, the bear itself is not mentioned in any Celtic legends, probably because it was not native to the islands. Pictures of it are seen in later manuscript illustrations by the monks. Artio was a bear goddess of the Celtic Gauls. It represents selfless actions.

Bees (*brech* in Old Irish; *beach* in Scottish Gaelic; *gwenynen* in Welsh): Bees were believed to come from heaven in both Ireland and Scotland. They brought secret wisdom with them, thus making honey an important product. The province of Munster listed honey as one of its assets.

Blackbird (Druid-dhubh): The Gaelic name of this bird links it solidly with the Druids. In Wales, it was connected with the goddess Rhiannon. The Birds of Rhiannon lived in the Otherworld. However, their influence crossed the boundaries and could affect humans by enchanting them to sleep with their song. The tale of Bran the Blessed tells of Bran's seventy followers entering into a state of suspended animation for seventy-two years on the island of Gwales, during which time they were serenaded by the Birds of Rhiannon.

Bull (Tarbh), **Cow** (Bó): Bulls appear frequently in Celtic myths. To the Celts, their cattle determined their wealth and food supply, so bulls and cows were very important. This importance is shown by the fact that there are over one hundred Gaelic words that relate to the cow. The Irish *Book of the Dun Cow* tells of a *tarbh feis*, or bull feast, performed at the election of a High King. Irish folklore tells of three supernatural cows that rise from the sea on occasion; one is white (*bó-finn*), one red (*bó-ruadh*), and one black (*bó-dhubh*).[6] Not only were cows and their milk important to wealth and the Celtic economy, the milk was also thought to have healing powers.[7] Goddesses such as Brigit and Bóann, and queens such as Medb, were associated with cattle. It was a primal symbol of strength and potency.

Cat (Caoit): There are eight words for *cat* in Irish Gaelic. Cats were not kept as pets by the Celts. They were viewed as very dangerous, supernatural creatures. The Cath Palug of Wales was the offspring of the supernatural sow Hen-Wen. Írusán was an Irish cat, as large as an ox, and known as the King of Cats. Senchán Torpéist, a chief poet of Ireland, went to the cave where the giant cat lived and recited a satire to him. Írusán rushed out of the cave, threw the poet onto his back, and ran away with him.

Crane (Corr): Legends say that this bird was associated with the Cailleach. The crane was a secret and magical bird. When Fionn mac Cumhaill was a child, his grandmother rescued him from danger by changing herself into a crane and carrying him away. Later, Fionn mac Cumhaill is associated with the Children of the Cailleach of the Temple, who are four cranes who bring him death.

Crow (Badbh), **Raven** (Bran): The crow was associated with the Irish war goddesses Macha, Badb, and Mórrígán. In Scottish tradition it is said that the crow has twenty-seven different cries, each of which relates to a different event.[8] It was considered to be a cunning and skilled messenger from the Otherworld, although tricky and ill-omened.

Deer (Abhach), **Stag** (Sailetheach): The deer mentioned in sagas were always the native Irish red deer, whose colors range from red-brown to gray. The only exception was the White Doe or White Stag that clearly were of Otherworld origin. Fionn mac Cumhaill's wife Sabha, who was an Otherworld being, assumed the form of a deer when she left the mortal world. Fionn's son Oisin was born of that union and was therefore considered to be half mortal, half deer. In Scotland there are stories of women who are able to change themselves into deer.

Stags were associated with horned gods, such as Cernunnos. The Irish goddess Flidais was called the mistress of deer and stags. Mórrígán often took the form of a stag when she tested heroes. Cernunnos is pictured on the Gundestrop Cauldron with stags by his side. Welsh literature tells of the Red Stag of Redynvre, which was one of the oldest living creatures. Stags, particularly white ones, frequently led mortals into the Otherworld.

Dragon: In Celtic myth this Otherworld creature is frequently called a worm or water serpent. It was a symbol of the Cailleach who ruled over winter, as well as representing the elemental power within the earth. The Druids spoke of tapping the dragon energy, or ley lines, in their magical work.

Eagle (Iolair): Eagles in Celtic tradition, particularly in Wales, were considered to be very magical. In the Welsh tale of Mabon, the Eagle of Cilgwry guides the searchers on the journey. In the Irish tale, *The Voyage of Maelduin*, the travelers watch as an ancient eagle renews itself in an Otherworld lake. In Welsh literature the eagle of Gwern Abwy is said to be the oldest creature in the world. Celtic tradition says that the eagle was one of the oldest animals. Highland chieftains still wear three eagle feathers in their bonnets as a sign of their rank.

Eel (As-chu): Thought to be as wise and full of inspiration as the salmon, the eel was also a protector. Certain Irish myths tell of eels that could turn into great destructive weapons when a hero handled them. The name of Gae-Bolga, the spear of Cú Chulainn, was derived from the eel. During one battle with this hero, Mórrígán turned herself into an eel.

Fox (Sionnach): The red fox is native to Ireland, although it is not always red. Sometimes it is a reddish-brown or reddish-gray color.

Goat (Gabhar): Goats were also native dwellers in the Irish mountains. Every year a goat is still crowned king of the Puck Fair in Killorglin, County Kerry.

Hare (Giorria): The Irish or blue hare is found only in Ireland. Related to the Arctic hare, it is small with white ears. At one time it was believed that old women turned into hares in May to steal milk. Hares were also associated with certain goddesses. Thus, it was taboo to hunt or eat the hare. In Britain certain tribes used the movements of a hare for divination.

Hawk (Aracos): The famous Hawk of Achill spoke to the poet Fintan and revealed that its knowledge of the world stretched back almost to the beginning of time.

Heron (Corr): In Celtic legends there is little if any difference between the symbolism of the crane and the heron.

Horse (Cab-all): The horse was a very important animal to the Celts. Not only did the Celts ride horses, but they also used them to pull chariots and to race in contests. These animals were said to originate in the sea or lakes and had the supernatural ability to speak. The two horses of Cú Chulainn, Liath Macha and Dubh Sainglenn or

Saingliu, rose out of a gray lake at Sliab Fúait; when Cú Chulainn died, Liath Macha shed tears of blood.[9] It was taboo for the Celts to eat horse-meat. In the Welsh tale of Branwen's marriage to the Irish king, Efnisien deliberately maimed the king's horses and thus started a war. The horse was associated with the goddesses Epona and Rhiannon.

In Britain there are fourteen hill figures of white horses carved into the earth. The oldest of these is the Uffington White Horse at Uffington Castle, Oxfordshire. It is 364 feet long.

Hound/Dog (Abach): In the Celtic world dogs were not kept as pets, but as guardians and companions for the hunt. The large, mild-tempered Irish wolfhound was one of the favorites. Hounds were believed to have the ability to understand anything said by a human. They also were thought to be easily influenced by the fairies. Legends tell of three green fairy hounds that were called Fios ("Knowledge"), Luath ("Swiftness"), and Tron ("Heaviness").

There are many myths that mention hounds, some of them supernatural. One of the best-known myths concerns Fionn mac Cumhaill and his pair of hounds. Fionn was a skilled hunter and prized dogs highly. Uirne, Fionn's sister, was changed into a dog for a time by a lover of her husband Illann. As a result of this temporary transformation, she bore human triplets and twin dogs. Fionn kept the hounds Sceolan and Bran, who were his favorites. In Wales at Carn Cafall, there is a strange print on a stone that folklore says was made by Arthur's hound Cafall.

In Wales there are stories that tell of the Cwn Annwn, or Otherworld Hounds, that belong to Arawn, King of the Underworld. These hounds are white with red-tipped ears and red eyes. In later times these hounds were associated with Gwyn ap Nudd, who leads the Wild Hunt. Hounds also accompanied the Goddess on Her sacred hunt; actually this Goddess-hunt was the origin of the later male-god-dominated Wild Hunt.

Many Irish and Welsh names are derived from the Gaelic word *cú*, which means "dog, hound." These include the great Irish hero Cú Chulainn (Cullan's hound), Con Cancness (dog without skin), Kentigern (hound king), and Cú Neglassus (gray dog).

Otter (Balgair): In Gaelic, the otter is known by two different names: *dobran,* "water-one," or *dobhar-chu,* "water-dog." The otter, a creature of both earth and water, was a powerful and magical creature of Celtic myth. All otters were considered invulnerable until the hero Muiredach killed one; he wore a mantle of this otter's skin to give him protection. Celtic folklore says that the otter is vulnerable only under its forearm or beneath its chin. For some unknown reason, this idea of the otter's good luck was transferred to "lucky" moles on the human skin; these moles were called *ball dobhrain.* An ancient strange and magical creature, the otter was one of the forms into which Cerridwen shifted when she chased Taliesin.

Owl (Ulchabhán; Scottish Gaelic, *cailleach*): A lunar bird associated with the night, wisdom, and great magic, the owl was the bird of the Welsh Blodeuwedd. It was thought to bear ill omens if sighted by day. The Welsh *Mabinogion* tale of "Culhwch and Olwen" speaks of the Owl of Cwm Cawlwyd; this bird is very ancient and full of wisdom.

Raven (Bran): Considered to be a bird of great power and magic, it was connected with the Irish goddess Mórrígán and the Welsh god Bran. The earliest depictions of ravens are found on the walls of prehistoric caves, where they seem to be speaking to humans. Ancient stories tell of the Druids predicting events from the behavior of ravens. In the Irish tale "The Wasting Sickness of Cú Chulainn," two ravens bring predictive messages to the hero. The raven was recognized as a bird that carried omens and prophecies, but was also the harbinger of death on the battlefields.

Salmon (Brionnfhionn): The salmon is always connected with wisdom and the acquisition of knowledge in Celtic stories. It is also associated with oracular powers. The Salmon of Assaroe is the most famous of this legendary fish and was said to be the oldest creature in the world.

The Irish and Scottish Celts highly prized the salmon above all other fish. It was frequently roasted and served with honey, for this fish was said to have magical and restorative powers. Salmon were also connected with sacred wells. Fionn mac Cumhaill gained his vast knowledge by eating the Salmon of Wisdom, which had grown very wise by eating hazelnuts that fell into the sacred well in which it lived. Both the Salmon of Wisdom at Linn Féic along the Boyne and the one at the falls of Assaroe on the Erne were caught and eaten by Fionn. In Welsh literature the oldest and wisest of living creatures was the Salmon of Llyn Llyw. The Welsh bard Taliesin was rescued from a salmon weir as a small child.

Seal (Rón): Seals were common along the Irish and Scottish coasts. In Ireland the gray seal with its dog-like snout is found along the seacoast, while the common seal with its round head lives in the estuaries. Many individuals and families still refuse to hunt or eat seals because their family history says they descended from a seal-woman. Seals that could transform into humans were called selkies.

Snake, serpent (Nathair): Snakes are not known in Ireland. However, they are recognized in Wales and parts of Scotland. The Welsh Druids once called themselves *nadredd*, "serpents." Patrick did not drive serpents out of Ireland, but rather persecuted the Druids and forced them to go underground. In Celtic art, and particularly on the Gundestrop Cauldron, are found depictions of the ram-headed serpent, a supernatural symbol connected with Cernunnos, god of the woodlands and Lord of Animals. The black buds of the ash tree resemble tightly coiled serpents. A first-century archaeological dig in Anglesey unearthed a Druidic ashwood wand with a spiral carved around it, a reference to the Druid connection with snakes.

Sow (Airc), **Boar** (*Torc* in both Scotland and Ireland; *baedd gwyllt* in Welsh): The Celtic languages use different words for wild pigs and for domesticated ones. A ferocious, aggressive animal to hunt, the Celts admired its strength and courage. Warriors in Scotland considered the boar's skin an appropriate dress. Many stories of pigs are found in both Irish and Welsh legends.

The pig is the only native farm animal found in Ireland. In both Ireland and Scotland, pigs were believed to have originated in the Underworld. This made pigs unpredictable and not to be trusted, although they were considered to be very powerful and magical. When Otherworld swine broke free of the Underworld and breached the gate of the Middleworld (Earth), they usually caused confusion and destruction, as in the tale of Mag Mucraime (Plain of Pignumbering).

Ailill, king of Connacht, and his queen Medb were faced with a disaster caused by runaway swine that entered the Middleworld from the

Caves of Cruachu. These pigs blighted the crops of corn and caused a decrease of milk production in the cows, even though their flesh did ease some of the hunger of the people. Ailill and Medb knew that something must be done or famine would strike their land. They marched their army to Fraechmag (Heatherfield) and chased the Underworld swine to Belach na Fert (the Pass of the Graves).

The Irish *Book of Invasions* tells of Torc Triath, king of the Otherworld pigs, while the Fenian stories relate the fierceness of Torc Forbartach.

In Wales, pigs were connected primarily with the goddess Cerridwen. In the *Mabinogion* tale of Pwyll, the Lord of the Underworld, Arawn, gave a herd of pigs to Pwyll as a special gift. There are also tales of the sow Hen-Wen who ate the beechnuts that fell from the Trees of Wisdom and the ferocious Twrch Trwyth who came from the Otherworld and was hunted by Arthur. Folklore says that Merlin kept a little pig that talked with him and imparted inspired visions, just as the White Boar of Marvan did for his master in Ireland.

In spite of this connection with the Otherworld, pork was considered a "food of the gods" and was favored by the Celts in both Ireland and Wales. However, in Ireland, the occupation of keeping pigs was the lowest position on the social scale.

In the Ardennes Forest, there was a Romano-Gaulish bear goddess named Arduinna. She was portrayed sitting on a boar and was frequently identified with the Roman goddess Diana. The Gauls also had a swine god named Moccus.

The Isle of Man has legends of the *arkan sonney*, called "lucky piggy" in English. This fairy pig was white with red ears, a typical description of fairy animals. It was said to be able to alter its size but not its shape. Although difficult to catch, it was believed to bring good luck to anyone who could hold it.

Squirrel (Iora): The red squirrel was a common inhabitant of conifer forests in Ireland.

Swan (Eala): The mute swan has always used Ireland as a breeding ground. This species builds big nests along the banks of rivers and lakes. The swan has always held a place of great mystical importance to the Celts. The bard or poet used the skin and feathers of swans to make her/his ceremonial cloak (called the *tugen*). It was believed that this aligned the bard with the language of the birds.

In Wales the swan was associated with communications with the Otherworld, while in Ireland they represented purity, beauty, and good luck.

The association of animals with the spiritual did not stop when Christianity took over in the Celtic areas. This association was simply transferred to the new "saints." One story relates that St. Gobhnat of Ballyvourny in County Cork discovered the place for her new monastery by following nine white deer. The enclosure of this monastery was later guarded by bees.

Some figures in myths and legends received their names from interactions with animals. For example, the hero Cú Chulainn, son of Dechtire, a mortal woman, and Lugh, a god, began his life with the name Sétanta. While visiting the smith Culann at Cuailnge with his foster father Conchobar, seven-year-old Sétanta is attacked by a huge, mean guard dog. The boy kills the dog, which leaves Culann without his prized hound or any protection for his compound. Sétanta offers to be Culann's hound until a new dog is raised. Thus, Sétanta becomes Cú Chulainn, or Culann's hound.

The legend of the Hawk of Achill also mentions several other supernatural animals: the solitary crane of Moy Léana, the eagle of Druim Brice, the crane of Inish Géidh, the stag named Blackfoot of Slieve Fuaid, the blackbird of Druim Seghsa, the blind salmon of Assaroe, and the white blackbird of Clonfert.

Symbols

The path of the mystic has symbols with deeper, multilayered meanings. The shaman must search during meditation for the most esoteric of these meanings, as they cannot be verbalized.

Oak: As an emblem of strength and long life, this tree was important and sacred to many ancient cultures. Among the Celts this importance was strengthened because of the mistletoe that grew on it and the lightning that frequently struck it. The oak was believed to be an earthly representation of the Tree of Life.

Salmon: In Celtic myth the salmon always is associated with wisdom gained from the Otherworld. It is also connected with sacred wells whose water flows directly from the Otherworld into the mortal world.

Snake: The serpent is an ancient symbol of wisdom. The Welsh bards referred to themselves as both Cerddorion ("sons of Cerridwen") and Nadredds ("adders" or "serpents").

Spiral: A symbol of the constantly moving energies of the universe and the serpent-energy of the stars, the spiral was a very sacred design to the Celts. Travelers into the Otherworld frequently follow a spiral or labyrinthine path.

Stone: The Celts did not often carve images of their deities. Instead, they believed that these deities frequently were represented by monolithic stones. Stones symbolized a place of primordial power, particularly Goddess power. They were one of the connections between the land itself and the Otherworld.

Torc: This piece of Celtic jewelry was made of strands of metal twisted together and formed into a circle. The circle represents the ultimate state of oneness, progression from time to timelessness, from the body-obsessed consciousness to the spiritual-centered subconscious.

Year Wheel: On one level the wheel with eight spokes is symbolic of time and the movement of karma, on another level it represented the movement of the Celtic Sacred Year. Each spoke signified a religious festival.

Stone Circle Meditation

Learning and practicing meditation is an absolute must for anyone on the Celtic spiritual paths. Regular meditation, not less than once a week, keeps you balanced and more able to cope with unexpected happenings. It also opens you to true messages from the ancestors, guides, and others from the Otherworld. These messages may come during meditation itself or through dreams.

For instructions on setting up a meditation space and taping the meditation, please refer to The Well of Slane Meditation in Chapter Three.

Stone Circle Meditation

Close your eyes and visualize a brilliant white light over your head. As you inhale deeply, feel this light coursing through your body, from your head down to your toes. Feel your muscles relaxing, beginning with your feet. The deep sense of peacefulness moves up through your legs, into your body and arms. You feel the tenseness flow out of the muscles in your shoulders, neck, and head. You are completely relaxed.

Before you now is a well. Take all the problems in your life and throw them into the deep darkness of the well. The problems are quickly carried far away from you. Leave them there, turn and walk away. You will be totally protected during this meditation. Absolutely nothing can harm you.

You are standing on a hill with a great circle of enormous stones before you. Thick forests of oak, ash, and fir surround the open place that contains the stone circle. A man and a woman stand in the center of the circle. They are dressed in long white robes, and each carries a tall staff with a flashing crystal on top. These are your guides for this journey.

You pass between two of the tall stones and walk to the center where the man and woman wait. As you stand before them, the woman touches your shoulder with her staff. The air begins to waver around you until the hill, the stones, and the forests disappear.

You are now standing at the entrance to a very large white

marble building. The building is surrounded by beds of bright flowers, gravel walks, and little fountains.

"Are you prepared to look into your past lives?" the man asks. "You cannot progress until you know what other lives and decisions brought you to this time and place."

"You will not be shown anything you cannot understand or handle," the woman says with a smile. Both guides take your arms and walk with you into the building.

Inside, a muted light comes through the high stained glass windows, falling in rainbow patterns on the white floor. The room is filled with tables and chairs, while the walls are lined high with shelves of books.

"This is the hall of Akashic records," the man says as they lead you to a table. "Here you will see into the past lives that have influenced your present life."

"Few have lived lives of greatness or fame." The woman smiles as she sits beside you at the table. "Do not expect to see something you already think you know. Open your mind to the truth, and see what is real."

The man places a large, leather-bound book on the table in front of you. "These are your lives," he says.

You open the book. You may see moving pictures inside, or strange writing and drawings or something like photos. The first few times you are in the hall of records you may be frustrated as you try to read the strange text or keep the pictures from moving too fast. Your guides can help you with this.

Do not be surprised if the majority of your past lives were lived as an ordinary person. Remember, it is ordinary people whose lives have the most impact on cultures, governments, and history, not the one-second-of-fame person.

Look for patterns of behavior and events between lives. This is a solid clue to what you may be facing today. Sometimes seeing the truth behind the events is enough to give you the determination and courage to break negative patterns.

When you have seen several lifetimes, your guides take you

back out into the gardens. They stroll down the paths with you, looking at the beautiful flowers and answering any questions you may have. Finally, they take you back to the stone circle.

When you are ready to leave, you look up to see a white stag waiting just outside the stone circle. You follow the stag back into the forest until you once again reach the well. You think of your physical body and find yourself within it. The meditation is ended.

Dress

Mystics wore ankle-length, white tunics. Sometimes these tunics had borders of purple or other colors. For ceremonies she/he often wore the skin of a white bull as a cloak and covered her/his head with a headdress of white feathers, complete with fluttering wings. The mystic wore or carried the *glain nadredd* ("adder stone" or "serpent glass") and gold ornaments.

For everyday wear, the mystic probably dressed in an ankle-length tunic of pale colors, leather shoes or boots, and a tartan-colored cloak. Her/his bag contained small quantities of herbs for healing, a set of ogham sticks, and any talismans or objects that were of great meaning to the individual.

---

1. The Gaelic word *cuigi*, or province, means a fifth.
2. L. H. Weston, *The Planet Vulcan.*
3. Alice Bailey, *Esoteric Astrology.*
4. Helena Paterson, *Celtic Astrology.*
5. Michael Bayley, *Caer Sidhe: The Celtic Night Sky.*
6. The colors of white, red, and black have been associated with the Triple Goddess since the earliest of civilizations.
7. In one Irish legend, the Pictish Druid Trosdane instructed the Irish army to use the milk of one hundred and fifty white cows to bathe their wounded.
8. The number twenty-seven is a multiple of the sacred number three: three times nine. If a flock of crows (*molmacha*) is calling all together, folklore says that no seer can understand their messages.
9. Some sources say that the hero's horses were named *Dubh-sron-gheal* and *Dubh-srannal*, while the horses of Fionn mac Cumhaill were named *Dubh-saoileann* and *Liath Macha.*

APPENDICES

Pronunciation Guides

Old Irish

Vowels

a, ai = like the "a" in gather

á, ái = like the "a" in law

áe, aí = like the "ai" in aisle

e, ei, éo, éoi = like the "e" in end

i = like the "i" in it

í, íu, íui = like the "e" in each

ía, íai = like the "i" in Ian

o, oi = like the "o" in odd

ó, ói = like the "o" in ode

óe, oí = like the "oi" in oil

u, úi = like the "u" in pull

ú, úi = like the double "o" in spoon

úa, úai = like the "e" in sewer

Consonants:

The consonants standing alone or in final positions are vastly different than those in English

b = (initial) as in beat; (final position) as the "v" in clover

c, cc = (initial) as in cat, and is never soft; (final position) as the "g" in dig

ch = as the Scottish word loch

d = (initial) as in dart; (final position) as the "th" in father

dh = as the "th" in there

f = as in fine

g = as in gift. "G" may also be guttural in some words

h = never pronounced as an initial

l, ll = as in leap or killer

m, mb, mm = (initial) as the "m" in mother; (final position) as the "v" in clever

n, nd, nn = as in nice

p = (initial) as the "p" in pal; (final position) as the double "b" in stub-born

r, rr = similar to the "r" in Sara, but with a little more roll to it

s, ss (when final or before a, o, or u) as in song; (when first letter or be-fore e or i) as in shine

t, tt = (initial) as in tank; (final position) as the "d" in pedal

th = thistle

Scottish Gaelic

Scottish Gaelic is similar to the Irish Ulster dialect but has more sounds that have no counterparts in English. The vowels are more irregular than those in other Celtic tongues.

Vowels

a = as in bath; (when before and after m, n) sounds like "v"

à = as in father; (when before and after m, n) sounds like "v"

ai = like the "e" in end

ài = as the "a" in father

ao = as the "u" in muse

aoi = as the double "e" in keen

e = as in end

è, èi = as the "a" in fare

ea = as the "a" in yard

i = as the "ea" in each; sometimes also like the "i" in it

io = as in it

o = as in pot

ò = as in more

oi = as in ode

u, ù, ùi = as the double "o" in spoon

Consonants:

b = as in beat

bh = as the "v" in Velcro, but also sometimes like a "u" or silent, depending upon its position in the word

c = as in cat

ch = (when before or after a, o, u) as in loch

ch = (when before or after e, i) as in the German word ich

chd = the "d" sounds like a "k"

d = like the "t" in tank

d = (when before or after e, i) as the "j" in jest

dh = silent when in a final position; other times similar to ch

dh = (when before or after e, i) like the "y" in yes

f = as in fine

fh = primarily silent

g = hard, as in girl

gh = similar to ch; sometimes silent

l = no comparable English sound in most positions

l, ll = (when before or after e, i) like the double "l" in million

m = as in mother but more nasal

mh = like the "v" in vile but more nasal

n = as in nice

n = (when before or after e, i) like the "n" in pinion

n = (when after c, g, m, t) similar to an "r"

ng = as in angle

p = as in pal

ph = as the "f" in fine

r, rr = as the double "r" in carry

s = (when before or after a, o, u) as in song

s = (when before or after e, i) like the "sh" in wish

sh = like the "h" in hope

t = aspirated like a "th"; (when before or after e, i) similar to the "ch" in chin

th = (initial) like the "h" in hope; other times silent or slightly aspirated

Wales

The Welsh language is very difficult to learn and frequently has pronunciations that sound nothing like the written word. Like Scottish Gaelic, Welsh has some sounds that have no English comparisons. There are also differences in North Wales and South Wales.

Vowels

a = several sounds, some as in father; others as the "o" in pot or the "a" in man

ae, ai, au = as the "ai" in aisle

e = like the "a" in Hayden. Sometimes like the "e" in end

ei, eu, ey = like the "i" in tie

ew = similar to the "ew" in stew

i = like the double "e" in peel. In some words like the "i" in it

iw = a "u" sound, like the "y" in yew, if at the beginning of a word. Like the "i" in rice, if at the end of a word

o = like the "o" in more; sometimes like the "o" in knot

oe, oi, ou = like the "oi" in oil

u = a variable sound, depending upon the consonants next to it. Often pronounced as the "u" in rug. However, it is also pronounced "thee" when in such combinations as Ddu.

y = like the double "e" in keen

yw = like the "ye" in yew

Consonants:

b = as in beat

c = as in cat

ch = as in loch

d = as in dart

dd = as the "th" in this

f = as the "v" in vile

ff = as the "f" in fine

g = hard as in girl

h = as in hope

l = as in leap

ll = a more aspirated "l"

m = as in mother

n = as in nice

ng = as in song

p = as in pal

ph = like the "f" in fine

r = slightly trilled like the double "r" in horrid

s = as in sing

si = like the "sh" in shin

t = as in tank

th = as in thin

w = similar to a "woo" or double "oo" sound

Major Celtic Deities

Pronunciations are only given where I feel comfortable with a phonetic translation. Any words without a phonetic pronunciation are those I am unsure of. However, I felt it important for the reader to know the word, whether or not they can pronounce it. The syllable given in italics in each word is the one that should be accented. Since Gaelic is much different than English, the pronunciations are only approximate.

Although a broad general pronunciation guide for the Old Irish, Scottish Gaelic, and Welsh languages is included, please understand that these are approximate only. Correct pronunciation can be gained only through a study course in the chosen Celtic tongue.

Most names and words are followed by the Celtic country in which they were used, such as Ireland, Scotland, or Wales. The term Gauls refers to the Continental Celts. For those words widely known in all Celtic areas, the word Celts alone is used. In the Welsh language, the word ap is sometimes called *ab* or *fab*, which means "son of," just as *mac* does in Irish and Scottish Gaelic.

Some of the names given will not be covered in the text. They are included to aid and enhance any further study the reader may wish to do on her/his own.

Áine of Knockaine (*aw*-nee): Ireland. As the goddess of love, she was also associated with the moon and Summer Solstice. She may have originally been a sun goddess. Described at various times as the wife or daughter of Manannán mac Lir, her fairy palace was said to be at Cnoc Áine or Knockainy in Munster. She was also connected with the well Tobar Áine near Lissan in County Londonderry and Cnoc Áine near Augher in County Waterford. She is associated with love, fertility, desire, crops, and cattle.

Airmid/Airmed (*air*-med or *air*-mit): Ireland. She was the daughter of Dian Cécht, the physician of the Tuatha Dé Danann, and the sister to Miach. A physician in her own right, Airmid helped her brother restore Nuada's severed hand. Her name translates as "measure of grain." When a variety of herbs grew from her brother's grave, she tried to catalog them, but her efforts were terminated by her jealous father. She is associated with herbal healing.

Angus mac Óg (moc og): Ireland. He was also known as Aengus, Aonghus, Angus of the Bruig, Óengus of the Bruig, and Angus mac Óc. The son of the Dagda and the goddess Bóann, his name means "young son." He was fostered by Midir, since his mother was married to Nechtan, not the Dagda. One of the Tuatha Dé Danann, his harp produced the sweetest music ever heard. Legend says that his kisses turned into birds that carried messages of love. Wherever he went, four swans circled over his head. His magical sword was named Móralltach. Because the Dagda stopped time from the date of his conception until his birth, Angus was also said to control time. His *bruig* or fairy mound was at Newgrange on the banks of the River Boyne. He is associated with youth and love.

Anu (an-oo)/**Ana**: Ireland. Sometimes she was called Búanann (the lasting one). A mother goddess of the Earth and plenty, she was considered to be the Mother of all the Tuatha Dé Danann and the greatest of all goddesses. She also ruled over cattle (security and prosperity), health, and fertility. At Summer Solstice, fires were frequently lit in her honor. Near Killarney on the border of Kerry and Cork, there are two hills still known as the Paps of Anu, *Dá Chích nAnann* in Irish Gaelic. Anu may be an aspect of Dana/Danu. Although she was said to have both malevolent and benevolent aspects, she is primarily associated with fertility, prosperity, and comfort.

Arawn (ar-awn): Wales. Called the Lord of Annwn, he ruled over the Underworld, which was a kingdom of the dead, not hell. He owned a magic cauldron and a herd of special pigs that he gave to Pwyll for his services of defeating his rival, Hafgan. His story is found in "Pwyll, Prince of Dyfed." He is closely related to Gwynn ap Nudd and is associated with death, rebirth, and karma.

Arianrhod (ar-*ree*-an-rod): Wales. A goddess of stars, sky, reincarnation, the full moon, and initiation, her name means "Silver Wheel or Disk." From her palace Caer Arianrhod or the Aurora Borealis, she ruled over time and karma, and was called Keeper of the Silver Wheel. Another name for her 'wheel' was the Oar Wheel, which was said to be a ship that carried the dead to Emania (Moon-land). Some legends say she was the mother of Lleu Llaw Gyffes and the sea god Dylan Eil Ton (Son of the Wave) by her brother Gwydion. She was the daughter of the goddess Don and the god Beli. She is associated with beauty, death, and reincarnation.

Badb (bive or bibe)/**Badhbh**: Ireland. Sometimes called "Red-Mouthed," her name has been variously translated as Boiling, Battle Raven, and Scald-crow, all signifying her attributes as a war goddess. In Gaul she was known as Badb Cath or Cauth Bodva. Her consort was a shadowy war god called Néit or Net. Sister of Macha, Nemain, and Mórrígan, she was one of a trio of war goddesses. In her aspect as a Mother Goddess, her cauldron produced a constant flow of life, wisdom, and inspiration. Lisbabe (*lios baidhe*, Badb's fort) in County Kerry near Aghadoe was named for her. She is associated with wisdom, inspiration, and enlightenment, and the symbols of cauldrons, crows, and ravens.

Banba (*ban*-ba): Ireland. She was part of a triad of obscure Sovereignty goddesses with Fódla and Ériu who used their powers to repel invaders to Ireland. This triad met with the Milesians soon after they landed. Although all three asked that their names be applied to the island, only Ériu's request was granted. This is also one of the poetic names of Ireland. Legend says she was married to Mac Cuill and the mother of Ogma. She is associated with the power of the land.

Blodeuwedd (*blod*-oo-eeth) (blow-die-eth) (Use both as there can be disagreement on pronunciation): Wales. Formed from flowers and nine separate elements by Gwydion and Math, she became the wife of Lleu. However, her betrayal of him with Gronw Pebyr caused Gwydion to turn her into an owl. Her name means "flower face." She is associated with lunar mysteries and initiations.

Bóann (*boo*-an)/**Bóand**: Ireland. Known as the goddess of the River Boyne and the mother of Angus mac Óg, Bóann means "She of the white cows." Her consort was a mysterious god named Nechtan, who guarded the Well of Segais. She is associated with seeking for knowledge.

Bran (brawn): Wales. The name Bran means "raven." He was also known as Bran Bendigeidfran/Bendigeid (ben-dig-*ide*-vran), or Bran the Blessed. This giant warrior was the son of the goddess Don and brother to Branwen. He owned a magic cauldron that would restore life to anyone placed inside it. He is associated with prophecy, the arts, the sun, music, and writing.

Branwen (*brawn*-oo-en): Wales. The daughter of Llyr and sister to Bran, she was known as the Venus of the Northern Seas. A goddess of love and beauty, the name Branwen is derived from the Welsh words *bran*, "raven," and *gwen*, "fair or white." She is associated with beauty and love.

Brigit (*bree*-itch or breet)/Brigid/Bride (breed): Ireland. A daughter of the Dagda, she was the goddess of fire, fertility, cattle, crops, poets, healers, smiths, and craftsmen. Sometimes listed as a triple goddess, she was associated with the festival of Imbolc. Legend says she had a son, Rúadán, by the Fomorian Bres. Under the name Bríg in one legend, she made the first keening or wailing for the dead in Ireland when her son Rúadán was killed by Goibniu during a great battle. Her all-female religious community (which consisted of nineteen priestesses called *Inghean an Dagha*) at Kildare kept a perpetual fire burning until it was taken over by Christians. One of her special symbols was, strangely enough, the snake. She is associated with healing, medicine, inspiration, divination, the arts, prophecy, smithcraft, brewing, animals, love, and occult knowledge.

Cernunnos (kerr-*noo*-nos): Celts. His name means "Hornéd One." He is portrayed on the Gundestrup Cauldron as a horned god, wearing antlers and surrounded by ram-headed serpents, stags, bulls, and other animals. Although he is Lord of the Animals, he is also connected with chthonic elements of the Otherworld and rebirth. The Druids called him Hu Gadarn. In his aspect as the Green Man, he was known in Old Welsh as Arddhu (The Dark One), Atho, and the Horned God. He is associated with virility, animals, the lands, woodlands, reincarnation, commerce, and wealth.

Cerridwen/Ceridwen (*kare*-id-wen): Wales. Her name probably is derived from *cyrrid*, "hooked," and *benyw*, "woman," thus giving the meaning as Crooked Woman. Representing a crone aspect of the Goddess, Cerridwen was a deity of inspiration and initiation. Her consort was the giant Tegid Foel. She is associated with initiation, death, regeneration, inspiration, magic, astrology, herbs, spells, and knowledge. Her most common symbols are the white sow and the cauldron.

Credne/Creidne: Ireland. A worker in bronze, brass, and gold, and a member of the smithing trio with Goibniu and Luchta, he helped forge weapons for the Tuatha Dé Danann in their great battles with the Fomorians. This triad was known as *na trí dé dána*, or the three craft gods of the Danann. He is associated with the arts, smithcraft, and warriors.

The Dagda (*dag*-da): Ireland. This name may be derived from an ancient Celtic word *dago-devos*, or "good god." This giant Tuatha Dé Danann was a rustic deity with a huge appetite for everything in life. He was also known as the Good God, Aedh (Fire), Ruad Rofessa (Lord of Great Knowledge), and Eochaid (ekka or *eo*-hee) Ollathair (All-Father). His magic harp was called Oak of Two Greens (*Daur-da-bla*) or the Four-Angled Music (*Coir-cethar-chuir*). He could play three kinds of music: sleep, laughter, and sorrow. He was also the guardian of the Undry cauldron brought from Murias. His gigantic club killed with one end and healed with the other. He also owned a black horse called Acéin (Ocean). When the Tuatha Dé Danann were defeated by the Milesians, the Dagda divided spiritual Ireland among them, giving each a *sídhe* or mound. Among his children were the sons Áed Minbhrec, Bodb Dearg, Cermait, Midir, and Angus mac Óg, as well as daughters Ainge and Brigit. He was tricked out of his *sídhe* (Bruig na Bóinne) by his son Angus mac Óg. He is associated with music, magic, the arts, protection, knowledge, prophecy, the weather, reincarnation, and prosperity.

Dana (*dan*-ah)/**Danu** (*dan*-oo): Ireland. A powerful Great Goddess, she was known as the mother of the Tuatha Dé Danann and may be similar to, or the same as, Anu. She is associated with magic, wells and water, prosperity, wisdom, and magic.

Dian Cécht/Diancécht (*dee*-an *keck*-t): Ireland. The great physician of the Tuatha Dé Danann, he made a silver hand with Credne to replace the one Nuada had lost in battle. Two of his children were Miach and Airmid. He is associated with medicine, healing, magic, and regeneration.

Don: Wales. This goddess was known as the Great Mother of the Welsh pantheon and is very similar to the Irish Dana or Danu. The name appears to mean "abyss of the deep sea." The Welsh knew the constellation of Cassiopeia as Llys Don. She is associated with wells, the elements, and healing.

Donn: Ireland. The name is derived from the Celtic word *dhuosno*, meaning the "dark" or "black" one. Known as the Lord of the Dead, this deity's house was called Tech Duinn (House of Donn), said to be located on one of the islands off the southwest coast of Munster. This island has a very unusual rock formation—a natural archway through which the sea flows with powerful force. All the dead were believed to pass through Donn's realm on the way to the Otherworld. If not the same deity as Bìle, Donn may be similar. He is associated with death and karma.

Dylan Eil Ton: Wales. This sea deity was the son of Arianrhod and the brother of Lleu. He left his father Gwydion at a young age and took to the sea. He was also called Son of the Wave. His symbol was a silver fish. The roar heard at the mouth of the River Conway in northern Wales is said to be his groaning. He is associated with the sea and all animals in it.

Epona (eh-*poh*-nah): Gauls. Known to both the Celts and the Romans as a horse goddess, she was called "The Great Mare" and "Divine Horse." The White Mare was a symbol of her powers. She was usually portrayed as riding sidesaddle and accompanied by a dog, a bird, and a foal. Acknowledged as a goddess of beginnings and endings, she carried the keys that opened the Otherworld to the dead. She is associated with fertility, maternity, healing springs, prosperity, and horses.

Gofannon/Govannon (go-vfan-an): Wales. A son of the goddess Don, he was the Welsh equivalent of the smith-god Goibniu and a patron of all smithing crafts. In Irish, gabha means "smith," while the Welsh word is gof. He is associated with blacksmiths, the making of weapons and jewelry, and brewing.

Goibniu (*gwiv*-noo): Ireland. This smith of the Tuatha forged the weapons by which the Fomorians were defeated. When wounded in battle, he was healed by water from the well of Slane. Legends say he had two brothers: Cian and Samhan. At the Otherworld feast of Fled Ghobhnenn, he served an ale that protected the drinkers against disease and death. Along with Luchta and Credne, he formed a triad of craft deities called *na trí dé dána*. Tradition says Goibniu's forge, *Cerdchae Ghaibhnenn*, lies east of Mullaghmast Hill in Glenn Treithin (*Treichim* in Old Irish) along the Kildare-Wicklow border. He is associated with regeneration, healing, the arts of smithing, magic, and protection.

Gwydion (*gwee*-dee-on): Wales. As one of the sons of the goddess Don, he was a master enchanter, the best storyteller in the world, and a many-skilled deity like the Irish Lugh. He was also the brother of Gofannon, Arianrhod, and Amaethon. He was an accomplished Druid, wizard, warrior, and bard. His symbol was a white horse. He is associated with shapeshifting, magic, spells, illusions, changes, and healing.

Gwynn ap Nudd (*gween* ap neethe): Wales. Known primarily in southern Wales, this Lord of the Underworld or of the Dead was believed to lead the Wild Hunt on stormy nights. Although a Welsh god, the entrance to his kingdom was said to be in Glastonbury Tor. In Scotland he is referred to as Arthur, a name which has nothing to do with the later legendary king; the name is derived from *ar ddu*, "the black one." He is associated with the fairies and Underworld journeys.

Lir (hlir)/**Ler:** Ireland. A sea deity, this god is the same as the Welsh Llyr. Some sources list him as the father of the sea god Manannán mac Lir; he was also the father of Fionnuala, Aed, Conn, and Fiachra, who were turned into swans by a jealous stepmother. In Old Irish the word *ler* means "sea." He is associated with hidden mysteries.

Lleu Llaw Gyffes (thlie thlaw guf-fies): Wales. Called "the fair one of the steady hand," he was the counterpart of the Irish Lugh. Legend hints that he was the son of Arianrhod by her brother Gwydion, twin to Dylan, and husband to Blodeuwedd. His aspects are similar to those of the Irish Lugh. He is associated with karma and reincarnation.

Lludd Llaw Ereint/Lludd/Nudd: Wales. A sky god, he was very similar to the Irish Nuada and was sometimes called Nudd. He was a son of Beli. He is associated with healing, incantation, and regeneration.

Llyr (thleer): Wales. This god's name means "of the sea." He was the mysterious father of Manawyddan by his wife Penardun, and Bran and Branwen by his wife Iweridd. Some sources say he was also known by the name Lludd Llaw Ereint (Silver Hand), which makes him similar to

Nuada of Ireland. He is associated with weather, the sea, and everything in the sea.

Luchta/Luchtaine (*loo*-ta): Ireland. A carpenter of the Tuatha Dé Danann, he was part of a triad of craft deities with Goibniu and Credne.

Lugh/Lug (loo): Ireland. Born to Cian of the Tuatha Dé Danann and Eithne of the Fomorians, he was the grandson of Balor of the Evil Eye, whom he later killed in battle. He was fostered by Manannán mac Lir of the Tuatha and Tailtiu, a warrior queen of the Fomorians. Lugh was guardian of the mystical spear of Gorias. He had many titles attached to his name: Lugh Lámfhota (of the Long Arm), Lug Samildánach (Many-Skilled), The Shining One, and The Fair-Haired One. He is associated with the sun, the arts and crafts, magic, strength, cunning, healing, journeys, prophecy, and commerce.

Macha (*mahk*-ah): Ireland. This goddess was one of a triad of battle goddesses with Mórrígán and Badb. She was also called Great Queen of Phantoms, Mother of Life and Death, Mania, and Battle Crow. She is associated with horses, dominance over males, cunning, sexuality, death, and protection.

Manannán mac Lir (ma-**naw**-nan moc leer): Ireland. A sea god of the Tuatha Dé Danann, he owned the Crane Bag, a magical coracle (little boat), and a cup of truth. He also possessed magical swine (whose flesh kept the Tuatha Dé Danann from aging), two spears named Yellow Shaft and Red Javelin, swords named The Retaliator, Great Fury, and Little Fury, a boat called Wave Sweeper, and a horse named Splendid Mane. His chariot horses could gallop over both land and sea. After the Milesians arrived and the Tuatha Dé Danann agreed to leave the Middleworld to them, Manannán prepared the sídhe for the Tuatha. He was closely connected with the Isle of Arran (Emain Abhlach) and the Isle of Man, but primarily ruled from Tír Tairngire (Land of Promise). Although his name is mac Lir, his father may have been the shadowy Allod. He is associated with ships, the seas, navigation, journeys, storms, the weather, magic, and commerce.

Manawyddan ap Llyr (man-ah-*ith*-an ap lir): Wales. A sea god and consort of Rhiannon, he was a cunning master craftsman and master magician. He is associated with magic, knowledge, and the sea.

Math Mathonwy (math math-*on*-oo-ee): Wales. The son of

Mathonwy, Math was a great king and the uncle of Gwydion, Gilfaethway, and Arianrhod. When Arianrhod cursed her son Lleu to have no mortal wife, Math and Gwydion created Blodeuwedd. He is associated with increasing wealth, magic, and enchantment.

Mórrígán (*moor*-ee-gon)/**Mórrígú** (*moor*-ee-goo): Ireland. Known by the titles of the Great Queen, Supreme War Goddess, Queen of Phantoms, and Specter Queen, this goddess reigned over the battlefield, but took no direct part. A shapeshifter, her favorite shape was that of a raven or crow. She was also part of a triad of goddesses related to war, death, and fate. This triad of the goddesses Badb, Macha, and Mórrígán were known as the Mórrígna. She is associated with war, revenge, magic, and prophecy.

Mórrígna/Mor-Ríoghna (*moor*-ug-nah): Ireland. This is the name of the triad of war and death goddesses, composed of Badb, Macha, and Mórrígán. This triad represented Fate.

Myrddin/Merlin: British Celts. The story of this great Celtic Druid and magician goes back much further than the Arthur sagas. He was originally called Myrddyn and was said to have an Otherworldly father. Later legends made him arch-mage and chief advisor to Arthur. He had a glass or crystal tower on Bardsley Island, where tales say he guarded the Thirteen Treasures of Britain. He is associated with psychic abilities, prophecy, divination, shapeshifting, healing, protection, magic, and protection.

Nuada/Nuadu (noo-ah-ha)/**Nuada Argetlám** (Nuada of the Silver Hand): Ireland. He was the great High King of the Tuatha Dé Danann until he lost a hand in battle against the Fir Bolgs. Then he was forced to abdicate because of the deformity. For a time he was known as Silver Hand, from the artificial hand made for him by Dian Cécht. He was able to resume his kingship when Miach and Airmid restored his physical hand. He was guardian of the shining sword from which none could escape, one of the treasures brought to Ireland by the Tuatha Dé Danann. He is associated with judgment, power, and knowledge.

Ogma (*og*-ma): Ireland. A son of the Dagda and a great warrior of the Tuatha Dé Danann, Ogma invented the sacred ogham alphabet. He was also known as Grianainech (of the Sunny Countenance) and Ogma Cermait (of the Honeyed Mouthed). During one battle with the

Fomorians, he captured the speaking sword of King Tethra. He ruled from the *sídhe* of Airceltrai, and was believed to be a god who conducted souls to the Otherworld. He is associated with dialects, eloquence, poetry, writing, inspiration, strength, magic, reincarnation, and war skills.

Pwyll (poo-*ill*): Wales. Known as the Lord of Dyfed, he once helped Arawn of the Underworld to defeat a deadly rival. Because of this association with Arawn, he was called Pwyll Pen Annwn (Pwyll, Head of Annwn). He married Rhiannon and was the father of Pryderi. He is associated with cunning.

Rhiannon (hri-*an*-non): Wales. Listed in sagas as the daughter of Hyfidd Hen, and called the Great Queen, she was associated with horses and birds. When her son Pryderi, by her first husband Pwyll, was stolen at birth, she was accused of his murder and had to carry visitors to the castle on her back until the child was miraculously returned. Her second husband was Manawyddan. The *Mabinogion* says that the Three Birds of Rhiannon can wake the dead and lull the living to sleep with their song. Her symbols are white horses and birds. She is associated with fertility, Underworld journeys, and enchantment.

Scáthach (*skaw*-thach): Ireland, Scotland. Her name translates as "Shadow" or "Shade." She was also known as Scáthach Buanand (Victorious). Associated with the Isle of Skye, Scáthach ran a martial arts school there and was the best warrior woman of all time. She taught all the great Irish heroes, including Cú Chulainn, to whom she taught the famous battle leap; she also gave him the deadly spear, Gae-Bolg. She is associated with the martial arts, strength, healing, magic, and prophecy.

Taliesin (tal-i-ess-in): Wales. The *Hanes of Taliesin* is a compilation of his beautiful poetry. He was a master magician and Chief of the Bards of the West. He is associated with shapeshifting, initiation, inspiration, writing, poetry, music, magic, and knowledge.

Minor Deities and Celtic Miscellany

Major deities were the more important ones that are frequently mentioned in Celtic myth and legend. Minor deities are infrequently mentioned and were less important.

Ábartach: Ireland. He was the son of the King of Tír Tairngire. His name means "feat-performing one."

Abcán: Ireland. This dwarf poet of the Tuatha Dé Danann owned a bronze boat with a tin sail, which he kept near the falls of Assaroe.

Abred: Welsh. This word is derived from the Welsh word meaning "to transmigrate." In ancient Welsh cosmogony, it was the innermost of three concentric circles of being. It is a synonym for Annwn, the Welsh Underworld.

Achill (ach-ill): Ireland. Legend speaks of the hawk of Achill that lived for thousands of years and could remember all Ireland's history from the beginning. This is also the name of a large mountainous island off the west coast of County Mayo.

Adammair (adam-mar): Ireland. Sometimes he is listed as the husband of the goddess Flidais.

Adar Llwch Gwin: Wales. This name is derived from the Welsh *llwch*, "dust or powder," and *gwin*, "wine." They were magical birds that belonged to Drudwas ap Tryffin and were often described as griffins. They were given to Drudwas by his fairy wife and could understand human speech.

Adder stone: Celts. Known in Wales as *glain nadredd* (glass of the serpent), it was a glass ball or amulet favored by the Druids. It was thought to be created from the bubbles produced by the mouths of breeding adders.

Áeb/Áebh/Aobh (ayv): Ireland. Derived from the Old Irish *Oíb*, "beauty," this was the name of the second of three wives of Lir. She was the mother of the four children who were turned into swans by her sister Aífe, who became Lir's third wife.

Áed (aye): Ireland. There are several men with this name in Irish legends. One was a son of the Dagda who seduced the wife of

Coincheann, another was the son of Eochair Lethderb, prince of Leinster. Two fairy women fell in love with Áed and took him away to a *bruig* for three years.

Áed Abrat: Ireland. This name means "light of the eye." He was the father of the goddess Fand, wife of Manannán mac Lir and he was skilled in singing healing songs.

Áed Minbhrec: Ireland. A son of the Dagda and a member of the Tuatha Dé Danann, he was wrongfully murdered by a jealous husband. Folklore says his sídhe was near Ballyshannon in County Donegal.

Aer (air): Wales. Goddess of the River Dee, this deity was also a deity of war and revenge.

Áer: Ireland. Derived from a word for "cutting" or "incising," in Old Irish literature this meant the verbal power of a bard to satirize or defame people.

Áes dána (ees *dah*-nah): Ireland. In Old Irish this means "people of the art," and was used to describe people who had a learned profession or trade in some form of art, such as poets, judges, metalworkers, woodworkers, and medical doctors.

Aí mac Ollamon/Aí mac Ollamain: Ireland. He was a poet of the Tuatha Dé Danann. His name means "poetic inspiration" or "learning."

Aíbell/Aoibheall/Aoibhell (*aye*-vil): Ireland. An Old Irish goddess or fairy queen who was associated with northern Munster and the O'Brien clan. Her fairy mound is said to be at Craig Liath near Killaloe, County Clare. Her name means "radiance, spark, fire." The goddess Clídna once turned her into a white cat.

Aífe/Aoife (*eef*-ah): Ireland, Scotland. The story of this Amazon warrior woman and her encounter with the hero Cú Chulainn, by whom she had a son Connla or Conlaí, is told in *Tochmarc Emire* (The Wooing of Emer). Known as the hardest woman in the world, she lived in Alba (Scotland) and, although listed as a sister to Scáthach and daughter of Árd-Greimne, was often in conflict with the great martial arts teacher.

Another Aífe was one of the wives of the god Lir. The daughter of Dealbhaoth, she was turned into a crane by a jealous rival for the love of Ilbrec. When she died, Manannán mac Lir made her skin into his mystical crane bag.

Ailbe (*ell*-veh): Ireland. She was one of the daughters of the fairy king Midir.

Aileach (*ahl*-ek): Ireland. The ruins of this major fortress in Ulster still stand about five miles northwest of Derry in County Donegal. Legend says it was built by the Tuatha Dé Danann and used by the three goddesses of Sovereignty (Banba, Fódla, and Ériu) with their husbands, Mac Cuill, Mac Cécht, and Mac Gréine. It was the seat of the Ó Néill kings until Murchertagh of Munster destroyed it in the early twelfth century.

Ailill mac Máta/mac Matach (*al*-yell moc *mat*-ah) (ah-*ill*-moc-*mah*-tah): Ireland. He was the King of Connacht and the husband of the warrior-queen Medb; the tale of their rivalry is told in the *Táin Bó Cuailnge* (The Cattle Raid of Cooley). His wife was a woman to be reckoned with; Medb had Conall Cernach kill Ailill after she caught him in a sexual embrace with another woman on May Day.

Aillén (ahl-*inn*): Ireland. He was a brother of the fairy queen Áine.

Aímend: Ireland. This sun goddess was the daughter of the king of Corco Loigde.

Alba (*all*-bah): Ireland, Scotland. This was the ancient name for Scotland, and is still the Scottish Gaelic and Modern Irish name for that country.

Alban (*all*-bahn): Wales, Cornwall. This is the Welsh name for Scotland.

Alban Arthuan: Celts. This is the Celtic name for the Winter Solstice.

Alban Eiler: Celts. This is the Celtic name for the Spring Equinox.

Alban Elved: Celts. This is the Celtic name for the Autumn Equinox.

Alban Heruin: Celts. This is the Celtic name for the Summer Solstice.

Albion: Celts. This was the ancient Celtic name for Britain.

Allod (ahl-*ehd*): Ireland. He is sometimes listed as the father of Manannán mac Lir. However, this is not likely, unless Allod was another name for the god Lir.

Amaethon/Amatheon (ahm-*aith*-on): Wales. This name is derived from the Welsh word *amaeth*, "agriculture" or "labor," thus making him an agricultural god or divine plowman. In Modern Welsh the word for farmer is *amaethwr*. A magician and a son of the goddess Don, he taught magic to his brother Gwydion. In Taliesin's poem, the *Cad Goddeu* (Battle of the Trees), Amaethon fought with Gwydion against Arawn, the king of Annwn. The war with Annwn was started because Amaethon stole a dog and a roebuck from Arawn. He is associated with agriculture, gardens, and plants.

Amairgin/Amairgen/Amergin (*ah*-mer-gin, with a hard g): Ireland. He was the major poet, judge, warrior, and Druid of the Milesians who invaded Ireland. He was also known as Amairgin Glúnmar (big-kneed). The *Book of Invasions* relates his famous incantation to Ireland just before the deciding battle with the Tuatha Dé Danann. His poetry, like that of the Welsh Taliesin, shows that he was a shaman. He is associated with enchantment, illusion, and knowledge.

Anam-chara (ah-num-*kahr*-ah): Ireland. This means "soul-friend," and is a term applied to a special person who prays over a dying friend.

Andraste (ahn-*drahs*-tay): British Celts. An Icenian victory goddess of the British Celts, she was worshipped by Queen Boadicea, who nearly succeeded in ridding Britain of the Romans.

Annuals of the Four Masters: Ireland. This is the English title for the Irish manuscript *Annála Rioghachta Éirann* (Annals of the Kingdom of Ireland), which was compiled from 1632 to 1636.

Annwn (aw-*noon*): Wales. Taken from the Welsh words *an*, "in," and *dwfn*, "the world," this is the Welsh name for the Underworld or Otherworld. Ruled by Arawn, it was not a place of punishment, but the site of ancestral power that mortals could visit. The Wild Hunt originated in Annwn. Legend also refers to this place as Caer Feddwid, "Court of Intoxication"; it was said to have a fountain full of sparkling wine. Another name is Caer Siddi, where old age and sickness are unknown. A magic cauldron is one of its fabulous treasures.

Aonbárr /Énbarr (*ahn*-varr): Ireland. Derived from *Aonbárr*, which means "unique supremacy," this magical horse belonged to Manannán mac Lir; it could gallop on land or sea.

Árd-Greimne (ard greem): Ireland, Scotland. He was the father of Aífe, who had a son by Cú Chulainn.

Artio (ahr-*tay*-oh)/**Dea Artio:** Gauls. This deity was the bear goddess of the Continental Celts.

Avagddu/Afagddu: Wales. The name means "utter darkness." He was the ugly son of the goddess Cerridwen. The potion Gwion Bach accidentally drank was meant for him.

Awen (ah-*oon*)/**Awenyddion:** Wales. Meaning "poetic or mantic inspiration," this is the word used to describe the power of poetic and bardic insight.

Balor (*bah*-lor): Ireland. He was the grandson of Néit, and King of the Fomorians. His daughter Eithne secretly slept with Cian mac Cainte of the Tuatha Dé Danann; their son Lugh killed Balor at the Second Battle of Mag Tuired. He is associated with strength, fear, and dark magic.

Bébinn (*beh*-vin): Ireland. Said to be a sister of the goddess Bóann, this early Irish deity was considered to be a patroness of birth and mothers in labor.

Belatucadros (bella-too-kadros): British Celts. A war god of Britain, he was revered in the northern areas; the Romans associated him with Mars. The horned god of the north, his name means "fair shining one."

Belenus (bell-*een*-us)/**Bel/Belinos:** Gauls. This was the sun god of the Continental Celts. Similar to Beli (Wales), this solar deity was a giver of light and a healer. He is associated with science, healing, hot springs, success, prosperity, fertility, farm animals, and purification.

Beli (*bell*-ee): Wales. The husband of the goddess Don, this god was a deity of death. He was often called Beli Mawr and was a later form of the Continental Belenus.

Beltane/Beltaine/Bealtaine (*bel*-tayn or *bal*-tinna): Ireland, Scotland, Isle of Man. A Celtic Fire Festival, it was held on May 1 and celebrated the fertility of all creatures and the land. The name means "fires of Bel."

Bendith y Mamau: Wales. This means "The Mothers' Blessing." These three goddesses were associated with the Triple Goddess of the Celts. The title is also a name for Welsh fairies.

Bíle (*bee*-leh): Ireland. Bíle was the powerful Irish deity of death and rebirth and the consort of Dana or Danu. The Beltane fires were lit in his honor.

Bile/Bili (plural): Ireland. This word means "large tree." In early

Ireland this was a specially designated tree that was believed to house elemental spirits or spirits of the ancestors.

Birds of Rhiannon: Wales. Traditionally, these were three blackbirds that perched in the Tree of Life in the Otherworld. Their singing guided souls into the Otherworld after death.

Black Annis: British Celts. Similar to the Cailleach Bhéirre of Ireland and the Cailleach Bheur of Scotland, this being was described as a blue-faced hag or crone who lived in a cave in the Dane Hills of Leicestershire.

Black Book of Caermarthen: Wales. This ancient book of Welsh poetry and legends was transcribed around 1250. Many of the poems are about Gwynn ap Nudd and Myrddin. It is called "black" because of its cover.

Blathnat (*blay*-nat): Ireland. She was the daughter of Midir, king of the Otherworld. Her father had a magic cauldron, which she helped the hero Cú Chulainn steal.

Blessed Islands: Ireland. According to legend, these were a group of Otherworld islands that lay to the west of Ireland. Otherworld beings and the mortal dead who were worthy lived there in a Celtic paradise.

Bodb Dearg (bohve dahrg): Ireland. The Otherworld king of the sídhe of Munster, he was also a son of the Dagda. His name translates as "Bodb the Red" or "bloody crow." He succeeded the Dagda as King of the Tuatha Dé Danann. He was said to have two residences: one at Loch Dearg near Killaloe in County Clare on the west bank of the River Shannon, and the other at Sídh ar Femen on Sliab na mBan (Slievenamon) in Tipperary. He was famed for his judgments.

Book of Aneirin: Wales. The Welsh title is *Llyfr Aneirin*. Some of the material in this ancient book dates from the ninth century. It contains the famous poem *Gododdin*.

Book of Armagh: Ireland. The Latin name of this text is Liber Ardmachanus. It was begun around 807 C.E. in Armagh, which was the seat of the Catholic primate of Ireland. The passages written in Irish are among the oldest still surviving.

Book of Ballymote: Ireland. The Irish name is *Leabhar Bhaile an Mhóta*. It was compiled around 1390 and contains historical material and bardic tracts on meter and grammar, as well as the key to the ogham alphabet.

Book of Conquest of Ireland: Ireland. The Irish name is *Lebor Gabála Érenn* and is commonly known as the *Book of Invasions*. It contains some of the very earliest Irish myths, legends, and genealogies.

Book of the Dean of Lismore: Scotland. This collection of old Scottish poetry was assembled by James MacGregor, Dean of the Isle of Lismore, in the early sixteenth century. This is the earliest and most extensive collection of Scottish ballads in existence.

Book of the Dun Cow: Ireland. The Irish name is *Lebor/Leabhar na huidre.* Compiled before 1106, the name is derived from its cover. Among its contents are the Ulster Cycle and the *Táin Bó Cuailnge* (Cattle Raid of Cooley).

Book of Fermoy: Ireland. Written in the mid-fifteenth century, and now housed in the Royal Irish Academy in Dublin, this text contains the *Altrom Tige Dá Medar,* or The Nurture of the Houses of the Two Milk Vessels. This story tells of the dispersal of the Tuatha Dé Danann to their mounds.

Book of Lecan: Ireland. The Irish title of this book is *Leabhar Mór Mhic Fhir Bhisigh Leacain.* It is sometimes called the Great Book of Lecan to distinguish it from another book of a similar name—the Yellow Book of Lecan. Compiled around 1150, it is considered to be one of the best sources of Irish myth and history.

Book of Leinster: Ireland. The Irish name is *Lebor Laignech or Leabhar Laighneach.* It was compiled after 1150 and is considered one of the best sources of Irish legends.

Book of Taliesin: Wales. This text is also known as the *Llyfr Taliesin* or the *Hanes of Taliesin.* Compiled around 1275, it contains more than sixty poems, including the Prophecy of Britain and *Cad Goddeu* (Battle of the Trees).

Bres (brehs): Ireland. The son of Balor, he was appointed king of the Tuatha Dé Danann until he was deposed because of his cruelty.

Bres mac Elotha (brehs moc *ehl*-uh-ha): Ireland. Although he was the son of Eri by a Fomorian king, he is not the same being as Bres, son of Balor.

Brí Léith (bree *lah*-th): Ireland. In Irish Gaelic *brí* means "hill." Now identified with Ardagh Hill in County Longford, this is the location of the fairy mound of Midir.

Brigantia (brig-ahn-*tee*-ah): British Celts. In the West Riding of Yorkshire, this deity was the goddess of the Brigantes and had similar equalities to the Irish Brigit. Her name means "High One."

Bruig (broo): Ireland. This descriptive word is connected with the fairy worlds in myth and legends. It refers to the interior of a fairy mound where fairies live together.

Bruigh na Bóinne/Bruig na Bóinne (*brooh* na *bone*-yeh): Ireland. Translated as "Place of the Boyne," this was said to be the Newgrange mound on the River Boyne, in modern Leinster near Stackallen Bridge. This mound is also called a fairy mound.

Buí (boo-ee): Ireland. Listed as one of the four wives of Lugh, this female may be the same as the Cailleach Bhéirre (the Hag of Beare). She is associated with a megalithic monument at Knowth in County Meath.

Cad Goddeu: Wales. Known as the *Battle of the Trees*, this short Welsh poem is in the *Book of Taliesin* and tells of the war between Arawn and Amaethon.

Cáer Ibormeith: Ireland. This woman was the daughter of Ethal Anubhail of the Tuatha Dé Danann of Connacht. Angus mac Óg fell in love with her in a dream. Later he learned that she was a powerful shapeshifter who spent alternate years as a swan. He found her at Loch Bel Dragon (Lake of the Dragon's Mouth) and correctly chose her from a group of 150 swans.

Caer Siddi: Wales. A great revolving castle of the Otherworld, or Annwn, Caer Siddi was believed to be surrounded by the sea and a series of fortified islands. Neither sickness nor old age was known there, and it was filled with enchanted music.

Cailleach (*kaw*-lik) **Bhéirre**: Ireland. This crone goddess was called the "Old Woman, or Hag, of Beare," a peninsula in southwest Ireland. At one time she formed a triad of goddesses with Cailleach Bolus and Cailleach Corca Duibhne. Sometimes called the Mountain Mother, she was said to give birth to the earth and everything on and in it, including the stones. Often called the Veiled One, she is associated with initiation, the moon, beginnings, change, death, disease, plague, and cursing.

Cailleach Bheur: Scotland, Isle of Man. An ancient mountain Mother Goddess with a blue face, her legend still lives today in northwest Scotland and the Isle of Man. The Scottish Gaels believe she controls the winter months and the weather.

Caílte (*kayl*-teh): Ireland. Also known as Caoilte (*kyl*-tah or *kwel*-che), this mortal man was a warrior of the famous Fianna; he was also a renowned poet. Legend says he killed the god Lir during a battle with the gods.

Caim (kaim): Ireland, Scotland. This is a protective prayer, usually with the goddess Brigit invoked, performed in conjunction with a magical circle drawn around people, animals, or objects.

Cairpre (*kair*-pra) mac Ethne: Ireland. He was a son of Ogma, grandson of Dian Cécht, and a famous bard and poet of the Tuatha Dé Danann. He was particularly noted as a powerful satirist.

Cauldron: Celts. Although several cauldrons are mentioned in Old Irish tales, the main cauldron was that of the Dagda, which was one of the four treasures brought to Ireland by the Tuatha Dé Danann. Another legendary Irish cauldron was stolen by Cú Chulainn and Cú Roí from a mysterious castle; this cauldron produced silver and gold. Famous Welsh cauldrons were those of Cerridwen, which gave initiation and inspiration, and of Bran, which gave rebirth. Cauldrons could give the qualities of life, death, initiation, inspiration, plenty, and wisdom.

Caves: Celts. Caves held great religious significance to Celts in all areas. They were believed to hold entrances to the Otherworld. Two of the more famous caves in Ireland are: Cave of Cruachan and the cave on an island in Loch Derg.

Ceithlenn/Ceithlionn (*ceh*-lyn): Ireland. The wife of the Fomorian Balor, she fought against the Dagda in the Battle of Moytura and was fatally wounded.

Cermait/Cermat (kehr-may): Ireland. This son of the Dagda bore a name that is the same as one associated with Ogma, "Honey-Mouthed." Lugh killed him when he caught Cermait with his wife.

Ceugant: Wales. This was the outermost of the three concentric circles of the Welsh Otherworld, and represented the concept of infinity.

Cian (*key*-an): Ireland. A son of Dian Cécht, he seduced Eithne, daughter of Balor, and fathered Lugh.

Clídna (cleevna)/**Clíodhna:** Ireland. One of three daughters of the

Druid Gebann, this goddess of beauty, also called "the shapely," was associated with County Cork. She lived in Tír Tairngire (the Land of Promise) until the mortal Ciabhán won her love; she drowned in a great wave. Her three brightly colored birds healed the sick with their music.

Cnú Deireóil: Ireland. The name means "little nut of melody," and refers to the dwarf fairy harper who accompanied Fionn mac Cumhaill. He had golden hair and his music lulled people to sleep.

Connla/Conlaí/Conlaoch (*kon*-la): Ireland. He was the son of Cú Chulainn and Aífe. Because of a *geas* put on him by his mother, he could not identify himself to his father and thus was slain.

Coventina (koh-ven-*tee*-nah): British Celts. A river goddess with triple aspects, her main temple was at Carrawburgh, Northumberland. She is associated with water and healing.

Co-walker: Ireland, Scotland. In Gaelic, this term is *coimimeadh*. This term was put into print by the Reverend Robert Kirk when he wrote his early essay on the fairy realms. Some writers call this an ethereal double or doppelganger, or the astral body. Other writers believe that this refers to an Otherworld companion, teacher, or guide.

Creiddylad (kred-*ee*-lahd): Wales. This is the name of the daughter of Lludd Llaw Ereint; her name means "flower face." See Blodeuwedd.

Creirwy: Wales. This beautiful female was the daughter of the goddess Cerridwen and the giant Tegid Foel.

Cruachain/Cruachan Ai (*croo*-ah-hahn eye): Ireland. Now known as Rathcroghan, it was the royal palace of King Ailill and Queen Medb. It lies between Belanagare and Elphin in County Roscommon.

Cuilenn: Ireland. In Irish this name means "wood of the holly tree." Cuilenn was a healer and the lord or fairy of a *sídhe* at Sliab Cuilenn (Slieve Guillion) in County Armagh.

Cú Chulainn (koo kulin): Ireland. The name means "Chulainn's hound." This great hero with shamanic powers trained under Scáthach.

Curcóg: Ireland. The daughter of Manannán mac Lir, legends frequently list her as a companion to Eithne, daughter of Balor. One myth says she led a company of women at Bruig na Bóinne.

Curragh (*kuh*-rah): Ireland. This is a hide-covered boat that looks like a painted rowboat; it has a broad beam and shallow draft with flat stern. The Welsh coracle (*cwrwgl*) is also a hide-covered boat, but is made over a rounded framework.

Cwn Annwn (*coon* ah-*noon*): Wales. Described as white with red-tipped ears and red eyes, these Otherworld hounds came out of the Underworld to join in the Wild Hunt. Their baying was thought to be a death omen. They are first listed in legend as the hounds of Arawn, Lord of the Underworld. Later they are associated with Gwynn ap Nudd.

Cyfarwydd (koo-*var*-oo-ith): Wales. This is the medieval Welsh name for a professional storyteller. Although a person with this title occupied a lower echelon of the bards, he was an esteemed teacher, storyteller, and magician. Such a storyteller is similar to the *seanchaidhe* (or *seanchaí*) of Ireland.

Cyhyreath (koo-*hir*-ith): Wales. The Welsh banshee is a form of the Scottish Caoineag, although originally she was a goddess of streams.

Cymric (*kim*-rik): Wales. Translated as "Welsh," this is the name the people of Wales call themselves.

Cymru (*kim*-roo): Wales. This ancient name for Wales was replaced by the Anglo-Saxons, who called it Welsh from the words *welisc* and *wealh*, which mean "foreigners." The correct name for the Welsh language is *Cymraeg*.

Dá shealladh: Scotland. It means "two sights" or "second sight," which is a description of being psychic.

Dál Riada (dall-ree-*ah*-dah): Scotland, Ireland. In the fourth century C.E. Conaire, the ruler of Munster, allowed his son Fergus mac Eirc and some of the people to leave the famine-stricken kingdom for Alba (Scotland). There, Fergus set up the kingdom of Dál Riada in Airer Gháilheal (Argyll), in the southern Highlands. For a time this kingdom included an area of Scotland, and the Glens of Antrim in Ireland. Legend says he asked his brother Muirchertach mac Erca to lend him the Lia Fáil for his coronation, then refused to return it.

Deosil: Celts. This is the act of walking or turning with the movement of the sun; turning to the right; clockwise. In Irish tradition, this is known as cor tuathal.

Dichetal do chennaib: Ireland. In Old Irish this means "an extempore incantation." This spell was composed by the *fili, ollams*, and

Druids, using the tips of the fingers. It may have been a kind of psychometry spoken in verse. The *ollam* had to be proficient in both the *dichetal do chennaib* and the *imbas forosnai*.

Diwrnach (doo-*run*-ohk) **Wyddel/Dyrnwch:** Wales. The name of the person who owned a magic cauldron that would not boil the food of a coward. This story is found in the ancient Welsh poem, the *Preiddeu Annwn*.

Dornbhuidhe: Ireland. This is the name of the *sídhe* of the mysterious Otherworld being called Uainebhuidhe (yellow-green). He sang magical songs accompanied by mystical birds.

Druim Caín: Ireland. This name is derived from the words *druim*, "ridge," and *caín*, "good, fair, beautiful." The *Lebor Gabála* lists this as the Fir Bolg name for the hill of Tara.

Dún (doon): Ireland. It means a stronghold or royal palace surrounded by an earthen wall.

Efnisien (ev-*ness*-yen)/**Efnissien/Evnissyen:** Wales. A half-brother to the deity Bran, his name means "lover of strife." He was a son of Penardun by Euroswydd and brother to Nisien the Peaceful. A vicious trickster, his malicious behavior caused a war with Ireland and the death of his half-sister Branwen.

Eiddilig Gor: Wales. This is the name of the shapeshifting dwarf of the Triads. He was called one of the Three Enchanters of the Isle of Britain.

Eithne: Ireland. This daughter of Balor, king of the Fomorians, mated secretly with Cian, producing the god Lugh.

Elatha (eel-*ah*-tah): Ireland. This name is derived from the words *elada* or *elatha*, which means "acquired skill or art." This Fomorian king, with his shoulder-length golden hair, came in a silver ship under the sea to woo and mate with Ériu; their son was Bres.

Emain Abhlach (*ehv*-in-ah-*valeh*): Ireland. Translated as "Emain of the Apple Trees," this was an island paradise ruled by the sea god, Manannán mac Lir.

Emain Macha (*ehv*-in *mah*-kah): Ireland. This was the ancient capital of Ulster and the royal seat of Conchobar mac Nessa. It is now the Navan Fort, located in County Armagh.

Emania (*ehu*-ahn-ya): Ireland, Wales. This Celtic "Land of the

Moon" was where the dead went. In later legends, this was sometimes connected with Emain Macha.

Eochaid (yohee): Ireland. This Irish sun god was called the "horseman of the heavens"; he carried a sword made of lightning and was described as having one eye or red eyes.

Eochaid Ollathair: Ireland. This title of the Dagda means "All-Father."

Ériu (err-i-*oo*)/**Éire** (*aye*-roo): Ireland. Legend says she was one of three goddesses of Sovereignty in Ireland. She was married to Mac Gréine, a son of Ogma. Her name was given to Ireland. She was associated with Uisneach.

Eryri: Wales. This is the name for Snowdonia, a mountainous region in northwest Wales; the name means "eagle top." The tallest peak in Wales is Snowdon, *Yr Wyddfa* in Welsh.

Esras/Urias: Ireland. He was the master of wisdom in the ancient city of Gorias.

Étaín (et-*ain* or *aid*-een): Ireland. A beautiful woman, she was both the wife of Eochaid Airem and the lover of the fairy king, Midir. Another of her names was Echraide, "horse-rider."

Étan (aye-din): Ireland. This patroness of crafts was a daughter of Dian Cécht and a wife of Ogma.

Falias (*fah*-lee-ahs): Ireland. One of the four ancient cities from which the Tuatha Dé Danann came, its master of great wisdom was known as Morfessa. The Lia Fáil came from there.

Fand (fahn): Ireland. This sea goddess is listed as one of the wives of Manannán mac Lir. Some sources say her mother was Flidais and her brother was Angus. Her name means "Pearl of Beauty," and she was connected with pleasure and healing.

Fedelm (feh-*delm*): Ireland. This woman prophet appears in *The Cattle Raid of Cooley*. She had beautiful blonde hair falling to her knees, gold-clasped sandals, and three irises in each eye.

Feis: Ireland. It means "festival." Irish legends report three great festivals that contain this word: Féis Temrach (Tara), Féis Cruachan (Croghan), and Féis Emna (Emain Macha). The gatherings at the celebrations of Tailltenn, Tlachtga, and Uisneach were fairs only.

Fer Fidail (fur fyahl): Ireland. Manannán mac Lir killed this powerful Druid, who had supernatural, or shamanic, powers.

Fer Í (fur-*ee*): Ireland. This magical harper was a foster son of Manannán mac Lir and the father of Áine. His music was so powerful and so enchanting that it could make people laugh, cry, or fall asleep.

Féth fíada (*fee*-fawh): Ireland. This phrase is derived from the Old Irish words *féth*, "mist or fog," and *fíada*, "lord or master." It is also known as *céo draoidheachte*, or "Druid's fog." This magical mist was raised to provide invisibility and the power to shapeshift into animals. Legend says that Manannán mac Lir bestowed this power upon the Tuatha Dé Danann and the Druids.

Fferyllt: Wales. Although this word is sometimes used to denote a fairy, it means "chemist" in Modern Welsh. In the myths, Cerridwen is said to have consulted the books of the Fferyllt when she prepared her cauldron of inspiration.

Fianna (*fee*-nah): Ireland. This warrior band was led by the hero Fionn mac Cumhaill. The band included several notable warrior women.

Fili/Filidh (*fee*-lyee): Ireland. This was a class of poets. Honored and respected in Irish society, it was their duty to know all of history, genealogy, and literature. The Brehon Laws state that the fili must study for twelve years to qualify for the position.

Findabair (*finn*-ah-var): Ireland. She was the daughter of Queen Medb and King Ailill.

Findias (*fin*-dee-as): Ireland. One of the four ancient cities from which the Tuatha Dé Danann came, its master of great wisdom was known as Uscias. Nuada's invincible sword came from here.

Finnbheara/Finnabair/Fionnbharr (*finn*-var): Ireland. This Tuatha Dé Danann was given the *sídhe* of Cnoc Mheada (Knockma, five miles west of Tuam), where he lived with his wife Úna or Oonagh. In folklore he became the King of the Connacht fairies and was said to have seventeen sons.

Fionn mac Cumhaill (finn moc cool): Ireland. A great hero of the Fenian Cycle of myths, Fionn and his band were much like the later knights of the Round Table in Britain.

Fios (fyos): Ireland. In Old Irish this means "ascertaining," while in Modern Irish it means "second sight." It was one of several early Irish terms for esoteric knowledge.

Fir Bolg (*feer*-bohlg): Ireland. The tribe of people who held Ireland until the coming of the Tuatha Dé Danann, their name literally means "men or people of the Builg." They consisted of three tribes: Domnu or Donn, Gaillion, and Bolg.

Fir (feer) **Chlis:** Ireland, Scotland. In Irish the word is *chlisneach*, while in Scottish Gaelic it is *na clis*; both terms mean "quickly, lively." This name means the "Nimble Men" or "Merry Dancers," a Celtic title given to the Aurora Borealis.

Flidais (flee-*daz*): Ireland. A goddess of forests and wild things, she rode in a chariot pulled by deer. She is associated with the land, wild animals, and shapeshifting.

Fódla/Fótla (*foh*-la): Ireland. She was one of three obscure Sovereignty goddesses who met the Milesians soon after they landed. She was married to Mac Cécht. In Celtic poetry, this is one of the names of Ireland.

Fomorians (foe-*moor*-ee-ans or fo-*vor*-ee-ans)/Fomorii: Ireland. The name means "dwellers under the sea." An ancient people said to live beyond the sea or under it, they were a strong force against the coming of the Tuatha Dé Danann to Ireland. Their king Balor was slain by Lugh at the Second Battle of Mag Tuired. In Irish myth the Fomorians represent evil and darkness and are associated with Tory Island.

Frecraid/Freagarthach: Ireland. Translated as "the Answerer," this sword belonged to the god Manannán mac Lir.

Gáe Assail: Ireland. This lightning spear of the god Lugh would return to his hand after thrown. It was one of the four treasures brought to Ireland by the Tuatha Dé Danann. To empower the spear with certain death, the wielder shouted "*ibar*" (yew) when throwing it.

Gae-Bulga (gay bool-gah): Ireland. This famous spear, whose name means "belly spear," was given to the hero Cú Chulainn by Scáthach. A deadly weapon, it opened into thirty barbs when it entered the body.

Gaidiar: Ireland. He is listed as a son of Manannán mac Lir and lived in Tír Tairngire.

Galan Mai: Wales. This is the Welsh equivalent of Beltane on May 1.

Geas, geis (gesh or geesh): Celts. This is a taboo or prohibition placed on someone, usually by the gods or someone in high authority, such as a king or religious leader. The plural is *gessa*, pronounced *gas*-ah. In Wales the geas is known as *ysgymunbeth*. In Ireland, the Druids had two curses or prohibitions they could place upon people: the geas and the *glam dicín*. The geas was placed on a particular person and was above human and divine jurisdiction; if that person broke the geas, it meant shame and outlawry. The *glam dicín* was more of a satirical incantation or curse for breaking divine or human laws, particularly murder.

Gebann (geh-*vahn*): Ireland. This is the name of the father of Clídna, the Irish goddess of beauty. He was also the chief Druid of Manannán.

Gilfaethwy (gil-*vyth*-oo-ee): Wales. He was one of the sons of the goddess Don and a brother of Gwydion.

Glain nadredd: Wales. See Adder Stone.

Glám dícenn: Ireland. This special satiric curse by a bard was considered powerful enough to kill a person or at least blister her/his face. Any victim of this curse was shunned by all society.

Glas Ghaibhleann/Ghaibhnenn: Ireland. The Fomorian king Balor stole this greenish-blue, magical cow from Goibniu the smith and took it to Tory Island. The Tuatha Dé Danann Cian retrieved it.

Glass Castle: Ireland. Known as Conan's Tower, it was built of glass or crystal by the Fomorians on Tory Island. When the Nemedians stormed the island, they slew the king, Conan mac Febar.

Gorias (*gor*-ee-as): Ireland. One of the four ancient cities from which the Tuatha Dé Danann came, its master of great wisdom was known as Esras or Urias. The invincible spear of Lugh came from here.

Grian (grahn)/**Grainne** (*grahn*-yah): Ireland. A sun goddess, her palace was said to be at Cnoc Gréine at Pailis Gréine (Pallas Green), in County Limerick.

Grianainech (*grahn*-yehk): Ireland. This title, which means "sunny countenance," was often applied to the god Ogma.

Gronw Pebyr: Wales. A lover of Blodeuwedd, he killed his rival, her husband Lleu Llaw Gyffes. However, Lleu was restored to life by

Gwydion. Thereafter, Lleu and Gronw fought a twice-yearly battle for supremacy.

Gundestrup Cauldron: This cauldron was discovered in a peat bog near the village of Gundestrup, Jutland peninsula, Denmark in 1880. It is one of the most celebrated of early Celtic metalwork and religious art, because part of its decoration includes the figure of the Lord of Animals.

Gweledydd: Wales. This is the Welsh name for "seer" or "prophet."

Gwion Bach (gween bahk): Wales. This was Taliesin's name before his initiation by Cerridwen.

Gwynfyd (*gween*-fyed): Wales. Translated as "Purity," this was the second of three Otherworld concentric circles in Cymric cosmology; it represents good over evil.

Gwythyr (*gwee*-theer): Wales. He was king of the Upperworld or heavens.

Hafgan: Wales. This name means "summer white." He was the Otherworld rival of Arawn of Annwn.

Hanes of Taliesin: Wales. This "History of Taliesin" was compiled from very old manuscripts of the late sixth century. It contains the poem-story of Gwion Bach and the goddess Cerridwen.

Hy Breasil/Bresal (hi *bres*-al): Ireland. An Otherworld realm that lies somewhere to the west of Ireland, this land was said to be ruled by King Breasil, known to the Irish as King of the World.

Hyfidd Hen: Wales. A king of the Underworld, some texts list him as the father of Rhiannon. The name Hen means "ancient."

Hywel Dda, Laws of: Wales. This compilation of laws is equivalent to the Brehon Law system in Ireland.

Ilaberg: Ireland. Sometimes listed as a son of the god Manannán mac Lir, he was said to rule the *sídhe* of Eas Aedha Ruaidh, which is the mount of Mullachshee near Ballyshannon, County Donegal.

Ildánach (*eil*-dan-ah): Ireland. Translated as "The Many-Gifted" or "All-Craftsman," this was one of many names applied to the god Lugh.

Imbas forosnai: Ireland. *Imbas* means "great knowledge, poetic talent, inspiration," and *forosnai* means "illuminates." The poets, especially the *ollam* as the highest rank of *fili* in early Ireland, had to have this gift of prophetic knowledge. Legend says that Scáthach made prophecies by using this gift.

Imbolc (imbolk)/**Imbolg/Oímelc:** Ireland, Scotland. This Celtic festival was celebrated on February 1 as the first lambs were born. Oimelc means "sheep's milk." This celebration was also known as *Feile Bhride*, or Brigit's Feast.

Imram (*im*-rahm)/**Imrama** (pl.): Ireland. Usually translated as "voyage," this term applied primarily to spiritual sea journeys through the Otherworld.

Inis Fáil (*in*-ish *fah*-ill): Ireland. This is another poetic name for Ireland.

Irnan: Ireland. She was one of the three daughters of Conaran the Tuatha who lived at Dún Conaran. Legend says that she and her sisters created a magic web to capture the Fianna.

Iweridd (yoo-*er*-ith)/**Iweriadd:** Wales. This name belonged to one of Llyr's wives and means "Ireland."

Labraid Luathlám ar Claideb (*loo*-reh *loo*-ah lav ar cleyev): Ireland. He was one of the fairy kings. His name translates as "swift sword hand," and he ruled Mag Mell, the Plain of Delight.

Lés/lésa (plural): Ireland. This is the name of the medicine bag carried by Irish Celtic healers.

Lia Fáil: See Stone of Fál.

Liban (*lee*-van): Ireland. A fairy woman, she was the wife of Labraid.

Lughnasadh (loo-*nah*-sah): Ireland, Scotland. This Celtic Fire Festival was held on August 1 to celebrate the season of harvest. It was named after the god Lugh (the son of the Tuatha Cian and the Fomorian Eithne) who instituted it in memory of his foster mother Tailtiu.

Mabinogion (mab-in-*oo*-geeon): Wales. This book of ancient Welsh legends was compiled from the White Book of Rhydderch, the Red Book of Hergest, and the Hanes of Taliesin.

Mac Cécht (moc keckt): Ireland. This name translates as "son of the plow." He was the husband of the goddess Fódla.

Mac Cuill (moc cool): Ireland. This name translates as "son of hazel." He was the husband of the goddess Banba.

Mac Gréine (moc grehn): Ireland. This name translates as "son of the sun." He was the husband of the goddess Ériu.

Mac ind Oc (*moc* en ogh): Ireland. This was one of Angus mac Óg's titles.

Mag (mahy): Ireland. This is an Irish word for "plain."

Mag Mell (mahy mel): Ireland. Translated as "The Pleasant Plain," this is part of the Otherworld and is a land of perpetual spring and sunshine. See Tír na nÓg.

Mag Tuired (mahy-*toor*-ah)/**Tuireadh:** Ireland. Sometimes written as Moytura, this translates as "The Plain of Towers." It was first the site of the battle between the Tuatha Dé Danann, led by Nuada, and the Fir Bolgs, led by Erc. Later it was the site of another battle, this time between the Tuatha Dé Danann and the Fomorians.

Maga (*mah*-yah): Ireland. She was a daughter of the love god Angus mac Óg.

Manannan Beg/Mac y Leirr: Isle of Man. This is the name of the Manx equivalent of the Irish Manannán mac Lir.

Matholwch (*math*-ol-ook): Wales. This was the Irish husband of Branwen, who mistreated her and started a war with her brother Bran.

Medb/Mabh/Maeve (*may*-v or meev): Ireland. This warrior queen was the consort of Ailill. Her name means "mead," but she was also called Queen Wolf and Drunk Woman. She is often portrayed as pale with long flowing red hair, wearing a red cloak, and carrying a flaming spear.

Miach (*mee*-ahk): Ireland. A physician and the son of Dian Cécht, he was a member of the Tuatha Dé Danann until his father killed him in a fit of jealousy after Miach restored Nuada's severed hand. He is associated with healing.

Midir (*mid*-ir or *meh*-yahr): Ireland. A son of the Dagda, he lived at the *sídhe* of Brí Léith (Slieve Callory), located west of Ardagh, County Longford.

Milesians (mil-*ease*-yans): Ireland. The name of Amairgin's people, they invaded Ireland and prevailed over the Tuatha Dé Danann.

Mog Ruith: Ireland. The name of this Druid or enchanter means "Slave of the Wheel." He was said to live on Valentia Island off the southwest coast of Munster, where he had a rowing wheel, much like a prototype aircraft.

Mór Muman: Ireland. Considered to be the ancestress of the royal houses of Munster, she was originally a sun deity whose throne was said to be in the western seas of Ireland.

Morfessa: Ireland. The master of wisdom from the city of Falias, his name means "Great knowledge." He gave the sacred coronation stone to the Tuatha Dé Danann.

Morfran: Wales. This is another name for Avagddu.

The Mothers/Matres: Celts. These triple Mother Goddesses were known in all Celtic areas and are related to the ancient Neolithic deities of Europe.

Moytura (moy-*toor*-ah): Ireland. This is a modernized version of Mag Tuired.

Murias (*moor*-ee-as): Ireland. One of the four ancient cities from which the Tuatha Dé Danann came, its master of great wisdom was known as Semias. The Dagda's cauldron of knowledge came from here.

Nantosuelta: British Celts. Her name means "winding river." She was the consort of the god Sucellus and linked with water.

Nechtan: Ireland. This deity was the consort of the goddess Bóann and the guardian of the Well of Segais.

Néit/Nét: Ireland. He was a very early, mysterious god of war. Listed as the husband of both Badb and Nemain, he was thought to be Fomorian.

Nemain: Ireland. This deity was a war goddess and one of the wives of Néit. She and four other goddesses were listed as those who hovered around battles. The others were Dea, Badb, Macha, and Mórrígán.

Nemeton: Celts. This word means "a sanctuary" or "sacred grove." The Old Irish word was *neimed*. This name can be found in Celtic place-names as far away as Turkey.

Niamh (*nee*-av) **Chinn Óir:** Ireland. The name of this goddess translates as "beauty, brightness," or "she of the golden head." She was the daughter of Manannán mac Lir and the lover of the hero Oisin, whom she led to Tír na nÓg.

Nicneven (nik-*neh*-veh): Scotland. Known as "Divine" or

"Brilliant," this Samhain goddess was believed to ride through the night with her followers on Halloween.

Nisien (*ness*-yen)/**Nissien/Nissyen:** Wales. A half-brother to the deity Bran, and brother of Efnisien, his name means "peace-maker."

Nos Galan-Gaeof (nohs gah-lan *gay*-ehf): Wales. This Welsh winter festival is the equivalent of the Irish Samhain.

Nuts of Wisdom: Ireland. In Irish legend, hazelnuts were believed to contain great wisdom. Nine hazel trees grew over the Well of Segais (sometimes called Conlaí's well). When their nuts dropped into the water, they caused bubbles of mystic inspiration to rise to the surface. The Salmon of Knowledge that lived in this well ate the nuts.

Ocean-Sweeper: Ireland. This magical ship, known in Gaelic as *aigéan scuabadoir*, was a gift from Lugh to Manannán mac Lir. Lugh brought it from the Otherworld because of its wonderful properties; the ship could read a man's thoughts and was propelled without sails or oars.

Ochall Ochne: Ireland. This was the name of the king of the sídhe of Connacht.

Ogam/Ogham (*oh*-am): Ireland. This earliest form of Irish writing was invented by the god Ogma.

Ollam/Ollamh/Ollave (*oh*-layv): Ireland. This Irish word describes a learned man of the highest rank of the fili, who had to study nine to twelve years and pass seven grades. This esteemed person was a poet, storyteller, historian, genealogist, and satirist.

Orna (*ohr*-nah): Ireland. Tethra, the Fomorian king, owned this talking sword until Ogma killed him at the Second Battle of Mag Tuired and claimed the sword.

Otherworld: Celts. Basically, the Celtic Otherworld consisted of the Upperworld (the sky), the Middleworld (various planes of existence in this world), and the Underworld (below the earth). However, there are also mentioned many subsidiary areas that do not fit completely into these planes. These areas range from the dark, brooding lands of the Fomorian islands to the pleasant, sunny areas of the Land of Promise. In both Ireland and Wales, it was believed that mortals could enter and live in any of these Otherworld lands.

Partholón: Ireland. He was the leader of the second wave of people to invade Ireland, according to *Lebor Gabála* (Book of Invasions).

Penardun/Panardun: Wales. This daughter of the goddess Don married Llyr and became the mother of Manawyddan.

Pencerdd: Wales. The name is derived from the Welsh words *pen*, "chief," and *cerdd*, "art." The title for the chief poet in Wales, the person holding this position had to have nine years training in grammar, metrics, and genealogy. It was similar to the Irish *ollam*.

Picts: Celts. They were known as the *Tuatha Cruithne* in Irish sagas and as *Priteni* in the Welsh tales.

Plant Rhys Ddwfn (rees doo-fn): Wales. The name is probably a corrupted version of *Pant yr Is-ddwfn* or *Plant Rhi Is-dwfn*, "Children of the King of the Underworld." This invisible land supposedly lies off the coat of Dyfed, Wales.

Pryderi (pri-*dare*-ee): Wales. The son of Rhiannon and Pwyll, he was kidnapped at birth by an evil creature from the Otherworld. His mother was accused of murdering him and made to carry guests on her back as punishment. However, Pryderi was found and raised by a man named Teurnon Twruliant and, years later, returned to his mother.

Ráth (rahth): Ireland. This word describes a circular earthen wall that surrounded ancient Irish strongholds.

Red Book of Hergest: Wales. Known in Welsh as *Llyfr Coch Hergest*, it was compiled around 1382–1410. It contains texts of the *Mabinogion*, as well as poetry, histories, and grammars.

Retaliator: Ireland. With the Gaelic name of *Díoltach*, it was one of three swords belonging to Manannán mac Lir; it never failed to kill once drawn.

Samhain (*sow*-en): Ireland, Scotland. This was the Celtic festival of the New Year and was held on the eve of October 31. Said to be ruled by the Cailleach, it was associated with the opening of the *sídhe* mounds and a thinning of the veil between worlds, thus making it possible to communicate with the dead. Today it is known as Halloween.

Samildánach (*sah*-vil-*dahn*-ahk): Ireland. Translated as "Of Many Talents," this was one of the many titles given to the god Lugh.

Seanchaidhe (shanakie): Ireland. This title was given to a professional storyteller or historian. The Modern Irish word is seanchaí.

Semias: Ireland. This master of great wisdom was from the city of Murias. He gave the Dagda his cauldron of plenty.

Sétanta (shay-*tant*-ah): Ireland. This was Cú Chulainn's childhood name.

The Sídhe (shee): Ireland, Scotland, Isle of Man. This term is used to describe the mounds or Hollow Hills in which the fairies (the Aes Sídhe or Daoine Sídhe) live. The Tuatha Dé Danann were the first to use these mounds after their defeat by the Milesians. The *sídhe* or mounds were said to contain entrances to Otherworld abodes.

Sinann (*shehn*-an): Ireland. This river goddess gave her name to the River Shannon.

Skye, Isle of: Ireland, Scotland. In Scottish Gaelic this is *An t'Eilean Sgiathanach* or the winged isle. It is also called the Misty Isle. The largest island in Scotland's Inner Hebrides, Skye is listed in legend as the home of Scáthach (*Sgáthaich* in Scottish Gaelic), the great warrior woman and martial arts teacher of many Irish heroes. The ruins of a fort on the island are called Dún Scáthaig in Irish, which means "Hill of Scáthach."

Sovereignty, Goddess of: Celts. These goddesses were connected with the power of the land. For a ruler to gain power in a land, he was required to marry one of these goddesses. Many times the marriage was consummated with a priestess of the particular goddess.

Stone of Fál (fahl): Ireland, Scotland. Known in Irish as the Lia Fáil (*lee*-ah *faw*-il), it literally means "Stone of Fál" or "Stone of Destiny." Narrow and tall as a full-grown man, this was Ireland's coronation stone that roared when the rightful king touched it. It was kept at Temuir (Tara). However, another similar stone (some say the same stone or part of it) was used at the coronation of the kings of Dál Riada, or Scotland. It was stolen by Edward I of England and taken to London.

Sucellus (soo-*kell*-us): British Celts. This Father God was also called "The God of the Mallet" and "Good Striker." Accompanied by dogs and carrying a mallet or hammer, this bearded deity was connected with abundance, success, and a sudden turn of fortune.

Tailtiu (*tile*-too): Ireland. A warrior queen of the Fomorians, she was also the foster mother of Lugh. She died of her labors of clearing the forest of Breg, which was named Tailtiu after her. Lugh instituted the festival of Lughnasadh in her honor.

Táin Bó Cuailgne (*toyn* bo *koo*-ile-nyeh): Ireland. In English this is the tale of the Cattle Raid of Cooley.

Tara (*tah*-rah): Ireland. In Old Irish this name was Temuir or Temair, and was derived from Téa, goddess and wife of Éremón who was the first Milesian High King. It defines the ancient capital of the Irish Celts and lay in County Meath. Archaeological dating at the site goes back to 2,000 B.C.E. Not so much a town as a religious and spiritual center, Tara was the main residence of the High Kings. Five roads led from Tara to each of the five provinces.

Taranis (tah-*rahn*-us): Gauls. Called the "Thunderer," this god ruled over storms, thunder, and lightning, and had a spoked wheel as one of his symbols.

Téa: Ireland. Myth says this queen of King Éremón of the Milesians gave her name to Tara. The Fir Bolg had earlier called the site Druim Caín.

Tech Duinn (chah doon): Ireland. Very similar in many ways to the Welsh idea of Annwn, Tech Duinn (the House of Donn) was a place of the dead said to lie off the southwest coast of Ireland. Donn, god of the dead, lived there.

Tech Midchuarta (chah mee-*hoot*-tah)/**Teach Miodhchuarta/** (*chah*-mee-*hoor*-tah): Ireland. This was the name of the great assembly hall of the ancient kings at Tara.

Tech Screpta/Teach Screpta: Ireland. A word for the libraries of ancient Ireland; those left after the destruction by Christian monks were mostly destroyed during the Viking raids.

Tegid Foel: Wales. This name is derived from the Welsh words *teg*, "beautiful," and *foel*, "bald." He was the giant of Pennllyn and the husband of the goddess Cerridwen.

Teinm laída: Ireland. This incantation or divination used by the *fili* means "chewing or breaking open the pith."

Temuir (*tahw*-ir): Ireland. This is the Irish spelling for the name for Tara.

Teutates (too-*tay*-teees)/**Toutatis/Totatis:** British Celts, Gauls. Known as "Ruler of the People," this god was a very old, powerful god of war.

Tir fo Thuinn: Ireland, Scotland. The correct phase in Scottish Gaelic is *Tír fa Thonn*. It means "land under the wave," or a sunken land, and is part of the Otherworld.

Tír na mBan: Ireland. The translation is "the Land of Women." This was thought to be a pleasant place with beautiful women who welcomed voyagers on journeys of seeking.

Tír na mBéo: Ireland. Known as the Land of the Living, this was an Otherworld place of everlasting life.

Tír na nÓg/Tír na nÓc (*teer* nah-nohg): Ireland. Translated as "the Land of Youth or Immortality," this Otherworld realm was a place where the gods and mortals lived together in beautiful peace.

Tír Tairngire (*teer tahrn*-gehr-eh): Ireland. In this Land of Promise, all desires and dreams can be fulfilled; another part of the Otherworld.

Torc Triath/Orc Triath: Ireland. This boar belonged to Brigit, the Dagda's daughter and was similar to the Welsh magical boar called Twrch Trwyth.

Tory Island: Ireland. This island off the northern coast of Donegal was the powerful stronghold of the Fomorians, according to ancient legends. Balor of the Evil Eye imprisoned his daughter in a glass or crystal tower on Tory Island, but Cian of the Tuatha Dé Danann rescued her; their son was Lugh. The name is derived from *torach*, which means "like a tower."

Trefuilngid Tre-Eochair: Ireland. A very ancient Otherworld being who predated creation, legend says he once appeared at an assembly at Tara to impart the correct history of Ireland. He was called "Triple Bearer of the Triple Key" and was associated with the shamrock and trident. Known as a master of all wisdom, this giant regulated the rising and setting of the sun. He was said to carry a tablet of stone in one hand and in the other a branch that contained fruit, flowers, and nuts.

Trioedd Ynys Prydain: Wales. This is the Welsh title for the manuscript known as The Triads of the Isle of Britain.

Túath (tooth or too-ath): Ireland. In early Ireland, this described a territorial unit, consisting of a population able to maintain 700–3,000 soldiers in an emergency.

Tuatha Dé Danann (*too*-ah-ha day *dan*-an): Ireland. This name encompasses all the Irish Celtic deities. They were the people of the goddess Dana or Danu who came to Ireland with four great treasures from the ancient lost cities. They fought against the Fomorians and Fir Bolgs for possession of Ireland, but retreated to the Otherworld or *sídhe* after they lost to the Milesians.

Twrch Trwyth (turk *trook*): Wales. Known as the Great Boar, he and his seven piglets terrorized Britain and Ireland until they were finally driven into the sea. Legend says he carried a razor, comb, and scissors in the hair between his ears.

Uaithne/Uathe: Ireland. This enchanted harp of the Dagda would only make a sound when summoned by him.

Úaman Sídhe: Ireland. This was the dwelling place of Ethal Anbúail, who was the father of Cáer. Cáer was the lover of Angus.

Uathach: Ireland, Scotland. A daughter of Scáthach, her name means "specter." When the hero Cú Chulainn was at the Isle of Skye, he slew her lover and took her as his mistress. In legend she was usually referred to as Uathach of the Glen.

Uí (*oo*-ee): Ireland. This is the Irish Gaelic word for "descendants," such as in the Uí Néill, meaning "the descendants of Niall."

Uisneach/Uisnech (*oosh*-nah): Ireland. In legend, the Hill of Uisneach (formerly Balor's Hill) was considered to be the geographic center of Ireland. Here, the great Stone of Divisions (Aill na Mireen) marked the point where the five provinces of Ireland met. It is now applied to the hill Usney or Ushnagh in County Westmeath.

Undry: Ireland. Sometimes named as Uinde ("act of beholding"), this magical cauldron of the Dagda could satisfactorily feed any number of people.

Uscias: Ireland. Legend says he was the master of wisdom from the ancient city of Findias. He gave Nuada the invincible Sword of Light.

Vates/Ovates: Ireland. This is a Latin word applied to one branch of the Druidic order.

Well of Segais: Ireland. This supernatural spring or well was considered to be the source of the River Boyne and a fount of supernatural knowledge. It was surrounded by nine hazel trees and was guarded by Nechtan, the husband of the goddess Bóann.

Well of Slane: Ireland. This is the well that Goibniu the smith used to heal himself after being wounded in battle.

White Book of Hergest: Wales. Called *Llyfr Gwyn Hergest* in Welsh, this book from the mid-fifteenth century contains the Laws of King Hywel Dda.

White Book of Rhydderch: Wales. Known as Llyfr Gwyn Rhydderch in Welsh, this collection of medieval prose was written down around 1325. It contains versions of the Mabinogion.

Widdershins: Celtic. This is the act of walking or turning against the movement of the sun; turning to your left; counter-clockwise. In Irish tradition, this is known as cor deiseil.

Wild Herdsman: Wales. He is described in the Welsh story The Lady of the Fountain as a black giant who guarded the beasts of the forest. He may be a form of Cernunnos.

Wild Hunt: Celts. An Otherworld phenomena known throughout the Celtic areas, this Hunt is said to take place only at night and often during storms. An Otherworld leader will ride through the skies with his men, accompanied by a pack of spectral hounds. They hunt down and capture those who have escaped punishment in the mortal world.

Yellow Book of Lecan: Ireland. The Irish name is Lebor Buide Lecáin. A medieval manuscript compiled around 1390, it contains The Wooing of Étaín, The Tragic Death of Aífe's Only Son, The Destruction of Da Derga's Hostel, and a version of The Cattle Raid of Cooley.

Ynys Afallon (in-is auf-lon): Wales. The name is derived from afall, meaning "apple." A island of perpetual youth in the western ocean, this name probably was the origin of the word Avalon.

Fairy Kith and Kin

Fairies and creatures associated with them are all inhabitants of the Otherworld. Their plane of existence lies very close to that of the earth occupied by humans, thus making it easy for them to come into our world. Originally, Celtic fairies were human-sized, not the tiny, winged entities promoted during Victorian times. The tiny fairies are actually nature spirits.

Áes sídhe (ees *shee*): Ireland. One of several Irish names for the fairies, it means "people of the mound or fairy hill." They were also called the Hosts of the Sídhe or People of the Hollow Hills, which actually referred to inhabitants of the Otherworld, not only fairies. Legend says they ride out in a great host on the eves of the four Fire Festivals: Samhain (October 31), Imbolc (January 31), Beltane (April 30), and Lughnasadh (July 31). At these times the Otherworld beings often communicate with mortals.

Báinleannán: Ireland. Derived from the Irish words *báine*, "pale or white," and *leannán*, "lover," this female spirit (white fairy lover) joined several questing heroes in their travels. See Leannán sídhe.

Banshee: Ireland. In Irish the correct spelling is *bean sídhe*, which means "fairy woman." It is a female spirit or fairy who foretells a death. The banshee is usually attached to certain families.

Bean nighe (bane nye): Scotland. In Scottish Gaelic this name is *nigheadaireachd*, or "washerwoman." Like the banshee, she appears as a death-omen. She is small, slender, and often dressed in green clothing. She usually haunts lakes and streams, where she washes bloody clothing.

Bócan (buckawn): Scotland, Ireland. In Scottish Gaelic this name is *bócan*, while in Irish it is *bauchan* or *bogan*. Although primarily known in Scotland, this dangerous sprite is also found in Ireland, North America, and Australia. It is a shapeshifting trickster.

Boctogaí: Ireland. Also called *bunadh beag na farraige* ("wee folk of the sea"), the name of these fairies of west Donegal may be a variant of *bocaidhe*. They are said to live in the sea and can be seen on the rocks and shore, their long yellow hair blowing in the wind. They are less friendly to humans than the fairies who live on land.

Brownie: Celts. This creature is called the bwca or bwbachod in Wales, the bodach in the Scottish Highlands, the fenodoree in Manx, and the pixies or pisgies in the West Country of England. They are solitary creatures who dress in brown. They will help if rewarded with a bowl of milk or cause malicious mischief if insulted. They do not like teetotalers or ministers.

Caoineag (konijack): Scotland. This is the Scottish Gaelic version of the Irish banshee. Her name means "Weeper." Tradition says that she was heard wailing the night before the massacre at Glencoe.

Clúracán (kloor-a-kawn): Ireland. One of the solitary fairies, it usually appears as a withered little man with a pink nose. He dresses in red with blue silk stockings and silver buckles on his shoes. He carries the *sparán na scillinge* (purse of shillings) and likes to raid wine cellars.

Coblynau (*kob*-ler-nigh): Wales. These small, ugly mine spirits are similar to the Knockers and often help miners find veins of ore.

Crodh Mara: Scotland. These fairy cattle that often mingled with ordinary cows gave three times the amount of milk.

Cú Síth (coo shee): Scotland. Known as a fairy dog, this creature was the size of a young bullock, but green in color. To see it is very dangerous.

Cyhyraeth (*ker*-her-righth): Wales. A form of banshee, and similar to the Irish banshee and the Scottish Caoineag, it is only heard before multiple deaths occur.

Daoine Sídhe (*dye*-ne *shee*): Ireland. This Irish name for fairies means "People of the Sídhe or Hollow Hills." They are more often referred to as the Good People or Gentry to avoid offending them. Originally, this term meant the Tuatha Dé Danann as well as the fairy folk.

Elves: Scotland. This Scandinavian form of fairy was added to Scottish legends with the invasion of the Vikings, just as it was in Ireland. In Scotland they became known as the Seelie (Blessed) and Unseelie (Unblessed) Courts who lived in Elfame.

Faery: Scotland. This title is used to refer to both the fairies and to the Otherworld realm they inhabit. Their realm is said to border closely on the human world, thus making it possible for humans to unwittingly stray into it.

Fairy: Celts. This name may be derived from the ancient word *fays*, meaning the Fates. Human-sized and without wings, these Otherworld beings frequently interact with humans. The small winged beings mistakenly called fairies are actually nature spirits. In Ireland many polite names are used when speaking of the fairies so as to avoid their displeasure. The correct name for fairy is *Sídhe* or *Sídeheog*. However, it is more common to hear such phrases as *daoine maithe* (good people), *daoine sídhe*, *áes sídhe* (people of the mound), or *daoine usisle* (the noble people or gentry). Tradition says fairies can bestow gifts of prophecy, healing, music, and other arts.

Fairy dart: Ireland, Scotland. The original Irish name for this is *gáe sídhe*. It refers to the flint arrowheads found near prehistoric ráths. The Celts believed that such darts, thrown by malicious fairies, caused swelling of the joints, hands, and feet.

Fairy dog: Ireland. This is usually the Cwn Annwn, but can also be a large, supernatural dog with white rings around its neck or the black dog that was said to haunt Slieve Mish in County Kerry.

Fairy herbs: Ireland, Scotland. Traditionally, these are the dandelion, eyebright, foxglove, yarrow, ivy, plantain, polypody of oak, and vervain.

Fairy mist: Ireland, Scotland. This mist that made people go astray was known as ceo sídhe in Irish Gaelic.

Fairy music: Ireland, Scotland, Wales. According to legends, this haunting and beautiful music could lure humans into the Otherworld. Some Irish music, such as the Londonderry Air, is said to have come from the fairies. In Irish this expression is *ceol sídhe*.

Fairy palace: Ireland, Scotland, Wales. In Irish this is *fáinne sídhe*; in Scottish Gaelic, *fáinne síth*; and in Welsh, *cylch y tylwyth teg*. It refers to a circle of dark grass in a lawn or meadow and is believed to be caused by fairies dancing there. Folklore says that if a human enters this ring after dark, she/he is compelled to join the wild fairy dances. This dancing can last for seven years or longer.

Fairy rock: Ireland, Scotland. This is a dolmen or megalithic stone.

Fairy sleep: Ireland, Scotland, Wales. In Irish this is *suan sídhe*. It is a deep sleep cast on a human by fairies; the affected person cannot awaken until a specified time.

Fairy stroke: Ireland, Scotland. This describes a sudden change in the physical or mental being of a human or an animal, usually a paralytic seizure. It is called *poc sídhe* in Irish. A person who can direct this malicious power is called a kinkishin (*cincís* in Irish).

Fairy tree: Ireland, Scotland. Traditionally, this is thought to be a thorn or hawthorn tree. However, fairies are also connected with the oak, ash, apple, hazel, alder, elder, holly, and willow.

Fairy wind, fairy blast: Ireland, Scotland. There are several Irish Gaelic phrases that describe this: *sídh gaoithe, sídh chóra, gaoth sídhe,* and *séideán sídhe.* Folklore says this is a sudden gust of wind or a small whirlwind, causing by the passing of a fairy host.

Fenoderee (fin-ord-*er*-ee)/**Fenodyree/Phynnodderee:** Manx. These are large, hairy, ugly brownies who rarely wear clothes. They can be helpful with heavy tasks.

Ferrish/Ferrishyn (ferrishin): Isle of Man. This is one of the Manx names for fairy. They can be one to three feet tall and are less aristocrat than the Irish fairies. Their hearing is said to be so keen that people take great care when speaking of them. They often hunt with the Cwn Annwn, or red-eared white Otherworld hounds.

Fuath (foo-ah)/**fuathan** (plural): Scotland. This is a general name for Highland monsters connected with water, lochs, rivers, and the sea.

Góbhan Saor, the Wright: Ireland. He was the master mason and architect for the fairies. His name may come from Goibniu.

Gwartheg y llyn (*gwar*-geth er thlin): Wales. These milk-white fairy cattle mingled with mortal cattle on occasion. They are the counterparts of the Scottish Gaelic crodh mara.

Gwrach y Rhibyn (gwratch er hreebin): Wales. A form of banshee, her name means "Hag of Warning."

Gwragedd Annwn (gwrageth anoon): Wales. These lake fairies sometimes gave skills to mortals and occasionally married them. One such fairy woman married a mortal man and started a famous line of Welsh physicians.

Ladi Wen, Y: Wales. Meaning "white lady," this apparition was often seen at Samhain.

Leannán Sídhe (lan-awn shee): Ireland. Known as the fairy mistress or lover, this fairy inspired poets and musicians. See Báinleannán.

Leprechaun (*lehp*-rah-kon): Ireland. This solitary Otherworld creature appears to be a form of the Fir Dhearga, or Red Men. Like them, he likes to play tricks on mortals. He is often the guardian of a treasure.

Mer-People: Celts. These water dwellers are frequently called Mermaids and Mermen. They sometimes lure fishermen to their deaths on rocks. The Irish equivalent is the Murdhuacha (muh-*roo*-cha) or Merrows.

Púca (pooka): Ireland. Anglicized as Pooka, this Otherworld sprite plays mischievous tricks on mortals, usually in the form of a horse. A very similar being is called the pwca in Wales.

Seelie Court: Scotland. Known as the Blessed (Good) Court of the Fairies, these Otherworld beings were usually benevolent to mortals. However, they were swift to take revenge for insults. They were said to ride from their mounds at the major Celtic festivals and take a circuit of the boundaries of their realm, much as the Áes Sídhe in Ireland were said to do.

Síthich (shee-ek): Scotland. In Scottish Gaelic this means "fairy" or "elf." In Highland legends this was a mischievous Otherworld being.

Síthiche: Scotland. This is the Gaelic word for the realm of fairy.

Sithein (*shee*-an): Scotland. This is the name for the outside of a fairy hill or barrow.

The Sluagh (*sloo*-ah) **sithe:** Scotland. It means a "host of fairies." Legend says the most formidable of these was the Host of the Dead (*sluagh na marbh*) who could be seen fighting in the sky on occasion. This Host could appear from any direction except the east, but boded no good for mortals. They were seen after dark and were thought to be able to pick up a person bodily and transport him great distances.

Speir-Bhean: Ireland. This Otherworld being was known as a vision-woman. Poets were apt to encounter her in lonely places. Their poems of these meetings were called *aislings*.

Tylwyth Teg (terlooeth teig), **y:** Wales. This is a Welsh term for the Fair Family, or fairies. Gwynn ap Nudd was their king.

Unseelie Court: Scotland. Known as the Unholy (Evil) Court of dark fairies to distinguish them from the Seelie Court, these Otherworld beings were not to be trusted by humans.

Resources

The following businesses are reliable sources for Pagan and magical materials. They sell a variety of products and ritual supplies. Although some catalogs are free, it is best to contact a business and ask about a catalog and its possible price.

Azure Green, P.O. Box 48, Middlefield, MA 01243-0048
Telephone: 413-623-2155
Fax: 413-623-2156
E-mail: AbyssDist@aol.com
Web site: www.Azuregreen.com
Candles, incense, stones, statues, jewelry (torcs), herbs, oils, mortars, books, cauldrons, daggers, chalices, robes, capes, wands, and many other items.

Creative Irish Gifts, 8157 Bavaria Rd., Macedonia, OH 44056-2252
Telephone Orders: 1-800-843-4538
Fax: 330-405-6500
Web site: www.shopirish.com
A good source for authentic Irish bodhrán drums, musical instruments, jewelry, and other products.

Crescent Moongoddess, P.O. Box 153, Massapequa Park, NY 11762
Telephone: 516-827-4399
E-mail: cresmoon@crescentmoongoddess.com
Web site: www.crescentmoongoddess.com
Handmade wands, chalices, incense, incense burners, cauldrons, candles, herbs, oils, books, daggers, jewelry, and capes. Many of the products she sells are handcrafted by Pagans.

The Irish Edition, P.O. Box 1700, 3424 White Mountain Hwy., North Conway, NH 03860-1700
Web site: www.theirishedition.com

Telephone Orders: 1-800-355-7268
Traditional Irish bodhrán drums, musical instruments, jewelry, and other products from Ireland.

Museum Replicas, Box 840, Conyers, GA 30012
Telephone Orders: 1-800-883-8838
Fax: 770-388-0246
Web site: www.museumreplicas.com
An excellent supplier of authentically reproduced swords, daggers, shields, ancient clothing, and jewelry.

Mystic Trader, 1334 Pacific Avenue, Forest Grove, OR 97116
Telephone: 1-800-634-9057
Fax: 503-357-1669
Statuary, incense, smudge sticks, musical instruments, and other Eastern items.

Sacred Source (JBL Statues), P.O. Box 163, Crozet, VA 22932
Telephone: 1-800-290-6203
Fax: 804-823-7665
E-mail: spirit@sacredsource.com
$2.00 catalog; Wide range of deity statues from many cultures around the world.

Bibliography

Acterberg, J. *Imagery in Healing: Shamanism & Modern Medicine.* Boston, MA: Shambhala, 1985.

Anderson, Rosemarie. *Celtic Oracles.* New York: Harmony Books, 1998.

Anderson, William. *The Green Man: The Archetype of Our Oneness With the Earth.* San Francisco, CA: HarperCollins, 1990.

Andrews, Ted. *Sacred Sounds.* St. Paul, MN: Llewellyn Publications, 1992.

Arrowsmith, Nancy and Moorse, George. *A Field Guide to the Little People.* New York: Pocket Books, 1977.

Bailey, Alice. *Esoteric Astrology.* 3 vols. New York: Lucis, 1976.

Bayley, Michael. *Caer Sidhe: The Celtic Night Sky.* UK: Capall Bann Publishing, 1997.

Bergin, Osborn. *Irish Bardic Poetry.* Ireland: Dublin Institute for Advanced Studies, 1970.

Berleth, Richard. *The Twilight Lords.* New York: Barnes and Noble, 1994.

Best, R. I. and Bergin, Osborn, editors. *Book of the Dun Cow (Lebor na Huidre).* Ireland: Royal Irish Academy, 1929.

Best, R. I., Bergin, Osborn, and O'Brien, M. A., editors. *The Book of Leinster.* Ireland: Dublin Institute for Advanced Studies, 1954–67.

Beyerl, Paul. *The Master Book of Herbalism.* Custer, WA: Phoenix Publishing, 1984.

Blavatsky, H. P. *The Secret Doctrine.* Wheaton, IL: Theosophical Publishing, 1979.

Bloomfield, M. W. and Dunn, C. W. *The Role of the Poet in Early Societies.* UK: D. S. Brewer, 1989.

Bluett, Anthony. *Things Irish.* Ireland: Mercier, 1994.

Bonwick, James. *Irish Druids and Old Irish Religions.* UK: Dorset Press, 1986. Originally published in 1894.

Bord, Janet and Colin. *Dictionary of Earth Mysteries.* UK: Thorsons, 1996.

Briggs, Katherine. *An Encyclopedia of Fairies, Hobgoblins, Brownies, Bogies and Other Supernatural Creatures.* New York: Pantheon Books, 1976.

Bryce, Derek. *Celtic Legends of the Beyond.* York Beach, ME: Samuel Weiser, 1999.

Buchman, Dian Dincin. *Herbal Medicine.* New York: Gramercy Publishing, 1979.

Campbell, Joseph. *The Masks of God: Occidental Mythology.* New York: Penguin, 1978.

_____. *The Mythic Image.* Princeton, NJ: Princeton University Press, 1974.

_____. *The Way of the Animal Powers.* New York: Harper & Row, 1988.

Carlyon, Richard. *A Guide to the Gods.* New York: Wm. Morrow & Co., 1982.

Carmichael, Alexander. *Carmina Gadelica.* Edinburgh, Scotland: Scottish Academy Press, 1972.

Chadwick, Nora. *The Celts.* New York: Penguin Books, 1991.

Chadwick, Nora and Dillon, Myles. *The Celtic Realms.* New York: New American Library, 1967.

Colum, Padraic, editor. *A Treasury of Irish Folklore.* New York: Wings Books, 1992.

Condren, Mary. *The Serpent and the Goddess: Women, Religion and Power in Celtic Ireland.* San Francisco, CA: Harper & Row, 1989.

Connolly, S. J. editor. *The Oxford Companion to Irish History.* UK: Oxford University Press, 1998.

Conway, D. J. *Animal Magick.* St. Paul, MN: Llewellyn, 1995.

_____. *By Oak, Ash and Thorn: Modern Celtic Shamanism.* St. Paul, MN: Llewellyn, 1995.

_____. *The Celtic Book of Names.* New York: Carol Publishing, 1999.

_____. *Celtic Magic.* St. Paul, MN: Llewellyn, 1990.

_____. *Crystal Enchantments.* Freedom, CA: The Crossing Press, 1999.

_____. *Lord of Light and Shadow.* St. Paul, MN: Llewellyn, 1997.

_____. *Magic of the Gods and Goddesses*. St. Paul, MN: Llewellyn, 1997. Originally titled *The Ancient and Shining Ones.*

_____. *Magickal, Mythical, Mystical Beasts*. St. Paul, MN: Llewellyn, 1996.

_____. *Moon Magick*. St. Paul, MN: Llewellyn, 1995.

Cook, Angelique S. and Hawk, G. A. *Shamanism and the Esoteric Tradition*. St. Paul, MN: Llewellyn, 1992.

Cooksley, Valerie Gennari. *Aromatherapy: A Lifetime Guide to Healing with Essential Oils*. Paramus, NJ: Prentice Hall, 1996.

Coon, Nelson. *Using Plants for Healing*. Emmaus, PA: Rodale Press, 1979.

Cotterell, Arthur. *A Dictionary of World Mythology*. New York: Perigee Books, 1979.

_____. *The Macmillan Illustrated Encyclopedia of Myths and Legends*. New York: Macmillan, 1989.

Cowan, Tom. *Fire in the Head*. San Francisco, CA: HarperSanFrancisco, 1993.

Cross, Tom P. and Slover, Clark H., editors. *Ancient Irish Tales*. New York: Barnes and Noble, 1969.

Crowley, Vivianne. *Celtic Wisdom*. New York: Sterling Publishing, 1998.

Cunliffe, Barry. *The Ancient Celts*. UK: Oxford University Press, 1997.

_____. *The Celtic World: An Illustrated History of the Celtic Race*. New York: Greenwich House, 1986.

Cunningham, Scott. *Cunningham's Encyclopedia of Magical Herbs*. St. Paul, MN: Llewellyn, 1986.

_____. *Magical Herbalism*. St. Paul, MN: Llewellyn, 1986.

Curtin, Jeremiah. *Myths and Folk Tales of Ireland*. New York: Dover Publications, 1975. Originally published in 1890.

Daley, Mary Dowling. *Traditional Irish Laws*. San Francisco, CA: Chronicle Books, 1997.

Davidson, H. R. Ellis. *Myths and Symbols in Pagan Europe*. Syracuse, New York: University Press, 1989.

_____. *The Seer in Celtic and Other Traditions*. Edinburgh, Scotland: John Donald, 1989.

Dexter, W. W. Ogam, *Consaine and Tifinag Alphabets*. Rutland, VT: Academy Books, 1984.

Dixon-Kennedy, Mike. *Celtic Myths and Legends*. UK: Blandford, 1997.

Doore, Gary. *Shaman's Path: Healing Personal Growth and Empowerment*. Boston, MA: Shambhala, 1988.

Eliade, Mircea. Translated by William Trask. *Shamanism: Archaic Techniques of Ecstasy*. Princeton, NJ: Princeton University Press, 1964.

Ellis, Peter Berresford. *Celtic Women: Women in Celtic Society and Literature*. Grand Rapids, MI: Wm. B. Eerdmans Publishing Co., 1995.

_____. *Dictionary of Celtic Mythology*. UK: Oxford University Press, 1992.

Enright, Michael J. *Lady With a Mead Cup*. Portland, OR: Four Courts Press, 1996.

Evans, Hazel. *The Irish Herb Basket*. Ireland: Gill & Macmillan, 1996.

Evans-Wentz, W. Y. *The Fairy Faith in Celtic Countries*. New York: Citadel Press, 1990.

Faraday. W. *Druidic Triads: The Wisdom of the Cymry*. Edmonds, WA: Sure Fire Press, 1984.

Ferguson, Diana. *The Magickal Year*. York Beach, ME: Samuel Weiser, 1996.

Ford, P. K., editor and translator. *The Poetry of Llywarch Hen*. Berkeley, CA: University of California Press, 1974.

Frazier, Sir James. *The Golden Bough*. New York: Macmillan, 1978.

Gantz, Jeffrey. *Early Irish Myths and Sagas*. UK: Penguin Books, 1981.

_____, translator. *The Mabinogion*. New York: Dorset Press, 1976.

Gerard, John. *The Herbal or General History of Plants*. New York: Dover Publishing, 1975. Originally published in 1633.

Gimbutas, Marija. *The Goddesses and Gods of Old Europe 7000–3500 B.C.* Los Angeles, CA: University of California Press, 1974.

Goldman, Jonathan. *Healing Sounds*. UK: Element, 1999.

Graves, Robert. *The Crane Bag and Other Disputed Subjects*. UK: Cassell & Co., 1969.

_____, editor. *The New Larousse Encyclopedia of Mythology*. UK: Hamlyn, 1978.

_____. *The White Goddess*. New York: Farrar, Straus & Giroux, 1966.

Gray, William G. *Magical Ritual Methods*. New York: Samuel Weiser, 1980.

Green, Miranda. *Celtic Goddesses*. New York: George Braziller, 1996.

————. *The Gods of the Celts*. Totowa, NJ: Barnes and Noble, 1986.

————. *Symbol and Image in Celtic Religious Art*. UK: Routledge, 1989.

————. *The World of the Druids*. UK: Thames & Hudson, 1997.

Gregory, Lady. *Visions and Beliefs in the West of Ireland*. New York: G.P. Putnam & Sons, 1920.

Grieve, M. A. *A Modern Herbal*. New York: Dover Publishing, 1982.

Guest, Lady Charlotte, translator. *The Mabinogion*. UK: J. M. Dent & Sons, 1913.

Halifax, Joan. *Shaman: The Wounded Healer*. New York: Crossroads, 1982.

Harner, Michael. *The Way of the Shaman*. New York: Bantam, 1982.

Heaney, Marie. *Over Nine Waves: A Book of Irish Legends*. UK: Faber & Faber, 1994.

Hippocrene. *Irish-English Dictionary and Phrase Book*. New York: Hippocrene Books, 1997.

Hopman, Ellen Evert. *A Druid's Herbal for the Sacred Earth Year*. Rochester, VT: Destiny Books, 1995.

Howard, Michael. *The Magic of the Runes*. New York: Samuel Weiser, 1980.

Humphreys, E. *The Taliesin Tradition*. UK: Black Raven Press, 1983.

Ingerman, Sandra. *Soul Retrieval: Mending the Fragmented Self*. San Francisco, CA: Harper & Row, 1991.

Jackson, Kenneth H. *The Oldest Irish Tradition: A Window on the Iron Age*. UK: Cambridge University Press, 1964.

Jones, Gwen and Thomas. *The Mabinogion*. UK: Dent, 1978.

Jones, Leslie Ellen. *Druid, Shaman, Priest*. UK: Hisarlik Press, 1998.

Kalweit, Holger. *Dreamtime and Inner Space: The World of the Shaman*. Boston, MA: Shambhala, 1988.

Keightley, Thomas. *The World Guide to Gnomes, Fairies, Elves and Other Little People*. New York: Avenel Books, 1978.

Kendrick, T. D. *The Druids*. UK: Methuen & Co. Ltd., 1928.

K'Eogh, John. Edited by Michael Scott. *An Irish Herbal: The Botanalogia*

Universalis Hibernica. UK: The Aquarian Press, 1986. Originally published in 1735.

Kerr, Ralph Whiteside. *Herbalism Through the Ages*. San Jose, CA: Supreme Grand Lodge of Amorc, 1969.

King, John. *The Celtic Druids' Year*. UK: Blandford, 1995.

Kinsella, Thomas, translator. *The Tain (The Cattle Raid of Cuailnge and Other Ulaid Stories)*. Ireland: Dolmen Press, 1969.

Kirk, Robert. Editor, Stewart Sanderson. *The Secret Commonwealth*. UK: D. S. Brewer, 1976.

Knott, E. and Murphy, G. *Early Irish Literature*. UK: Routledge & Kegan Paul, 1966.

Kondratiev, Alexei. *The Apple Branch: A Path to Celtic Ritual*. Cork, Ireland: The Collins Press, 1998.

Lahr, Jan, editor. *The Celtic Quest in Art and Literature*. New York: Welcome, 1999.

Larrington, Carolyne, editor. *The Feminist Companion to Mythology*. UK: Pandora, 1992.

Leo, Alan. *Esoteric Astrology*. New York: Astrologer's Library, 1978.

Logan, Patrick. *The Holy Wells of Ireland*. UK: Colin Smythe, 1992.

Lonigan, Paul R. *The Druids: Priests of the Ancient Celts*. Westport, CT: Greenwood Press, 1996.

Lover, Samuel and Croker, Thomas Crofton. *Ireland: Myths and Legends*. UK: Senate, 1995.

Macalister, R.A.S., editor and translator. *The Book of the Invasions of Ireland (Lebor Gabala Erenn)*. Ireland: Irish Texts Society, 1938–54.

MacCana, Proinsias. *Celtic Mythology*. New York: Peter Bedrick Books, 1991.

MacCulloch, J. A. *The Celtic and Scandinavian Religions*. Westport, CT: Greenwood Press, 1973. Originally published in 1948.

_____. *The Religion of the Ancient Celts*. UK: Constable, 1991. Originally published in 1911.

Mackenzie, Donald A. *Scottish Folk-Lore and Folk Life*. Glasgow, Scotland: Blackie & Son, 1935.

MacKillop, James. *Dictionary of Celtic Mythology*. New York: Oxford University Press, 1998.

MacManus, Diarmaid. *Irish Earth Folk*. New York: Devin-Adair, 1959.

MacManus, Seumas. *The Story of the Irish Race*. Old Greenwich, CT: Devin-Adair, 1978.

MacMathuna, Seamus and O'Corrain, Ailbhe. *Irish Dictionary*. UK: HarperCollins, 1995.

Mag Fhearaigh, Críostóir. *Ogham: An Irish Alphabet*. New York: Hippocrene Books, 1998.

Mann, N. R. *The Celtic Power Symbols*. UK: Triskele, 1987.

Markale, Jean. Translated by Jon Graham. *The Druids: Celtic Priests of Nature*. Rochester, VT: Inner Traditions International, 1999.

Martel, Hazel Mary. *What Do We Know About the Celts?* New York: Peter Bedrick Books, 1993.

Maternus, Firmicus. *Ancient Astrology Theory and Practice*. NJ: Noyces Press, 1975.

Matthews, Caitlin. *The Celtic Book of the Dead*. New York: St. Martin's Press, 1992.

_____. *The Celtic Tradition*. UK: Element, 1989.

_____. *The Elements of the Celtic Tradition*. UK: Element Books, 1989.

_____. *The Aquarian Guide to British and Irish Mythology*. UK: The Aquarian Press, 1988.

_____. *The Encyclopaedia of Celtic Wisdom*. UK: Element Books, 1994.

Matthews, John, editor. *The Bardic Source Book*. UK: Blandford, 1998.

_____. *A Celtic Reader*. UK: Aquarian Press, 1990.

_____. *The Celtic Shaman*. Rockport, MA: Element Books, 1991.

_____. *The Celtic Shaman's Pack*. Rockport, MA: Element Books, 1995.

_____, editor. *The Druid Source Book*. UK: Blandford, 1997.

_____. *Fionn MacCumhain*. UK: Firebird Books, 1988.

_____. *The Song of Taliesin: Stories and Poems from the Books of Broceliande*. UK: Aquarian Press, 1991.

_____. *Tales of the Celtic Otherworld*. UK: Blandford, 1998.

_____. *Taliesin: Shamanism and the Bardic Mysteries in Britain and Ireland*. UK: Aquarian Press, 1991.

Matthews, W. H. *Mazes and Labyrinths: Their History and Development*. New York: Dover Publications, 1970. Originally published in 1922.

McAnally, D. R., Jr. *Irish Wonders.* New York: Gramercy Books, 1996.

McNeill, F. M. *The Silver Bough.* Edinburgh, Scotland: Cannongate, 1989.

Meadows, Kenneth. *Shamanic Experience: A Practical Guide to Contemporary Shamanism.* Rockport, MA: Element Books, 1991.

Morgannwy, Iolo. *The Triads of Britain.* UK: Wildwood House, 1977.

Murphy, Gerard. *Saga and Myth in Ancient Ireland.* Ireland: Cultural Relationships Committee of Ireland, 1961.

Murray, Liz and Colin. *The Celtic Tree Oracle.* New York: St. Martin's Press, 1988.

Neumann, Erich. *The Great Mother: An Analysis of the Archetype.* Princeton, NJ: Princeton University Press, 1974.

Newark, Tim and McBride, Angus. *Ancient Celts.* Hong Kong: Concord Publications, 1998.

O'Boyle, S. *Ogam, The Poet's Secret.* Ireland: Gilbert Dalton, 1980.

O'Brien Press. *The Celtic Way of Life.* Ireland: The O'Brien Press, 1997.

O'Driscoll, R., editor. *The Celtic Consciousness.* Edinburgh, Scotland: Cannongate, 1982.

Ó hÓgáin, Dáithí. *The Hero in Irish Folk History.* Ireland: Gill & Macmillan, 1985.

————. *Myth, Legend and Romance.* UK: Ryan Publishing, 1990.

————. *The Sacred Isle: Belief and Religion in Pre-Christian Ireland.* Cork, Ireland: Boydell Press, 1999.

O'Kelly, Michael J. *Newgrange Archaeology.* UK: Thames & Hudson, 1982.

O'Rahilly, T. F. *Early Irish History and Mythology.* Ireland: Dublin Institute for Advanced Studies, 1946.

Parry-Jones, D. *Welsh Legends & Fairy Lore.* New York: Barnes and Noble, 1992.

Patch, H. R. *The Other World.* Cambridge, MA: Harvard University Press, 1950.

Paterson, Helena. *The Celtic Lunar Zodiac.* St. Paul, MN: Llewellyn, 1997.

————. *The Handbook of Celtic Astrology.* St. Paul, MN: Llewellyn, 1994.

Pennick, Nigel. *Magical Alphabets*. York Beach, ME: Samuel Weiser, 1992.

_____. *The Pagan Book of Days: A Guide to the Festivals, Traditions, and Sacred Days of the Year*. Rochester, VT: Destiny Books, 1992.

_____. *The Sacred World of the Celts*. Rochester, VT: Inner Traditions, 1997.

Purce, Jill. *The Mystic Spiral: Journey of the Soul*. New York: Thames & Hudson, 1974.

Reade, W. Winwood. *The Veil of Isis, or Mysteries of the Druids*. New York: Peter Eckler, 1964.

Rees, Alwyn and Brinley. *Celtic Heritage*. UK: Thames & Hudson, 1961.

Rose, Jeanne. *Herbs & Things*. New York: Grosset & Dunlap, 1973.

_____. *Jeanne Rose's Herbal Body Book*. New York: Grosset & Dunlap, 1976.

Ross, Anne. Edited by V. Newal. "The Divine Hag of the Pagan Celts," *The Witch Figure*. UK: Routledge & Kegan Paul, 1973.

_____. *Druids, Gods and Heroes From Celtic Mythology*. New York: Schocken Books, 1986.

_____. *Everyday Life of the Pagan Celts*. UK: Routledge & Kegan Paul, 1970.

_____. *The Pagan Celts*. Totowa, NJ: Barnes and Noble, 1986.

Ryall, Rhiannon. *Celtic Lore and Druidic Ritual*. UK: Capall Bann Publishing, 1994.

_____. *Symbols of the Ancient Gods*. UK: Capall Bann Publishing, 1998.

_____. *Weaving a Web of Magic*. UK: Capall Bann Publishing, 1996.

_____. *West Country Wicca*. Custer, WA: Phoenix Publishing, 1989.

Scott, Gini Graham. *Shamanism and Personal Mastery*. St. Paul, MN: Paragon House, 1991.

Sharkey, John. *Celtic Mysteries: The Ancient Religion*. UK: Thames & Hudson, 1991.

Sjoo, Monica and Mor, Barbara. *The Great Cosmic Mother: Rediscovering the Religion of the Earth*. San Francisco, CA: Harper & Row, 1987.

Skene, W. F., translator. *The Four Ancient Books of Wales*, 2 vols. New York: AMS Press, 1984-5.

Smith, A. G. and Kaufman, William. *Life in Celtic Times*. New York: Dover Publications, 1997.

Smith, Charles Hamilton. *Ancient Costumes of Britain and Ireland: From the Druids to the Tudors*. UK: Bracken Books, 1989. Originally published in 1814.

Somerville-Large, Peter. *Legendary Ireland*. Boulder, CO: Roberts Rinehart Publishers, 1995.

Spann, David B. *The Otherworld in Early Irish Literature*. MI: University of Michigan, 1969.

Spence, Lewis. *The History and Origins of Druidism*. UK: Aquarian Press, 1971.

_____. *The Magic Arts of Celtic Britain*. New York: Dorset Press, 1992.

_____. *The Mysteries of Britain*. Philadelphia, PA: David McKay Co., 1972.

Squire, Charles. *Celtic Myth and Legend*. New York: Newcastle Publishing, 1975. Originally published in 1905.

St. Clair, Sheila. *Mysterious Ireland*. UK: Robert Hale, 1994.

Stahl, Carl W. Vulcan: *The Intra-Mercurial Planet*. CO: V. Z. Enterprises, 1968.

Stevens, J. and L. S. *Secrets of Shamanism*. New York: Avon Books, 1988.

Stewart, R. J. *Celtic Gods, Celtic Goddesses*. UK: Blandford, 1992.

_____. Robert Kirk: Walker *Between Worlds*. UK: Element Books, 1990.

_____. *The Underworld Initiation*. UK: Aquarian Press, 1985.

Stone, Merlin. *When God Was a Woman*. New York: Harcourt Brace Jovanovich, 1976.

Talbot, Rob and Whiteman, Robin. *Brother Cadfael's Herb Garden*. Boston, MA: Little, Brown & Co., 1996.

Thompson, C.J.S. *Celtic Healing: The Healing Arts of Ancient Britain, Wales, and Ireland*. Edmonds, WA: Sure Fire Press, 1994.

Tresidder, Jack. *Dictionary of Symbols*. San Francisco, CA: Chronicle Books, 1998.

Van Gelder, Dora. *The Real World of Fairies*. Wheaton, IL: Quest Books, 1999.

Vescoli, Michael. Translated by Rosemary Dear. *The Celtic Tree Calendar: Your Tree Sign and You*. UK: Souvenir Press, 1999.

Walkley, Victor. *Celtic Daily Life.* New York: Quality Paperback Book Club, 1997.

Webb, D. A., Parnell, J., and Doogue, D. *An Irish Flora.* Ireland: Dundalgan Press Ltd., 1996.

Weston, L. H. *The Planet Vulcan.* AZ: American Federation of Astrologers, n.d.

Wilde, Lady. *Irish Cures, Mystic Charms and Superstitions.* New York: Sterling Publishing, 1991.

Wilde, Lyn Webster. *Celtic Women in Legend.* UK: Blandford, 1997.

Wildwood, Chrissie. *The Encyclopedia of Aromatherapy.* Rochester, VT: Healing Arts Press, 1996.

Williams, I. (English version by J. E. Caerwyn Williams). *The Poems of Taliesin.* Ireland: Dublin Institute for Advanced Studies, 1975.

Williamson, R. *The Craneskin Bag: Celtic Stories and Poems.* Edinburgh, Scotland: Cannongate, 1979.

Yarwood, Doreen. *The Encyclopedia of World Costume.* New York: Bonanza Books, 1986.

Yeats, W. B. and Gregory, Lady Isabella Augusta. *A Treasury of Irish Myth, Legend and Folklore.* New York: Avenel Books, 1986. Originally published in 1888.

Zaczek, Iain. *Ancient Ireland.* UK: Collins & Brown, 1998.

_____. *Chronicles of the Celts.* New York: Sterling Publishing, 1996.

Index

BOOKS BY THE CROSSING PRESS

Ghosts, Spirits and Hauntings

Ghosts, specters, phantoms, shades, spooks, or wraiths-no matter what the name, Patricia Telesco will help you identify and cope with their presence. Whatever you encounter, Patricia would like you to relate to it sensitively and intelligently, using this book as a guide.

$10.95 • Paper • ISBN 0-89594-871-0

The Language of Dreams

Patricia Telesco outlines a creative, interactive approach to understanding the dream symbols of our inner life. Interpretations of more than 800 dream symbols incorporate multi-cultural elements with psychological, religious, folk, and historical meanings.

$16.95 • Paper • ISBN 0-89594-836-2

A Woman's I Ching

By Diane Stein

A feminist interpretation of the popular ancient text for diving the character of events. Stein's version reclaims the feminine, or yin, content of the ancient work and removes all oppressive language and imagery.

$16.95 • Paper • ISBN 0-89594-857-5

All Women Are Psychics

By Diane Stein

Women's intuition is no myth; women really are psychic. But your inborn psychic sense was probably suppressed when you were very young. This inspiring book will help you rediscover and reclaim your dormant psychic aptitude.

$16.95 • Paper • ISBN 0-89594-979-2

Channeling for Everyone: A Safe Step-by-Step Guide to Developing Your Intuition and Psychic Awareness

By Tony Neate

This is a clear, concise guide to developing our subtler levels of consciousness. It provides us with safe, step-by-step exercises to prepare for and begin to practice channeling, allowing wider states of consciousness to become part of our everyday lives.

$12.95 • Paper • ISBN 0-89594-922-9

Clear Mind, Open Heart: Healing Yourself, Your Relationships and the Planet

By Eddie and Debbie Shapiro

The Shapiros offer an uplifting, inspiring, and deeply sensitive approach to healing through spiritual awareness. Includes practical exercises and techniques to help us all in making our own journey.

$16.95 • Paper • ISBN 0-89594-917-2

Fundamentals of Hawaiian Mysticism
By Charlotte Berney

Evolving in isolation on an island paradise, the mystical practice of Huna has shaped the profound yet elegantly simple Hawaiian character. Charlotte Berney presents Huna traditions as they apply to words, prayer, gods, the breath, a loving spirit, family ties, nature, and mana.

$12.95 • Paper • ISBN 1-58091-026-2

Fundamentals of Jewish Mysticism and Kabbalah
By Ron Feldman

This concise introductory book explains what Kabbalah is and how study of its text and practices enhance the life of the soul and the holiness of the body.

$12.95 • Paper • ISBN 1-58091-049-1

Fundamentals of Tibetan Buddhism
By Rebecca McClen Novick

This book explores the history, philosophy, and practice of Tibetan Buddhism. Novick's concise history of Buddhism, and her explanations of the Four Noble Truths, Wheel of Life, Karma, Five Paths, Six Perfections, and the different schools of thought within the Buddhist teachings help us understand Tibetan Buddhism as a way of experiencing the world, more than as a religion or philosophy.

$12.95 • Paper • ISBN 0-89594-953-9

The Heart of the Circle: A Guide to Drumming
By Holly Blue Hawkins

Holly Blue Hawkins will walk you through the process of finding a drum, taking care of it, calling a circle, setting an intention, and drumming together. She will also show you how to incorporate drumming into your spiritual practice. She offers you an invitation to explore rhythm in a free and spontaneous manner.

$12.95 • Paper • ISBN 1-58091-025-4

The Native American Sweat Lodge: History and Legends
By Joseph Bruchac

To deepen our understanding of the significance of sweat lodges within Native American cultures, Bruchac shares 25 relevant traditional tales from the Lakota, Blackfoot, Hopi, and others.—Booklist

$12.95 • Paper • ISBN 0-89594-636-X

Peace Within the Stillness:
Relaxation & Meditation for True Happiness
By Eddie and Debbie Shapiro

Meditation teachers Eddie and Debbie Shapiro teach a simple, ancient practice which will enable you to release even deeper levels of inner stress and tension. Once you truly relax, you will enter the quiet mind and experience the profound, joyful, and healing energy of meditation.

$14.95 • Paper • ISBN 0-89594-926-1

Physician of the Soul: *A Modern Kabbalist's Approach*
to Health and Healing

By Rabbi Joseph H. Gelberman with Lesley Sussman

In a self-awareness program suitable for all faiths, internationally renowned Rabbi Joseph Gelberman reveals wisdom drawn from Jewish mysticism. Exercises in meditation, visualization, and prayer are discussed to promote harmony in mind, body, and soul.

$14.95 • Paper • ISBN 1-58091-061-0

Pocket Guide to Celtic Spirituality

By Sirona Knight

The Earth-centered philosophy and rituals of ancient Celtic spirituality have special relevance today as we strive to balance our relationship with the planet. This guide offers a comprehensive introduction to the rich religious tradition of the Celts.

$6.95 • Paper • ISBN 0-89594-907-5

Pocket Guide to Meditation

By Alan Pritz

This book focuses on meditation as part of spiritual practice, as a universal tool to forge a deeper connection with spirit. In Alan Pritz's words, Meditation simply delivers one of the most purely profound experiences of life, joy.

$6.95 • Paper • ISBN 0-89594-886-9

Pocket Guide to Self Hypnosis

By Adam Burke, Ph. D.

Self-hypnosis and imagery are powerful tools that activate a very creative quality of mind. By following the methods provided, you can begin to make progress on your goals and feel more in control of your life and destiny.

$6.95 • Paper • ISBN 0-89594-824-9

Shamanism as a Spiritual Practice for Daily Life

By Tom Cowan

This inspirational book blends elements of shamanism with inherited traditions and contemporary religious commitments. An inspiring spiritual call.—Booklist

$16.95 • Paper • ISBN 0-89594-838-9

To receive a current catalog from The Crossing Press
please call toll-free, 800-777-1048.
Visit our Web site: **www.crossingpress.com**